Oliver Gru

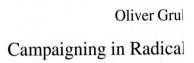

Campaigning in Radical

Studien zur politischen Kommunikation
Studies in Political Communication

herausgegeben von
edited by

PD Dr. Jens Tenscher
(Universität Trier / University of Trier)

Band / Volume 11

LIT

Oliver Gruber

Campaigning in Radical Right Heartland

The politicization
of immigration and ethnic relations
in Austrian general elections,
1971–2013

LIT

Published with the financial assistance of
the Faculty of Social Sciences of the University of Vienna
the Austrian Political Science Association
the City of Vienna, MA 7 Wissenschaftsförderung

Bibliographic information published by the Deutsche Nationalbibliothek
The Deutsche Nationalbibliothek lists this publication in the Deutsche
Nationalbibliografie; detailed bibliographic data are available in the Internet at
http://dnb.d-nb.de.

ISBN 978-3-643-90517-8

A catalogue record for this book is available from the British Library

©LIT VERLAG GmbH & Co. KG Wien,
Zweigniederlassung Zürich 2014
Klosbachstr. 107
CH-8032 Zürich
Tel. +41 (0) 44-251 75 05
Fax +41 (0) 44-251 75 06
E-Mail: zuerich@lit-verlag.ch
http://www.lit-verlag.ch

LIT VERLAG Dr. W. Hopf
Berlin 2014
Fresnostr. 2
D-48159 Münster
Tel. +49 (0) 2 51-62 03 20
Fax +49 (0) 2 51-23 19 72
E-Mail: lit@lit-verlag.de
http://www.lit-verlag.de

Distribution:
In the UK: Global Book Marketing, e-mail: mo@centralbooks.com
In North America: International Specialized Book Services, e-mail: orders@isbs.com
In Germany: LIT Verlag Fresnostr. 2, D-48159 Münster
Tel. +49 (0) 2 51-620 32 22, Fax +49 (0) 2 51-922 60 99, E-mail: vertrieb@lit-verlag.de

In Austria: Medienlogistik Pichler-ÖBZ, e-mail: mlo@medien-logistik.at
e-books are available at www.litwebshop.de

Contents

List of tables and figures

Acknowledgements

This book is based on a study conducted as part of my dissertation project at the University of Vienna. On the road to completing the project and turning it into a book I received a lot of invaluable support and advice for which I wish to express my gratitute to a number of people and institutions.

First and foremost I am deeply indebted to my supervisor Sieglinde Rosenberger who advised me all the way during my dissertation project and provided me with a healthy dose of encouragement. Moreover, I received immense scholarly support from my colleagues at the University of Vienna. Sarah Meyer offered repeated expertise, necessary critique and invaluable moral support for which I am immensely grateful. Florian Walter helped me with important comments on the study's framework and methods. Julia Mourão Permoser, Teresa Peintinger and Alexandra König gave me valuable comments on various parts of this book. Great personal gratitude goes to Petra Herczeg for bringing me into acadamia as much as for supporting me in times of doubt. I also thank Maximilian Gottschlich for offering me excellent working conditions over the last years.

Evidently, I received crucial support from other institutional contexts as well. Thus, I would like to thank the Austrian Academy of Science, and in particular Gabriele Melischek and Josef Seethaler, for integrating me into a research project that has constituted the grounds of this book, as well as Melanie Magin for being a propelling colleague during that period. I am also highly grateful for Tim Bale to have shared his insight and expertise during my fellowship at Queen Mary University which has been of immense value and helped me sharpen the perspective on party competition that is documented in this book. Sincere thanks also go to the series editor, Jens Tenscher, for giving early advice on the study's structure and offering an outstanding opportunity to share my findings in this book series on political communication. In the final steps to completing this book, Hannes Hambrecht helped me enourmosly by proof-reading the manuscript while Marie-Therese Pekny designed the book's cover in a fabulous way.

As any researcher I also owe a great debt of gratitude to the institutions that offered the resources and contexts for this book to become published. Therefore, I would like to thank the Leibniz-Institut für Sozialwissenschaten (GESIS) and Bruno Hopp as well as the Austrian National Library for their help with the allocation of my data basis. Moreover, I am highly indebted to the Faculty of Social Sciences at the University of Vienna, to the Austrian Society of Political Science and to the City of Vienna for the funding I received for this book.

Last but not least, I would like to praise my parents for everything they have provided during the last decades. This work is dedicated to them as much as to those who could not live to see these pages. Thank you.

Vienna, April 2014

1.   Introduction

In recent decades, migration and ethnic relations have emerged as contentious political issues in most European democracies. Despite the differing histories of ethnic diversity and traditions of immigration across Europe, intense public debates about these issues and about the political regulation of rights, duties and restrictions have become a common theme, with dominant frames of interpretation travelling across national borders (Mahnig/Wimmer 2000; Joppke 2007). This marked increase in public attention is both reflected and intensified by a lively political debate involving political authorities, (inter)national courts, non-governmental organizations, affected groups, and, not least, political parties. It has given rise to public debates that intermingle topics such as cross-border migration, asylum and refugees, ethnic diversity, and the many facets of migrant and minority integration, and often all of these different aspects are lumped together by means of references to "others", "aliens" or "foreigners" (Roggeband/Verloo 2007). Though these discursive strands obviously developed at different rates in different historical periods, they have accumulated into a complex political field that, nowadays, is increasingly important in structuring political preferences.

Among the arenas for this public debate on migration and ethnic relations, one forum has been instrumental in raising and spreading the salience of these issues and distributing interpretive schemes across national contexts: the realm of party competition (Schain et al. 2002: 3-4). Political parties have become key voices in the increasingly contentious debate, forwarding all manner of stances on questions of migration and ethnic relations. Most prominently, anti-immigrant perspectives and claims for cultural hegemony have been catalyzed by the rise of radical right parties (Betz 1993/1994), but pro-immigrant and multicultural stances have also been voiced, mostly by left-libertarian and liberal parties (Lahav 2004). On the other hand, the behavior of mainstream parties both left and right of the political center has long been characterized by ambivalence, both in their engagement as well as in their policy stances. Hence party competition has grown to serve as a microcosm mirroring competing perspectives within a society, with political parties increasingly attaching the issues of migration and ethnic relations to their agendas. But parties do not only reflect already existing preferences among electorates. In fact they vitally stimulate these discussions and preferences themselves, turning from mouthpieces into generators of political sentiments.

Interestingly, for a long time scholarly research on immigration underrated the significance of political parties (Triadafilopoulos/Zaslove 2006: 171; Bale 2008: 316; Duncan/van Hecke 2008: 432). This longstanding reluctance is particularly baffling in light of the fact that today, political parties play a crucial role all across Europe as much in framing migration and ethnic relations as in placing them on the political agenda (Schain 2008: 465). The reasons for this reluctance stemmed partly from the early assumption that mainstream parties would avoid politicization of the issue because the boundaries for a legitimate debate were narrow and because detailed information on patterns and consequences of immigration was scarce (Freeman 1995: 884-887). In part it was also owed to the perception that the actual leeway for policies to be promoted by political parties was limited by liberal and human rights principles (Soysal 1994: 7-8). Thus, with traditional mainstream politics emphasizing other policy fields, the systematic inclusion of party politics in research on migration and ethnic relations was neglected long into the 1990s.

In recent years, however, a growing number of authors have called for closer scrutiny of the role of political parties, especially that of anti-immigrant radical right parties, "as critical nodes" in the realm of migration and ethnic relations (e.g. Perlmutter 1996; Minkenberg 2001; Schain 2006/2008). The crucial influence that political parties exert on both the discussion and the regulation of migration and ethnic relations in Western democracies has since become a lively strand of research acknowledging that migration phenomena do not exist independently of their political discussion but rather are controlled, framed and perceived through politics (Messina 2007: 55). Thus bringing parties back into the study of migration and ethnic relations "helps us to understand the importance of changing preferences, their relation to strategic interests, and the means by which they are activated in policy-making processes" related to these issues (Triadafilopoulos/Zaslove 2006: 189).

As part of this deepening scholarly interest, several authors have pointed out transformations of traditional cleavage patterns and new conflicts whose growing relevance has come to structure party competition, with migration and ethnic relations playing an important part in these developments (Inglehart 1990; Betz 1993; Kitschelt 2001; Kriesi et al. 2006). Of the party families, anti-immigrant radical right parties have received the most attention due to their role in pushing migration and ethnic relations onto the political agenda as well as to their ability to influence the policies of governing parties (Green-Pedersen/Odmalm 2008; van Spanje 2010) and occasionally even implement policies themselves by gaining office (McGann/Kitschelt 2005; de Lange 2007; van Spanje/van der Brug 2008).

The role of mainstream parties has come under systematic scrutiny only in the last few years as a result of the success of anti-immigrant parties that started in the late 1990s and eventuated in radical right government participation (such as in Italy, Austria, Denmark, Norway and the Netherlands; see de Lange 2012). Since then, the role of center-right parties has been addressed in a number of studies (Eatwell 2000; Downs 2001; Bale 2003; 2005; Meguid 2005 and 2008), and recently the hitherto-neglected role of center-left parties has attracted some scholarly interest as well (Art 2007; Bale et al. 2010), while systematic evaluation of pro-immigrant parties has remained scarce. This recent strand of research has been oriented on a number of core questions that are the guiding questions for this book as well: When do political parties add migration and ethnic relations to their agendas? How can their politicization be analyzed systematically? Where do parties position themselves in a controversial policy field that cuts across several government portfolios? Which motives can be identified as driving forces of parties' behavior, and what are the rational strategies of politicization linked to these different motives? What roles do the different politicization channels available in electoral competition play in these considerations?

This book addresses these research questions on the basis of an in-depth country study and suggests a conceptual framework for the analysis of electoral party competition on the issues of migration and ethnic relations. Its central objective is to contribute to the understanding of existing concepts of party politicization of these issues. It focuses on the supply side of competition, thus on the inputs offered by parties' political communication efforts, while demand-side factors (dealing with the opportunities and constraints created by voter preferences) are considered only from an explanatory perspective. The book integrates literature from studies on party politics, political communication, and immigration in order to develop a conceptual framework based on the following three considerations.

Firstly, it conceptualizes an instrument that is suitable for the identification of party politicization patterns, i.e., the ways in which parties emphasize and frame the issues or subtopics of a debate. Approaching politicization as a process of "publicly addressing an issue in the light of its political regulation", the design will be based on three concepts joining different strands of literature, i.e. *issue salience, subtopics* and *positions* (Downs 1957; Budge/Farlie 1983; Carmines/Stimson 1993; Petrocik 1996; Benoit/Laver 2006; Meguid 2008; Jäger/Maier 2009), and the argument that parties strategically adapt these aspects of their politicization out of competitive considerations. That is, in order to tap into a particular political issue, parties may increase their issue emphasis in general, highlight the importance of certain specific subtopics over that of others, or change their stances on the issue in question.

Secondly, since these strategies of politicization are expected to vary among different party types and changing competitive conditions, this study develops an explanatory framework for party politicization of migration and ethnic relations. To this end, it integrates theoretical arguments from recent literature on party goals with work dedicated specifically to the issues of migration and ethnic relations (eg. Strøm 1990; Müller/Strøm 1999; Downs 2001; Bale 2003/2008; Meguid 2008; Green-Pedersen/Odmalm 2008; Bale et al. 2010). Suggesting a combined framework that considers party ideology and issue ownership as well as motives of vote maximization and coalition considerations, the study is able to explain individual party behavior from a longitudinal perspective. Additionally, since party competition does not take place in a vacuum but is rather vitally embedded in external socio-structural circumstances, consideration is also given to the impact of these circumstances on the overarching politicization patterns.

Thirdly, the book contends that the electoral arena is the crucial locus for identifying parties' core values and strategies in the debate on migration and ethnic relations, and that electoral competition incorporates a variety of campaign channels serving different communicational goals and needs in the campaigning process. This multi-dimensionality of the electoral arena raises questions about how different campaign channels correspond to different patterns of politicization, and whether certain types of parties are more capable of maintaining campaign consistency than others (Maarek 1995; Blumler et al. 1996; Adams et al. 2006; Kriesi et al. 2009; Williams 2009). To answer these questions, the study compares programmatic communication as provided by election manifestos with the day-to-day campaigning shown in parties' press releases.

These three conceptual considerations are examined empirically by means of a longitudinal country study (George/Bennet 2004; Gerring 2004) of Austrian general elections from 1971 to 2013. The case of Austria was selected on the basis of several theoretical considerations. Firstly, since 1945 the Austrian party system has developed in a characteristic way for democracies in Europe, turning from a narrow, party-centric system characterized by high party loyalty and partisanship into a more heterogeneous party spectrum competing on increasingly diverse issues (Plasser/Ulram 2006; Müller 2006). Secondly, Austria has a long history of cultural diversity reaching back to the Habsburg era, and furthermore, due to its geopolitical situation, it experienced characteristic immigration and asylum inflows following 1945 (Fassmann/Münz 1995). Thirdly, the prominent role of the radical right Freedom Party of Austria (FPÖ) since the mid-1980s has made the Austrian case a standard example for research on anti-immigrant parties (Luther 2000; Pelinka 2002). Fourthly, the comparatively high rates of attentiveness and skepticism of the Austrian population regarding the questions of migration and ethnic relations have further fuelled political controversy (Rosenberger/Seeber 2011).[1] All of these factors together make Austria an informative case for the analysis and evaluation of party strategies in electoral competition on migration and ethnic relations.

The longitudinal analysis presented in this book traces the development of these contentious political issues under changing socio-structural conditions while examining the adaptations of parties' strategies to changing competitive contexts; thus it integrates these strands into a single reciprocal model explaining patterns of party politicization in Austria. By focusing on the electoral arena, it aims to reveal the dynamics of competition in contemporary party politicization on migration and ethnic relations and thus seeks to illustrate the role of these issues for parties' strategic considerations.

---

[1] Each of these considerations will be illustrated more thoroughly in the discussion of the case in Chapter 3.

The structure of the book

The book approaches these objectives in six steps, which yields the following structure of chapters.

Following this introduction, Chapter 2 offers a condensed review of the main theoretical arguments regarding party motives, issue competition and the particular role of the issues of migration and ethnic relations for electoral party politicization. It begins with a discussion of the goals that parties pursue in inter-party competition and an introduction to the spatial concepts used to describe and analyze issue politicization (2.1). Subsequently, it explores the strategic politicization options available to parties in these spatial concepts and examines these general considerations in the specific context of migration and ethnic relations while consulting the recent literature on this subject (2.2). Finally, the chapter characterizes the context of the electoral arena, compares the campaign communication channels available to political parties, and makes assertions about the differences in politicization between programmatic and day-to-day party campaigning (2.3).

Chapter 3 introduces the case of Austria as the subject of investigation. It begins by sketching the socio-structural inputs giving rise to these issues, such as the history of immigration to Austria since the 1960s and the development of public opinion vis-à-vis these questions (3.1). Subsequently, it focuses more closely on the internal circumstances influencing the strategies in party competition, i.e. the number and strength of relevant parties, their ideological foundations, and potential coalition scenarios (3.2). The recognitions regarding both external and internal factors of competition are condensed into concise hypotheses that are to guide the succeeding analysis and that will be revisited in the book's final empirical chapter.

Chapter 4 outlines the methodical design applied in this study, recapitulating the process of data selection and the operationalization of politicization by means of three analytical variables: issue salience, subtopics and positions. It discusses experiences from previous content analyses of migration and ethnic relations as well as the issue categories devised for them, and condenses these categories into a coding scheme for analyzing subtopics. Furthermore, the chapter documents the approach used to quantify salience and proximity in party competition, contrasting advantages and disadvantages of various existing approaches. Finally it discusses the usefulness of both deductively and inductively developed codes for policy positions on migration and ethnic relations, indicating the need for the integrated approach underlying this study.

Chapter 5 presents the first, qualitative findings produced by this study. After introducing the concept of framing and the characteristics of the combined approach for the development of strategic discursive frames, it discusses the various policy frames represented in the debate on migration and ethnic relations that are identified as a result. As a result, a set of eleven policy frames which portray the standpoints represented in party politicization from the 1970s on at a moderate level of abstraction is developed. These frames are grouped into an either liberal or restrictive spectrum of party discourse and form the foundation of a quantitative content analysis of politicization in Austrian electoral competition, the findings of which are discussed in the succeeding chapter.

Chapter 6 presents the empirical results of the longitudinal analysis, comparing the quantitative findings on the programmatic and day-to-day campaign channels used for electoral politicization. The first section collects data on the overall salience of migration and ethnic relations issues and traces their history in Austrian party competition. Additionally, it focuses on individual parties in order to explicate the strategic use of issue emphasis in inter-party competition (6.1). The second section of the chapter discusses specific issue preferences (subtopics) in Austrian party discourse on migration and ethnic relations. It locates the topical center of the debate and differentiates between the topical emphasis in the politicization efforts of individual parties in order to indicate which aspects dominate the debate on these issues (6.2). Finally, the chapter focuses on parties' core policy positions on migration and ethnic relations by indicating the relevance of the policy frames idenitified in chapter 5. Frames are arranged on a bipolar scale in order to show parties' positions and movements; additionally, focusing on parties' individual frames of politicization reveals discursive coalitions between competing parties as well as the dividing line that bisects the Austrian party spectrum (6.3).

To finally close the circle with the preceding chapters, chapter 7 synthesizes the study's explanandum and explanans. It evaluates the conjectures generated in the theoretical chapters on the basis of the empirical findings and assesses the applicability of the assumptions that guided the research design. In doing so, the chapter discusses the explanatory power of the various factors suggested in chapters 2 & 3, including those with additional potential. This synthesis is used to suggest a heuristic model for explaining party politicization of migration and ethnic relations.

The final chapter recapitulates the findings produced by this study, it highlights the book's principal contributions to the current debate on party competition on migration and ethnic relations, and it raises questions that remain for future research.

The book not only reaches out to scholars of party politics, political communication and migration studies but also aims to address an interested, non-academic audience. Accordingly it grants considerable room for background explanation wherever this is deemed necessary though, hopefully, withouth overcomplicating the flow of reading.

2. Compete and campaign: Conceptualizing electoral politicization of migration and ethnic relations

Migration and ethnic relations are characteristic phenomena of societies past and present. They shape the composition of people bound together in social and political entities, thereby stimulating and transforming conceptions of national community. However, their translation into politically relevant issues is by no means a natural, obvious process. In fact, a central concern of political research is when and how social phenomena turn into politically relevant issues and become subject to political regulation. With the emergence of modern democracies starting in the 19th century, the process of organizing societies into democratic polities became linked to a specific type of actor, namely political parties. Parties adopted a central role in delivering the input necessary for the political executive to implement the interests of its *demos*, and despite certain indications of their decline (Clarke/Stewart 1998; Drummond 2006; Whiteley 2011; van Biezen et al. 2012), they still continue to fulfill this core function today. In contrast to other intermediary actors (such as syndicates, unions, NGOs, grassroots, etc.), political parties address a broad range of issues and have become the main source for recruiting legislative and executive personnel in most Western democracies. Thus analysis of parties' politicization not only reveals socially relevant issues within a polity, but also indicates which issues are most likely to become objects of policy regulation in the first place. Moreover, in the increasingly media-saturated Western democracies, party politicization has become a major means of political orientation both for the electorate and, even more importantly, for journalistic gatekeepers by virtue of highlighting the relevance of particular sets of policy questions and thereby setting a political agenda (Konstantinidis 2008; McCombs 2008; Hopmann et al. 2010).

The present study uses *party politicization* to refer to a party-induced process of publicly addressing socially relevant issues according to the need for their political regulation (Zürn 2011; de Wilde/Zürn 2012). It is not limited to the narrower meaning of 'mobilization' commonly used in political sociology to refer to the process of stimulating people, groups, classes, etc. to engage in specific forms of political action (e.g. Rothschild 1981; Olzak 1984; Vanden 2003).[2] It also differs from its usage in other research contexts, in which politicization can denote 'functional competences' in order to address the responsibility of the political system as opposed to other systems such as jurisprudence, economy, etc. – either by describing a process of competence shifts toward political authority

---

[2] For example, in his book "Ethnopolitics", Joseph Rothschild sketches politicization as follows: "To politicize ethnicity is (1) to render people cognitively aware of the relevance of politics to the health of their ethnic cultural values and vice versa, (2) to stimulate their concern about this nexus, (3) to mobilize them into self-conscious ethnic groups, and (4) to direct their behaviour toward activity in the political arena on the basis of awareness, concern, and group consciousness" (Rothschild 1981: 6).

as opposed to juridification, economization, etc. (e.g. Schulze 2006), or referring to growing political influence and control in other systems (e.g. Ronge 2003). Finally, the study's use of the term politicization also differs from that of authors who use it in a broader sense to refer to all phases of the policy cycle (e.g. Hooghe/Marks 2008). Although these approaches are obviously closely linked to the concept of politicization that underlies this study, it is nevertheless important to isolate the issue-related aspect of the term, since publicly addressing an issue with regard to its political regulation need not necessarily be tied to mobilization attempts or competence shifts. This study argues that it is crucial to maintain a distinction between setting an issue on a political agenda and whether and how the issue is finally submitted to the actual process of policy and law-making. Thus the agenda setting and framing aspects of politicization have to be isolated in analysis, particularly when focusing on the electoral arena, since building a political agenda is as much a central characteristic of political parties as influencing public and media agendas is (McCombs 2008).

As a consequence, this study relies on a concept of issue competition in electoral contexts that is well established (Robertson 1976, Budge/Farlie 1983, Carmines/Stimson 1993; Petrocik 1996; Budge et al. 2001; Green-Pedersen 2007a): the notion that party competition is a struggle over issues, i.e. it consists of identifying and promoting winning issues, avoiding or depoliticizing disadvantageous issues, and undercutting opponents' issues. Hence the electoral race, especially, is tied to this notion of issue competition, which at its root is opposed to that of positional competition (prototypically suggested by Anthony Downs), wherein parties compete on the same set of issues by promoting different positions. However, a number of studies have demonstrated that these two notions need not necessarily be mutually exclusive, but rather may be merely different aspects of competition (Riker 1996; van der Brug 2001; Green-Pedersen 2007a; Green-Pedersen/Mortensen 2010). Accordingly, this book builds on this dual notion and thus integrates both dimensions into a single coherent concept of party politicization as a competition over issues and positions alike. This necessitates a thorough discussion of the conditions that structure this process, which is why the theoretical framework explains the main characteristics of political parties as electoral agents, as well as the factors that can affect parties' politicization strategies.

This chapter will solidify this theoretical basis in three steps. In the first step, it will introduce conceptions of party goals, i.e. what motivates parties in electoral competition (section 2.1). Based on these, it will then discuss basic theories on the strategies used by parties in their competition for issues and positions (section 2.2). Thirdly, these general hypotheses will be applied to the specific issues of migration and ethnic relations to develop assumptions about the patterns of politicization that might be expected in these policy fields (section 2.3).

2.1   Part of a system: Individual parties in party competition

With the spread of early types of modern political parties, the character, functions and organization of these growing entities became the subject of scholarly discussion. Although initially it focused primarily on "cadre parties", the predominating early form, (Krouwel 2012: 4), the debate anticipated key elements of the motives and limitations of party behavior that have remained valid up to the present. Functionalist views regarded the emergence of political parties as a response to growing competition of group interests in ever-expanding and diversifying societies and as performing specific functions for a polity, such as establishing links between society and government, informing people about and involving them in public matters, stimulating discussion, suggesting policies, but also providing representatives for the parliament and government (Morse 1891: 18-19). Explicitly affirmative perspectives, such as the Burkean definition of the political party as "a body of men united for promoting by their joint endeavors the national interest upon some particular principle in which they are all agreed" (Burke 1899: 530), viewed political parties as champions of social realignment and disseminators of political ideas. On a more skeptical note, however, even in the early debates on political parties it was quite common for cadre parties to be accused of patronage and corruption, while some critics were disapproving of their partisan purblindness (e.g. Richardson 1892; Lilly 1900).

Such remarks persisted even after the ascent of mass parties in the 20th century. Although a number of processes (e.g. the global diffusion of democracy, universal suffrage, and the need to organize larger electorates and parliamentary groups) led to significant changes in political parties over the last century (Duverger 1954: XXIV; Krouwel 2012), many of the underlying premises of party behavior still remain unchanged. Thus while ideology and their capacity to aggregate, stimulate and convert political issues in accordance with basic ideological principles is one vital aspect of political parties' activities, another involves strategic bargaining, maneuvering, and sacrificing principles or personnel to gain or preserve a powerful position. This antagonism has been influential for contemporary concepts of party behavior which systematize and integrate it into a framework of goals of modern parties in electoral competition, as will be elucidated in the discussion that follows.

2.1.1 Party goals: The tension between ideology and power

Although parties in the modern age differ from their precursors in various regards, with respect to parties' underlying goals, a number of contemporary authors have departed from the antagonism set forth above in analyzing the motivations driving political parties' strategies. Hence the debate in the twentieth century was shaped by two influential "party paradigms": "the rational-efficient model and the responsible parties model" (White 2006: 9). Each articulates specific forms that party goals may take, which in recent years have been elaborated into more systematic, coherent models (Strøm 1990; Müller/Strøm 1999; and Wolinetz 2002).

Rational choice concepts and the pursuit of power

Among the most influential paradigms of party behavior, the "rational-efficient model" is linked to Anthony Downs' seminal work, "Economic Theory of Democracy" (1957), which generated a comprehensive and systematic model of political competition based on economic considerations.[3] Grounded on earlier economic models of competition (Hotelling 1929; Smithies 1941), Downs' approach fruitfully combined a spatial perspective with behavioral approaches to party politics. By treating both political parties and voters as rational actors with limited choices, the paradigm focuses on strategic considerations and likely outcomes of these actors' decisions (Robertson 1976: 23). Obviously, there are various formal simplifications that must be made in order for the predictions of rational choice models to apply. Firstly, they have to treat the party as a homogeneous actor ("whose members agree on all their goals instead of on just part of them", Downs 1957: 25-6). Secondly, voters are modelled according to a "proximity logic" which assumes that a rational voter will choose the party closest to him/her on a given political dimension. Inversely, a rational party has to ensure the proximity of its own issue positions to those of "its" voters in order to secure their support.

Within this framework, actors are expected to behave strategically based on rational assessment of options and goals, which is why rational choice theories must outline initial assumptions about what, at bottom, motivates these actors (Budge/Laver 1986: 485). Since in two-party systems maximizing electoral success and winning elections is the major means to attain government responsibility, Downs originated an understanding of party goals known as *vote seeking behavior* (Müller/Strøm 1999: 8). Its most important conclusion is that political ideologies must be treated as the "means to power", since political parties should not be mistaken as "agents of specific social groups or classes; rather, they are autonomous teams seeking office *per se* and using group support to at-

---

[3] Economic theories of party behavior had obviously been expressed before, although never in such a systematic way. A famous example is Schumpeter's (1942: 283) analogy between political parties and department stores: "[...] all parties will of course, at any given time, provide themselves with a stock of principles or planks and these principles or planks may be as characteristic of the party that adopts them and as important for its success as the brands of goods a department store sells are characteristic of it and important for its success. But the department store cannot be defined in terms of its brands and a party cannot be defined in terms of its principles. A party is a group whose members propose to act in concert in the competitive struggle for political power."

tain that end" (Downs 1957: 97).[4] Securing a maximum of popular support thus becomes the main objective guiding the competitive strategies of parties, which accordingly attempt to identify the issues and positions that promise the largest share of the electorate.

Particularly in the realm of coalition theory, the notion of a vote-seeking strategy is juxtaposed with a perspective that subordinates vote-seeking to the objective of gaining executive power, a distinction that is already present in Downs' work but not pursued systematically. *Office-seeking behavior* puts its "primary emphasis on securing government office, even if it is at the expense of policy goals or maximizing votes. Office-seeking parties either seek to hold power alone, or more realistically (in the context of the systems in which they operate) to share power with others" (Wolinetz 2002: 152). This differs from a vote-seeking strategy both in the resulting policy positions as well as in the mode of confrontation with opponents. In party systems that necessitate the formation of coalition governments, an office-seeking party should try to remain a viable coalition partner and thus should temper its electoral attacks on potential partners and avoid policy claims that make it seem like an intolerable coalition partner while still gaining sufficient votes to be a relevant force (Wolinetz 2002: 152). Thus the distinction between vote-seeking and office-seeking behavior stands out most prominently when comparing two-party systems with multi-party systems. While maximizing votes brings an automatic increase in chances of gaining office in two-party contexts (thus making office-seeking merely a function of successful vote-seeking behavior), these strategies become diverging options in multi-party settings (Adams et al. 2004: 589).

What unites office-seeking and vote-seeking concepts of party behavior is that they subsume parties' policy choices under strategic conceptions of power (either in terms of electorate size or in terms of governing authority). A scholarly examination of party politicization, then, must to consider the basic conditions prevailing in party competition (such as the number of competing parties, their expected strength, their coalition potential, etc.); sections 3.2.2 and 3.2.3 will carefully evaluate these variables in the Austrian case.

Ideology and policy pursuit

In sharp contrast to the strategies derived from a rational-efficient paradigm, another theoretical approach highlights how political parties develop as actors and attempt to achieve specific political goals or ideology in a broader sense: "*Policy-seeking parties* are issue-oriented and, quite simply, give priority to their policies" (Wolinetz 2002: 150).[5] Scholarly conceptions of policy-oriented party

---

[4] Interestingly, Downs himself already points to the discursive nature of ideological formations, defining them "as a verbal image of the good society and of the chief means of constructing such a society" (Downs 1957: 96).

[5] Italics inserted by author and not present in the original text.

goals have come from various directions. Such suggestions can be found in early definitions of political parties (Burke 1899), but also characterized theories from the 20th century, such as the "responsible parties school". Stimulated by Schattschneider's (1942) work on political parties and party government, it argued that only competition between parties responsible for programs to which they committed themselves could lead to an effective party system (APSA 1950: 18). Hence, parties sticking to a "coherent set of ideas" would not only offer clear choices to voters in issue-based electoral competition, but could also be held accountable for their policy output once they were in office (White 2006: 10). Another stimulus for policy-oriented concepts came from coalition studies, in which they were developed to overcome the "policy-blind axioms" of earlier studies on government and coalition building that underrated the importance of ideological proximity in this process (Strøm 1990: 567).

Most prominently, however, a concept of policy-oriented behavior is inherent to cleavage theory, which argues that social conflicts, demands and pressures become effectively translated into democratic politics only through the formation of political parties (Lipset/Rokkan 1967: 5). Political parties, then, are just one potent kind of actor among others that associates a social divide with a particular set of values or identities and brings them into the political realm (Sartori 1990: 169-70). Cleavages, which serve as important distinctions between social groups based on fundamental socio-structural characteristics, are used as much to appeal to a common identity shared by the members of such a group as to translate such a collective identity into an "organizational expression, whether through a political party, a trade union, a church, or some other body" (Mair 2006: 373). Thus issue preferences and positions turn into characteristic hallmarks for political parties by which they can be categorized into different ideological or party "families". These preferences structure party behavior, especially within the context of competition, and political parties "apply these ideologies to the issues of the day in order to generate preferred solutions, which they advocate in election campaigns as one way of attracting or consolidating their vote" (Budge 2006: 422).

Such a conception expects the policy positions of political parties to remain relatively stable along existing social cleavages and to change only as a consequence of transformations in the cleavage structure. Although political cleavages are characterized by continuity,[6] they are liable to weaken or change under certain circumstances, such as an erosion of the real-world conditions on which they are founded, weakening of the common identity of affected social groups, or decreasing interest on the part of organizations in translating the conflict

---

[6] This is because cleavages usually remain stable and basic patterns of the political system –
    such as the electoral system, parliamentary system, and institutional setting – favour the
    cleavages of those parties that were founding powers of the system and continue to trans-
    late them into actual politics.

(Mair 2006: 374; Mair et al. 2004: 3). Given that voters more readily switch between parties than across cleavages (Mair 2006: 373-4), established parties may be pressured by the emergence of new or revived cleavages and other parties addressing them. Thus the distinction between mainstream and niche parties has grown to be of vital importance for comprehending contemporary issue-based party competition. In recent decades many Western democracies have witnessed growth in their available electorates and situations in which formerly minor parties have achieved considerable competitive strength (Mair et al. 2004: 5). For these niche parties, such as Green or radical right parties, for example, it has become a winning formula to identify new, appealing issues and to popularize these issues and positions accordingly (Riker 1986; de Lange 2007; Meguid 2008; de Vries/Hobolt 2012). By raising the salience of new lines of conflict they are able to carve out their own ideological niches in which established mainstream parties at the center-right and center-left (such as Labor or Social Democratic parties and Conservative or Christian Democratic parties [Adams et al. 2006: 513]), have not declared particular ideological interests. From this perspective, then, party behavior is mainly based on the pursuit of issues and policy positions that reflect the core values and belief systems of a political party. Thus parties' ideological foundations and policy preferences constitute the main explanatory factor. In section 4.2.1 this perspective is discussed in more detail and applied to the Austrian party system.

Of course, these different types of party objectives – votes, office and policy – represent ideal types that hardly ever exist in their pure form. While every party needs some core of ideology that it will not sacrifice to its thirst for power, parties can hardly be effective if they solely and unchangingly promulgate their core positions regardless of the electoral will or the issue positions of their competitors.[7] Hence parties will consolidate and develop these goals; the more established the party, the more clearly its objectives will be formulated. And while there may be examples of the successful integration of all three objectives, the most common situation is instead one of trading off one goal against the others (Müller/Strøm 1999: 11-2; Wolinetz 2002: 153). Changes to party goals are most likely to occur when the patterns of the competitive system, e.g. the electorate's preferences, the composition of the party spectrum, the competitors' strength, or the dominant lines of conflict, are in flux. Under such changing conditions of competition, the options for political parties to adapt their behavior are manifold. As Mair et al. (2004) point out, established parties may choose not to respond at all, either because they are not aware of these changes or because they underestimate their importance (Mair et al. 2004: 10). If, on the other hand, parties do correctly identify important changes in the electoral system and increasing competitive pressure as calls to action, they may, for example, redefine

---

[7] This circumstance is obviously much more pronounced in multi-party systems than it is in two-party systems.

their primary electoral target groups, abandon lost voters, or define new targets in the electoral arena. In a multi-party system they may also respond on the inter-party level by modifying their stances toward their opponents (e.g. by creating new alliances or inciting controversy with other parties) in order to attract new voters and to broaden their coalition perspectives. Whatever strategic response a party might choose, it generally implies changes in the selection of issues or policy positions, or both (Mair et al. 2004: 10).

As issue-based party competition is the focus of this study, the following sections will examine how these different motives might be expected to translate into electoral politicization strategies. The first step in this direction is to clarify how party politicization in electoral competition can be captured in the first place. What are the main indicators of parties' strategic use of political issues in competition? The next section lays a basic foundation by examining spatial perspectives on party competition and discusses how they might be used to grasp politicization.

2.1.2 Spatial perspectives on party competition

While a party can be analyzed as a single entity by itself, in order to evaluate party competition it is necessary to expand the perspective to a party's location in the broader picture of the party system. As Sartori (1976: 44) emphasized, the etymology of the term "party" itself indicates the idea of a part of a larger whole, a party system shaped by the interaction between multiple parties. Most commonly, party system analyses examine the number of competing parties, their strength, their ideological positions, the issue dimensions on which competition takes place, and the party coalition options (Blondel 1968: 183; Wolinetz 2006: 53). A party system, then, comprises the interactions between organizations that show a certain degree of persistence, i.e. that are institutionalized and tied to specific electorates that they claim to represent (Mainwaring/Torcal 2006: 205).

Spatial perspectives have come to play an essential role in the observation of party competition. They have not only emerged as the best tool for party politics scholars to model and analyze competition among parties within a system, but are also the most widespread way of talking about politics in the general public: it is common for people to speak of "where key actors stand on substantive matters at issue" (Benoit/Laver 2006: 11). Analyzing politics in terms of parties' positions on specific political issues allows the comparison of their positions to identify similarities and differences. Spatial representation of the political arena usually states the degree of similarity between actors' positions in numerical terms. Since this provides researchers with the means to measure changes in the positions of political parties as well as the electorate, a spatial lens has become the most widespread approach in contemporary research on party competition (Laver/Hunt 1992; Budge et al. 2001; Bara/Weale 2006; Volkens et al. 2013).

Therefore, much scholarly effort has been devoted to measuring and modelling competition in spatial terms, most prominently using the left-right (spatial) analogy.[8] Although there is no inherent necessity of using a (bipolar) spatial analogy to describe patterns of party competition, its widespread use is mainly the result of three factors: "historical accident, ease of visualization and, by now, convention" (Laver/Hunt 1992: 11). The analogy has been used as a means to capture the arrangement of competing interests in politics and their gradual movements toward one or the other of two extreme poles. Its application has been extended to ideological lines of conflict in party competition other than the traditional left-right axis, and also expanded into multi-dimensional spaces, though always founded on the basic premise that "most policy preferences can be described as having a particular position on a line, or dimension, joining the two ideological poles" (Laver/Hunt 1992: 12-3). Of course, since the very beginning, the use of spatial analogies of party competition has also met with criticism, often focusing on the oversimplification of single-dimensional models, or even objecting that "political complexities cannot be mapped spatially at all" (Budge 2006: 423). Indeed, policy dimensions will always remain only approximations of reality, i.e. scientific models that represent an interrelation of points on axes defined by the scholar. It is exactly due to this "relativity" of spatial maps of political competition that their designs can vary significantly between different approaches (see Chapter 4).

Nonetheless, since the aim of this book is to longitudinally compare party positions and shifts on the particular issues of migration and ethic relations, a spatial perspective serves as the best available tool for this task. However, a spatial description of party competition is no more than a means to describe patterns of conflict, and in itself offers no cogent information about parties' motives and strategies within these spaces. Thus, in order to develop assertions about parties' actual strategies of electoral politicization of migration and ethnic relations, subsequently we need to link these spatial frameworks to theories about how parties utilize issues and positions to compete in the struggle over policy, votes and office.

Downs' standard model of party competition

As mentioned previously, analyses of rational party behavior in spatial terms generally reference Anthony Downs as an originator of standard spatial models of party competition. His confrontational conception of party competition as the struggle between different positions within a space defined by the dominant is-

---

[8] Stemming from the historical seating arrangement in the post-revolutionary French Constituent Assembly of 1789 (with conservatives placing themselves to the right of the Chair and radicals to the left), the distinction between left and right, together with the notion of an undefined political centre, has become an established way of describing both positions of political actors as well as citizens' preferences (Laver & Hunt 1992: 8-9).

sues of a polity has influenced spatial analysis up to the present day. In connection with this approach, Downs has also become influential for his perspective on how vote-seeking parties will likely behave within this framework of competition. Based on the proximity argument (that voters opt for the parties closest to their own positions), his most frequently quoted assertion is the "median voter theorem", which states that in two-party competition, parties will move toward each other, a pattern that eventually leads to what has been described as "Tweedledum-Tweedledee" political competition between center-oriented major parties offering voters little choice. For the individual parties, such a centripetal strategy is a rational decision because they can expect that even if they move toward the center, extremist voters on their side of the spectrum will still prefer them over the opponent. By moving toward the opposite side of the spectrum, a party thus enlarges its voter spectrum.[9]

In a multi-party setting, however, the expectation of centripetal party behavior becomes problematic, mainly because the maneuvring room for parties becomes tighter and they are less mobile, since they cannot make ideological leaps over their neighbors (Downs 1957: 122). Conversely, multi-party settings provide no incentive for parties to converge ideologically, as the number of lost voters roughly equals the number of voters gained. Therefore Downs asserted that "in multi-party systems, parties will strive to distinguish themselves ideologically from each other and maintain the purity of their positions; whereas in two-party systems, each party will try to resemble its opponent as closely as possible" (Downs 1957: 126). With some restrictions,[10] Sartori (1976) made similar predictions of party behavior, arguing that two-party systems differ from multi-party systems in that the latter are characterized by centrifugal dynamics, with parties moving toward the fringes of the party spectrum.[11] In a comparison of

---

[9] Admittedly, Downs qualified the argument by adding an "elastic demand at each point of the scale", considering those voters at the extremes who might detach themselves if a party's identity becomes too centrist (Downs 1957: 116-7). These limitations prevent parties from converging past the point at which they lose more voters at the extremes than they gain at the center.

[10] Sartori (1976: 346) notes that, even in two-party systems, a median-voter argument may be applied only under certain conditions: most importantly that the undecided voters are moderates and not extremists, and that the parties compete in the same issue-space.

[11] Sartori sketched similar conditions for party systems including two, three and four parties, arguing that the "competitive configuration of three-partism remains bipolar" (Sartori 1976: 348) and that four-party systems are merely "subdivided, or doubled, representation[s] of the two-party scheme", i.e. that they retain a centripetal pattern of interaction (ibid.). According to Sartori, the critical threshold for a shift towards a centrifugal pattern is reached with five or more parties, for the space is enlarged and the competition within such a space allows for greater mobility. Sartori describes this shift as the turn from "moderate" to "polarized pluralism", and argues that the emergence of three or more poles in combination with a relevant center makes convergent behavior ineffective, the presence of relevant extreme parties at the poles stimulating intensified polarization. However, as Sar-

twenty parliamentary democracies, Andrews/Money (2009) empirically demonstrated the accuracy of Sartori's prediction by presenting evidence that an increasing number of parties leads to greater ideological dispersion.[12]

These traditional assumptions have obviously been subject to critique and modification both on empirical as well as theoretical grounds. Conflicting findings (for a discussion see Budge 2006: 426-7) have raised questions about some of the early standard spatial assumptions. For example, the basic motive of rational-efficient party behavior was cast in doubt by early observations that the policy positions of political parties tend to be more extreme than those of their voters (Converse 1975). Moreover, findings from longitudinal studies of post-war democracies showed that parties (at the election level) do not converge, but rather stick to relatively stable issue positions in multi-party as well as two-party systems (Budge 1994; Adams 2001). Thus the presumption that parties would orient toward the median voter did not prove to be valid, and party behavior fitted instead into a cleavage-based model. McDonald et al. (2004b) supported these findings with further empirical evidence and concluded that party responses were more strongly linked to ideology than to any other factor. Adams et al. (2004) also highlighted the importance of parties' ideologies, although they additionally assigned a significant role in influencing parties' policy positions to public opinion, especially in the case of "disadvantaged parties", i.e. parties that adjusted their ideologies when public opinion clearly shifted away from their previous position. In addition to the conflicting empirical findings, objections have also been raised from a conceptual standpoint that focus either on spatial designs in general (e.g. criticizing the insufficiency of unidimensional rational models for capturing complex political behavior; see Green/Shapiro 1994) or on the type of party competition described, as most convincingly presented by "directional models" and "salience theory" of party competition.

Conceptual extensions and alternatives

As regards the conceptual level, important extensions of standard spatial concepts arose out of "directional models" of party competition, which were developed by Matthews (1979), Rabinowitz/MacDonald (1989), and Macdonald et al. (1991). Their objections to previous models hinged on assertions that the issue criteria by which voters evaluate parties vary rather than being uniform and, even more importantly, that voters have no precise policy interests but rather simply favor one side of an issue debate over the other (Macdonald et al. 1991: 1108). Thus a directional model makes no room for a variety of policy positions

---

tori emphasizes, the potential for expansion and polarization is limited, because eventually a party spectrum will either collapse due to overstretch or begin to shrink once more (Sartori 1976: 348.)

[12] This increase levels off at five parties; dispersion remains the same or may even decrease in party systems with six or more parties.

on an issue continuum; instead every issue is conceptualized as a dichotomous choice around a neutral center position. Unlike the median voter theorem, directional models assign relevance to the direction of divergence, since voters might not evaluate a party at all if it holds a centrist position on an issue. Accordingly, parties are expected to take strong positions on issues and to avoid the center in order to increase mobilization (Macdonald et al. 1991: 1107). Moreover, voters are expected to choose only those parties which they consider most likely to advocate policy changes in their preferred direction, leading to greater party divergence rather than convergence in politicization (Hinich et al. 2004: 37). Consequently, the anticipated behavior should more closely match a model of "conflict- or cleavage-oriented politics" (Macdonald et al. 1991: 1126), in which parties put more emphasis on "their" core electorate's policy issues and directions and prioritize voter affect over rational cost-benefit calculations. However, empirical evidence of the comparative tenability of proximity and directional models does not clearly favor one over the other. While Macdonald et al. (1991) asserted the superiority of the directional model, empirical evidence from other studies suggests that although party positions in European democracies usually deviate from a median voter position, they are not as polarized as the directional model would suggest (Dalton 1985; Iversen 1994; Adams/Merrill 1999; Karp/Banducci 2002). Hence the debate over proximity vs. directional models has remained lively up to the present day and is only ever conciliated by suggestions of combined or unified approaches (Iversen 1994; Merill/Grofman 1999; Green-Pedersen 2007a).

A very similar critique of the Downsian model stems from another strand of research, namely "salience theory" (most prominently implemented by the Comparative Manifesto Project, CMP, see Budge et al. 2001; Klingemann et al. 2006). Here, emphasis is put not only on changes in party proximity, but also on parties' manipulation of favorable policy dimensions in general. The core argument of salience theory is that different parties are associated in the different policy areas with generally desirable goals. Consequently, parties' competitive strategies might be better described in terms of the different priorities they attach to specific issues than by a confrontational interpretation of parties holding different positions on all policy issues (which is in fact the core assumption underlying unidimensional left-right scales). According to Budge/Farlie (1983), parties follow a strategy of "selective emphasis", highlighting mainly those issues that correspond with the qualities ascribed to them by voters and addressing unfavorable issues only marginally, if at all. These perceived competences have been captured by the concept of "issue ownership" (Carmines/Stimson 1993; Ansolabehere/Iyengar 1994; Petrocik 1996), which refers to a political party's "reputation for policy and program interests, produced by a history of attention, initiative, and innovation toward these problems, which leads voters to believe that one of the parties (and its candidates) is more sincere and committed to doing something about them" (Petrocik 1996: 826). Admittedly Budge/Farlie

(1983) pointed to the possible links to confrontational models and salience theory, arguing that the two models of party competition are not mutually exclusive, but they assigned a greater role overall to "selective emphasis" (Budge/Farlie 1983: 270).

Regardless of the ambiguous empirical evidence, both directional models and salience theory highlight the importance of the emphasis a party grants to a certain issue. Moreover, both concepts expect centrifugal behavior to be the predominant mode in electoral politicization because center positions are ill-suited for voter mobilization. This supports the conjecture that ideology and cleavage-based "issue ownership" might be the major points of reference for parties in choosing their competition strategies, in particular when considering their limited information regarding voters' actual will (Pardos-Prado 2011). A party can compensate for these uncertainties by sticking to its core ideology, since that ideology serves as a benchmark or orientation for both politicians and voters: "As it often defines itself by contrast to other ideologies, it provides a way of defining and partitioning policy space and of indicating the broad area within which a particular party should take its position" (Budge 1994: 446).

To sum up, so far a number of factors have been identified that influence and structure party behavior on any given issue dimension of political competition. Not only do spatial models of issue competition describe the "proximity" between voters' and parties' issue positions as a crucial factor, but when informed by "directional models", they also account for the direction of divergence. Since movement toward a centrist position carries the risk of losing voters, whose preferences for policy directions are usually diffuse, directional models anticipate centrifugal, divergent tendencies rather than convergent party behavior. However, as noted by salience theory, these expectations do not hold true for every issue with every party. In fact, different strategies for different parties are to be expected depending on whether or not an issue is associated with a party's ideological profile (i.e. whether it possesses *issue ownership*). If not, it is more probable that the party will, instead of shifting its position, seek to avoid addressing an issue at all (which may not be possible if an issue is of enormous actual significance to a society).[13]

---

[13] It is important though to keep in mind that the nature of politicization varies between different phases of the political process. While inter-election periods are characterized by a more complex and issue-specific way of dealing with policy fields (in legislatures and governments), election periods of course bring a compression of both issue complexity and issue diversity. As a consequence, not only might the debate about any single issue be condensed to general position markers, but also the competition as a whole might be compressed "into one unidimensional left-right space" (Budge 2006: 429-30).
For a more detailed discussion of the different channels of electoral politicization, see Chapter 3 of the present study.

Starting from these preliminary inferences from theories on spatial competition, it is possible to design an integrated approach for analyzing politicization: various examples have been suggested in recent years. Thus the next section is dedicated to discussion of an integrated model of party politicization and the extraction of analytical tools for the purposes of this study (2.2.1), and applies those tools to the particular context of migration and ethnic relations, linking to recent literature on party strategies in that context (2.2.2).

2.2 Party politicization of migration and ethnic relations: An analytical framework

It is apparent that party competition in contemporary democracies can be analyzed on various levels, with politicization being only one instrument among many. However, issue competition, i.e. the contest over which issues will dominate the political agenda (Green-Pedersen 2007a), has become an increasingly important factor in party competition in recent decades. Electoral campaigns have become far more issue-based in the sense that parties do not simply respond to "'natural' changes in the electorate" but rather try to popularize new and winning issues themselves at the cost of established parties, which seek "to defend the importance of their old issues" (Mair et al. 2004: 6-7). Similarly, Meguid (2008) pointed to the important shift in electoral circumstances since the early spatial models of Anthony Downs, arguing that from the 1970s on Western European democracies have produced patterns "of issue-based party competition [...] where voters cast their ballots based on policies, rather than class loyalties or partisanship" (Meguid 2008: 23-4). In many European democracies this transformation was accompanied by a rising number of political parties addressing new political issues and cleavages to attract a similarly rising number of "realigning" voters (Dalton et al. 1984; Mair 1990). These newly emerging niche parties were particularly keen on those issues that cut across established cleavages, which is why much of their attention has been centered on migration and ethnic relations. As a consequence, models of politicization that not only integrate the levels of politicization mentioned above (issues & positions), but also reflect the particularities of competition between mainstream and niche parties are of especial importance for an analysis in the context of migration and ethnic relations.

2.2.1 Toward an integrated model of politicization: Combining issues and positions

In order to meet these requirements, first of all, suggestions for integrated concepts that include the role of both issues and positions alike are necessary. As Green-Pedersen (2007a: 610) pointed out, "[e]ven though issue competition and positional competition are different forms of competition, they do not exclude each other." On the contrary, they may very well be linked as two aspects of one complex process of party competition. On a similar note, Meguid (2008) suggested an integrative approach to party competition for the age of increasingly mobile voters, whose decisions to support or abandon a party are shaped by three basic considerations: a) whether a "party's issue is considered salient, or important", b) whether a "party's position on a given issue is attractive", and c) whether a "party is perceived to be the rightful 'owner' of that policy stance" (Meguid 2008: 24). By integrating the three aspects of salience, position and ownership into one model, Meguid aimed to overcome the deficiencies of standard spatial theory.

Based on these three pillars, Meguid described party politicization, and in particular competition between mainstream parties and niche party challengers, as an interaction of three strategic options, two of which *(I / II)* involve altering the party's position on the issue in question. When a political party is confronted with opponents trying to politicize certain issues to its disadvantage, it is limited to two options: "[...] movement toward *(policy convergence)* or movement away from *(policy divergence)* a specific competitor", which Meguid termed an *accommodative strategy* (I) and an *adversarial strategy* (II), respectively (Meguid 2008: 24). However, positional shifts in themselves are insufficient as long as they are communicated only marginally, which is why they need to be linked to an increase in salience in order to signal the issue's relevance; otherwise, the shift may not be taken into account by voters (Meguid 2008: 24-5). The role of salience in positional shifts opens up a third strategic option: to downplay the relevance of the issue by simply depoliticizing it. In order to avoid debate on issues that might be unfavorable to a party's profile, depoliticization using a *dismissive strategy* (III) often becomes even more promising than directly dealing with an opponent's positions. A dismissive strategy of depoliticization thus goes beyond the choice of focus on issue positions by referencing a party's issue ownership (or credibility) on a specific policy issue and acknowledging the fact that voter decisions are heavily influenced by perceptions of who owns the issue in question. This fact has been overlooked by the proximity model of standard spatial theory, which assumes indifference on the part of voters to their policy options as long as those options are equidistant (Meguid 2008: 26). The role of ownership is of particular importance in competition between mainstream and niche parties: While mainstream parties generally draw on a broad spectrum of issues, the opportunities of niche parties are usually limited to a narrow range of issues that are orthogonal to traditional issues; hence establishing salience for these new issues is vitally important to niche parties' success (ibid.).

Meguid's distinction between position, salience and ownership together with her threefold set of strategies offers a strong basis for analyzing individual party politicization of issues, and is in line with the models of other scholars who highlight salience and position as primary instruments of strategic competition over political issues. William Downs' (2001) analysis of mainstream parties' responses to radical right success, for example, very generally distinguished between strategies of *engagement* (i.e. "co-opting" or "collaborating") and *disengagement* (i.e. "ignoring" or "isolating"), arguing that among the various levels of party response,[14] convergence in discourse would be the first sign prior to any actual collaboration. More recently, Bale et al. (2010) have also suggested a model for party behavior when a new political issue or party emerges on the stage of party competition, distinguishing three types of strategies for established parties similar to those discussed by Downs and Meguid. According to them, an old party that is disadvantaged by the emergence of a new issue might attempt to "defuse" the issue in order to cut the competitive ground out from under the new party opponent. If, however, an established party engages with a new competitor, it must choose between two options, either maintaining an oppositional stance or adopting an issue position that approximates that of the new competitor. Table 1 collects these various models and heuristically extracts the common denominators in the way they describe party behavior when new issues are emphasized by new parties.

Table 1:   Issue-based strategic responses to an opponent's success

Downs (2001)	Ignoring	Isolating	Co-opting	Collaborating
Meguid (2008)	Dismissive strategy	Adversarial strategy	Accommodative strategy	
Bale et al (2010)	Defuse	Hold (opposing position)	Adopt	
Heuristic description	Party downplays the salience of the issue by depoliticizing it	Party challenges the opponent by overtly politicizing opposing issue positions	Party aligns its issue positions & the ascribed issue salience toward the opponent's preferences	

Note: This table is of heuristic nature and aims to pin down the common denominators of the strategies outlined by the various models. Thus not every feature of each strategy is considered; only a rough description of their common thrust is given.

These response strategies, obviously, are only useful to those parties which originally lack ownership of the newly introduced issue and which are obliged to respond to its emergence and successful emphasis by a challenger. Conversely, parties that do possess ownership from the start will continue to stick to the issues that help them to carve out their niche as long as they do not suffer serious setbacks. This is an important distinction between mainstream and niche parties in the context of migration and ethnic relations.

---

[14] An analysis of party response strategy can focus on "bargaining impacts" (i.e. an actor's capacity to influence the process of government building), on "policy impacts" (i.e. measurable shifts of policy output that can be linked to an actor's ability to pressure governing parties or to participate in governing coalitions itself), or on "discourse impacts" (i.e. a measurable shift of policy formulation strategies).

Linking party motives to strategies of politicization

Strategies of politicization, obviously, are no end in themselves. They are means to achieve the underlying party goals that drive parties' calculations in inter-party competition. Thus this study argues, that in order to comprehend party politicization it is crucial to link these two dimensions more clearly than has been done in previous studies. Do parties purely promote their core ideologies? Do they respond to previous gains or losses at the ballot box? Do they factor in even potential chances of entering government coalitions? Drawing a line between parties' underlying motives in competition and their strategies of politicization helps to make parties' competitive behavior more comprehensible. This study attempts a typology of party politicization in the context of emerging issues that includes both niche and mainstream parties (which is summarized in Table 2).

Building on the foundation of the concept of issue ownership, a party can generally be linked to a specific set of issues that are attached to its ideology and profile. It will likely accord high salience to issues that it owns, and its position on those issues will remain clear-cut and in accordance with the party's core ideology. As long as it prioritizes a policy-seeking motive, it will have no incentives to change its approach and thus will stick to its position and level of emphasis, a strategy that can be labeled *ideological emphasis* (thus this is the default strategy of newcomer parties exploiting new issues). Even prioritizing a vote-seeking or office-seeking perspective, a party will maintain its default strategy as long as it continues to be rewarded with an increasing vote share or improving chances of becoming part of a government coalition or both (1&2). Only when its ideological emphasis either turns out to be costly at the ballot box or diminishes the party's attractiveness as a coalition partner will it be forced to change its strategy. In either case, it will most likely avoid changing its position (as this would interfere with its ownership) and instead cut the salience of the issue in its appeals in order to overcome the experienced deficits (3&4): a strategy of *depoliticization*.

The more interesting and difficult case, however, is when a party lacks ownership of the issue. In this case the most obvious strategy is to depoliticize a disadvantageous issue, which is the default strategy for established parties vis-à-vis emerging issues that cut across traditional cleavages. When other parties succeed in politicizing a new and unfamiliar issue, however, an established party has three different options for strategic competition: It may continue to depoliticize the issue, it may actively confront the new competitor by increasing salience and taking oppositional stances, i.e. a strategy of *adversarial politicization*, or it may join the competitor in its high-salience politicization of a common issue position, i.e. a strategy of *accommodative politicization*. These strategies are mediated by the party's underlying motives, since parties likely to sacrifice their previous positions and emphasis in the face of changing patterns of competition are primarily those driven by vote-seeking and office-seeking motives, whereas parties that prioritize policy will be largely unperturbed. If vote-seeking considerations prevail, accommodative politicization is most likely to come from those parties that have suffered the most from voter migration to the challenging party (6), whereas otherwise a party will most likely continue to depoliticize the issue as long as it remains itself unaffected by serious voter defection (5). Conversely, if office-seeking considerations and coalition potential are the predominant driving motive, accommodative politicization is only to be expected if the joint coalition potential between a party and its challenger increases (7), whereas parties will most likely opt for adversarial politicization if they are threatened by an opposing coalition that includes the challenger (8). In most of the literature, this distinction is traced back to the parties' ideological proximity, i.e. whether the challenger is an ideological neighbor or opponent, since both the shared electorate and the coalition attractiveness is more of a factor in the former case than in the latter.

Table 2:   Party politicization of emerging political issues – a typology

Previous electoral experience	Politicization strategy
Niche parties (by default *Ideological emphasis*)	
1: Increase in party vote share 2: Increase in party's coalition options	*Ideological emphasis*
3: Decrease in party vote share 4: Decrease in party's coalition options	*Depoliticization*
Mainstream parties (by default *Depoliticization*)	
5: Gains in party vote share	*Depoliticization*
6: Losses in party vote share (vis-à-vis main challenger) 7: Increase in party's coalition options (vis-à-vis main challenger)	*Accommodative politicization (vis-à-vis main challenger)*
8: Decrease in party's coalition options (vis-à-vis main challenger)	*Adversarial politicization (vis-à-vis main challenger)*

Note: Table classifies the strategies available to a party based on previous electoral outcome. It considers only those niche parties which have an ideological interest in the emerging issue (since any others are of less relevance in competition on this issue).

In the next section, these expectations will be linked to concrete examples of party strategies on the particular issues of migration and ethnic relations. Thus the section tackles the following questions: What are the patterns of ownership as regards issues of migration and ethnic relations? Which parties are put under pressure by opponents emphasizing these issues? How will these parameters determine individual parties' strategies of politicization? By discussing recent literature and its conflicting conclusions regarding party strategies in the realm of migration and ethnic relations, the section underlines the need for a more coherent framework to link parties' motives to their strategies of politicization on these particular issues.

2.2.2 Politicization of migration and ethnic relations: Lessons from previous research

In recent decades, migration and ethnic relations have become major issues across Western democracies, and political parties have been strongly linked to this development. As Triadafilopoulos/Zaslove (2006: 189) put it, "[...] immigration is an issue which parties on the left and right can use to define their identities, engender coalitions, or co-opt rivals". Thus if we neglect to think of political parties as critical nodes for migration politics and especially politicization, we overlook major actors responsible for "the increasingly deep cleavages on migration-related issues in contemporary liberal democracies" (ibid.). Perusing the scholarly literature on parties and migration, however, it becomes strikingly evident that the vast majority of analysis departs from one particular angle of the political spectrum, which has become a sort of heartland of party politicization of migration issues: anti-immigrant radical right parties.

The contagion thesis as a common reference

Among the authors engaged in research on party competition on migration and ethnic relations, many have tied the growing politicization of these issues to the emergence of increasingly active radical right parties all over Europe (e.g. Kitschelt/McGann 1997; Downs 2001; Bale 2003; Norris 2005; Schain 2006). It has to be critically remarked here that this predominant focus on anti-immigrant parties and their impact has obscured somewhat the potential effects of pro-immigrant parties, which began to appear in Western democracies around the late 1970s (Triadafilopoulos/Zaslove 2006; Meyer/Peintinger 2011). Due probably to their more limited success in shaping party discourse than radical right parties, the role of Green and libertarian parties has only recently come to greater prominence in party-related research on migration politics. Emerging anti-immigrant parties, on the other hand, were already receiving considerable scholarly attention in the late 1980s, such as that to the French National Front's impact on the rhetoric of established parties and in particular of the center right (e.g. Schain 1987). Since then, a number of authors have carried on the debate, even though until the 1990s there remained some expectation that mainstream parties would stick to a "hidden consensus" and depoliticize migration in order to organize policy as far away from public attention as possible (Freeman 1995: 884). Confronted with evidence to the contrary, however, Harmel/Svasand (1997: 335) concluded that the success of anti-immigrant parties had in fact caused a general shift to the right among established parties during the 1990s, and the underlying finding of discursive contagion was explicitly confirmed by Pettigrew (1998: 95). Eatwell (2000: 423-4) strengthened this point by stating that the radical right had only been legitimized through political discourse becoming increasingly "contaminated by its themes, notably ones related to immigration". Minkenberg (2002: 18-9) similarly emphasized that extreme-right parties effectively transformed political discourse in Western European democracies, including mainstream parties' statements on migration and ethnic relations,

whereas Norris (2005: 263-9) further substantiated the magnitude of the contagion effect, particularly on European center-right parties. After the turn of the
millennium, authors began to focus more actively on mainstream parties' behavior and the electorate itself, highlighting the effects of competition between center-right and radical right parties (as well as the center right's advances toward
the radical right) on the voters' evaluations of radical right parties (van der Brug
et al. 2005: 560-1). In some cases, center-right mainstream parties even man-
aged to effectively curtail the radical right's success, once their own ideology
had shifted to the right (Carter 2005: 131-5).

Thus investigations of a contagion effect of European anti-immigrant parties on
party competition in general as well as on center-right parties specifically have
been a rewarding branch of research for the development of theories on party
behavior as well. However, as Schain (2008: 469) pointed out, "the strategic decisions of [both] the left and the center-right are made in the context of a party
system, in which the decisions of one influence those of the other. The emergence of a party of the extreme right vastly complicates this strategic relationship". The success of radical right parties in politicizing migration and ethnic
relations has affected the remaining party spectrum in more ways than early research on mainstream party contagion suggested. As a consequence, in the last
decade, the ongoing and increasing success of radical right parties in European
democracies in shaking off their previous pariah status and even being included
in government coalitions (such as in Italy, Austria, Denmark, Norway, and the
Netherlands; see de Lange 2012) has stimulated scholars to develop more systematic approaches to analyzing parties' strategies, in particular those of mainstream parties, in the context of migration and ethnic relations.

Center-right parties and their neighborly relations

Among the first scholars to systematically develop a framework for mainstream
party responses to radical right party success, Downs (2001) developed a five-
part model. He demonstrated empirically that in stable electoral environments,
Belgian local councilors with re-election ambitions chose to disengage from (i.e.
to ignore, isolate or legally restrict) the radical right pariah, whereas in cases
with greater electoral pressure, the willingness to engage (i.e. to co-opt or cooperate with) the radical right was much higher; thus office-seeking considerations
outweighed ideological concern for "clean hands". Building on this finding,
Bale (2003) similarly tried to pin down issue-specific strategies of center-right
parties under radical right pressure, again expecting them – being the closest
ideological neighbors to radical right parties – to be the first respondents to radical right success. He hypothesized that the increase in the number of post-
millennium right-bloc coalitions in European countries was preceded by a convergence of center-right parties toward their radical right counterparts, despite
the risk of helping to legitimize radical right positions on immigration and even
raising their salience (Bale 2003: 70). Drawing on qualitative observations, Bale
concluded that at least three out of five countries (Austria among them) had wit-

nessed a center-right convergence and subsequent cooperation with radical right positions (Bale 2003: 78).

Boswell/Hough (2008) reminded readers that for center-right parties, occupying the anti-immigrant space between themselves and their radical right opponents might offer more risks than gains: Not only are they in danger of losing some of their legitimacy among moderate center-right and clerical voters; they also risk programmatic dissonance by contradicting human rights commitments, business interests and supranational freedom of movement agreements; not to mention the risk of it diminishing their practical credibility once the gap between rhetoric and viable action becomes too wide. Despite these risks, Boswell/Hough's analysis of the German center-right Christian Democratic Union (CDU) showed that the party had implemented an increasingly restrictive profile on migration since the 1990s despite the fact that there hasn't even been a serious, continuous electoral threat on the German radical right.

On a similar note, van Kersbergen/Krouwel (2008: 399) portrayed politicization of immigration as a "double-edged sword" for center-right parties in the Netherlands: While they might benefit from these issues, given that they traditionally possess some ownership of restrictive approaches to national identity and questions of law & order (and can also rely on an electorate that, by and large, supports these approaches), these tendencies might also go against core values of the center-right, such as economic liberalism and Christian charity, entailing the risk of "ripping the centre-right apart". If the balance was easier to maintain before, without radical right parties exploiting these issues, the Dutch case demonstrates that center-right parties' positions become far more critical once there is serious pressure from the radical right. However, in line with Boswell/Hough (2008), van Kersbergen/Krouwel (2008) observed that shifts toward restrictiveness and assimilationism on the part of the two dominant Dutch center-right parties had started long before radical right parties' success, and that thus they cannot be reduced simply to reactions to successful radical right parties. Rather, these shifts were part of an attempt by the center right to capture some of the growing right-wing electorate, which favored tough stances against foreigners and had been encouraged to do so even more by the waxing Dutch radical right parties. Thus, while van Kersbergen/Krouwel agreed with the conclusion that the center right's dallying with overt restrictiveness vis-à-vis migration is a natural – vote-seeking – temptation in many countries, they also underlined that wherever the radical right has successfully promoted these issues, center-right parties have further intensified their efforts to pursue.

Once a radical right party has grown to such a size that it becomes a potential kingmaker, these considerations may also be shaped by other, coalition-focused calculations. Green-Pedersen/Odmal's (2008) comparison of Swedish and Danish center-right parties, for example, gave strong evidence for the significance of coalition politics in center-right parties' strategies on migration. Trying to explain the markedly more restrictive approach in Denmark (notwithstanding the similarities between the two countries' societal contexts), they concluded that the Danish center right's shift toward restrictiveness that started in the 1990s resulted from its need to treat the radical right as a potential partner in government coalitions. The Swedish center-right parties, on the other hand, never faced a similar threat; on the contrary, they were forced to maintain a center-right alliance in order to fortify their position. Thus, as Schain (2008: 469) noted about this coalition-focused aspect, "because of its strategic position within the party system, the extreme right is capable of ensuring that the centre-right parties are incapable of gaining office, [...] not unlike what powerful Communist parties did in France and Italy during the post-war period." As a result, center-right parties' competition strategy promises to remain one of engagement with the radical right for the foreseeable future.

The intricate role played by center-left parties.

On a different flank of the issue from that of the political right, center-left parties are equally prone to engage in competition over migration and ethnic relations. For example, Garner (2005) mentioned that anti-immigration is a core value not only for radical right and center-right parties but occasionally for center-left parties as well, and not necessarily because of radical right successes. Using evidence from the United Kingdom, she demonstrated that restrictive immigration policies (at times coupled with racist overtones) had already existed long before the new radical right emerged all over Europe (Garner 2005: 124-5) and that in the context of electoral politics, particularly, the issue of immigration has emerged as "a topic that cuts across traditional affiliations" (Garner 2005: 126).

However, as most scholars agree, even for center-left parties', successful radical right mobilization creates a factor worthy of consideration. Accordingly, Bale (2003: 71) explained that the significant overlap between center-left parties' electorate and groups targeted by the radical right (especially among less educated blue-collar workers in urban areas, who are the first victims of unemployment and may be alarmed about immigrants competing on the labor market) exerts pressure on center-left parties to engage in competition on migration and ethnic relations. Duncan/van Hecke (2008: 434) pointed out a similar problem, namely that for the center-left "there is a tension between representing the interests of the native working class and wider concerns about social justice."

However, Schain (2008: 468) qualified the importance of this internal conflict of values among center-left parties, arguing that "although the working-class reaction to newly enfranchised immigrants has certainly been a problem for parties of the left, it has been relatively rare that the left has supported restriction and exclusion." On the contrary, he asserted that when center-left parties supported restrictive measures, they most often did so to achieve a consensus with the center-right in an attempt to depoliticize the issue, whereas when they actively politicized immigration, they mostly did so in order to promote inclusive policies (ibid.). Moreover, Schain recalled another, often disregarded motive of center-left parties: As the left is more likely to benefit from the immigrant vote than the right, inclusive appeals derive not only from leftist ideological core values (solidarity, egalitarianism, etc.) but oftentimes serve the strategic purpose of increasing the size of its voter base by mobilizing immigrant electorates (Schain 2008: 468). Thus from a vote-seeking standpoint, there are arguments leading in both directions of engagement, raising the questions of the conditions under which center-left parties will respond to radical right politicization of migration and ethnic relations, to what degree they will do it, and in which direction. In his comparison of eleven countries between 1994 and 2004 Van Spanje (2010) offered some empirical evidence to suggest a shift toward restrictiveness by demonstrating that, although there is a positive correlation between radical right party success and a general shift of other parties toward restrictive positions, there is no evidence whatsoever that contagion effects are stronger on center-right parties than on other parties. Instead he concluded that even far-left parties (Greens and Communists) are in danger of giving up their liberal or multicultural positions (Van Spanje 2010: 16).

Meguid (2008: 357) suggested another, rather coalition-centered argument that issue-based competition is not reserved for ideological neighbors but represents a strategic tool for non-proximate competitors as well. For example, center-left parties may employ "single-issue adversarial tactics" vis-à-vis the radical right's immigration claims in order to apply pressure to the center-right mainstream party opponent that is closer to it. Recently Bale et al. (2010) supported this argument, highlighting the fact that aside from the center-left's vote-seeking concerns caused by the overlap in the radical right's and social democrats' electorates, another striking problem has become apparent in the last two decades: While on the one hand successful radical right parties help to raise public awareness for issues traditionally 'owned' by the right, on the other hand, and strategically even more importantly, radical right parties also "facilitate the formation of centre-right governments" and thereby indirectly create more options for the center-right mainstream competitor while hampering the office-seeking ambitions of the center left (Bale et al. 2010: 410-1). From this perspective, handling the radical right presence becomes an important strategic consideration that center-left parties have to take into account, accepting that their center-right conservative neighbors and the radical right share an ideological foundation that is contrary to the solidarity-based and egalitarian values of most social democratic parties (van Kersbergen/Krouwel 2008: 402; Bale et al. 2010). However, the empirical findings of their four-country comparison turned out quite ambivalent: While their observations showed differing social democratic responses to radical-right pressure in each of the four countries, varying in "the substance, the scope or the pace of that response", the authors concluded that "the response of centre-left parties is determined not just by the populist far right itself but also by the behavior of the mainstream right and of their left and/or liberal competitors, as well as by actual and potential dissent within their own ranks" (Bale et al. 2010: 423). This variety of factors thus leads to different responses when center-left parties try to balance making slight positional adaptations with not giving up too many of their core values and their credibility (ibid.).

These remarks demonstrate that with regard to center-left parties, so far both the theoretical explanations and the empirical findings are less clear-cut than with regard to center-right parties. It can be concluded, though, that across European democracies "the extreme right – even where it has not gained governmental power – has developed agenda-setting influence that goes far beyond what its percentage of the vote would indicate. While the left has not been immune from this influence, the impact has been primarily on the centre-right, and has prevented centre-right parties and governments from developing more flexible and/or open policies on immigration/integration" (Schain 2008: 469).

Integrating the fragmented state of the art

Summing up, the literature on strategic party behavior in the context of migration and ethnic relations has produced several predictions about the strategies of different kinds of parties. While the strategies described for radical right parties are more or less stable (in the sense that they are expected to adopt highly salient anti-immigrant positions), various scenarios have been suggested for the remaining party spectrum. For center-right parties, the expected response to anti-immigrant politicization is an accommodative (converging) strategy combined with increased salience of the issues. The logic behind this is that, due to voter-emigration to the radical-right opponent, center-right parties need to articulate stronger (law & order) statements in order to retain or recapture disaffected voters (Downs 2001; Bale 2003). A similar response is expected from an office-seeking standpoint, since a right-bloc coalition effectively increases the center-right's chances for government responsibility (Bale 2003). With regard to center-left parties, on the other hand, the predictions vary. While Meguid (2008) predicts an adversarial strategy at odds with that of the radical right intended to put the center-right competitor under pressure and prevent majorities from forming on the right, Bale et al. (2010) instead expect center-left parties to give up their adversarial tactics in light of increasing radical-right pressure on their own electorate and eventually opt also for accommodative (converging) strategies in an attempt to regain voters lost to the radical right. Finally, with regard to leftist parties, only few explicit predictions can be found in the literature, in part because until recently their role has received less scholarly attention and in part because analogous strategies to those of radical-right parties can be expected from some far-left parties (i.e. stable strategies of high-salience but pro-immigrant positions).

These remarks make it clear that there is still a need to substantiate the literature on issue-based strategies of competition of political parties in the context of migration and ethnic relations: Predictions have been advanced and validated irregularly for the various types of parties (with center-right parties being the most debated ones and center-left and far-left parties being somewhat disregarded). Thus certain questions have not been addressed sufficiently so far, such as whether a potent actor on the far left opposing radical right politicization can increase pressure on mainstream parties on the other side of the party spectrum. In this case, not only would center-left parties be more cautious in adopting issue positions close to those of the radical right, but center-right parties would also have to weigh the danger of a majority of the left bloc in striving for a right-bloc majority (Triadafilopoulos/Zaslove 2006). What is most evident from this discussion is the need for an integrated approach that manages to take into account the unequal conditions for the different parties and more systematically considers the differing motives driving parties' politicization strategies.

The goal of this book is to help clarify existing lines of inquiry, which have already elucidated – at times more implicitly, at others more explicitly – the various motives that drive parties' competitive behavior, the most important ones being *party ideology*, *vote maximization* and *coalition evaluations*. These underlying motives accord with the behavioral concepts discussed in chapter 2.1.2 of *policy-seeking behavior* (prioritizing ideological positions or specific policy interests over maximizing votes and pursuing office), *vote-seeking behavior* (using issue management and adapting policy positions to win more votes), and *office-seeking behavior* (sacrificing policy interests and potential voters for the sake of improving chances of entering a majority coalition). On the other hand, this distinction is somewhat academic, since, as has been emphasized by Müller/Strøm (1999: 11-2) and Wolinetz (2003: 153), hardly any party is driven solely by a single one of these motives. On the contrary, the reality is characterized by an interplay of different motives whose relative weights may change over time. As a consequence, section 3.2 will show in detail which intrinsic elements of party competition can be identified as major influences on parties' motives as well as the corresponding strategies of politicization. Beyond that, some explanatory factors, such as socio-structural developments and the influence of public opinion on issues of migration and ethnic relations, have received less attention in the debate so far. In order to integrate them into the explanatory framework of this study, section 3.1 will discuss these contextual aspects of migration and ethnic relations in Austria.

Before that, however, the arena of competition under consideration in this study needs to be defined more specifically. Party competition takes place in a variety of arenas, each with its own internal logic and at times demanding a strategy that contrasts with a party's strategy in other arenas. Thus the next section will delineate the concept of electoral campaigning, discuss its relevance within the greater context of party competition, and distinguish between different campaign channels and the roles they play in parties' election campaigns.

2.3   Electoral campaigning: The apex of political communication

The previous sections discussed concepts of party behavior and strategies of politicization both from a broad theoretical perspective as well as with specific regard to the issues of migration and ethnic relations. So far, however, no comments have been made about the arena of competition under consideration. It is important to clearly distinguish between different loci of political competition, however, because they present different strategic limitations and possibilities for party competition. What is central to the present study is the very specific context that is created by electoral competition. Especially for emotionally charged issues such as migration and ethnic relations, the electoral arena is arguably the sphere most crucial to an analysis of party politicization, as it condenses parties' preferences and emphasis to their prototypical cores. However, the electoral arena in itself poses different demands on parties' campaign activities.

Thus this section is dedicated to two goals. Firstly, it discusses the conditions obtaining in the electoral arena as opposed to other arenas of political competition (2.3.1). Secondly, it deconstructs electoral campaigns into diverse communicational goals that political parties must pursue in their campaign efforts. The section thus suggests a closer study of different campaign channels, and initiates a discussion on the diverse roles of programmatic and day-to-day campaign communication in parties' politicization strategies (2.3.2).

2.3.1   The electoral arena as party environment

Political parties compete in a number of different contexts, with each of these contexts constituting a particular framework for political action (Wolinetz 1988: 5-6). Accordingly, Panebianco (1988: 207) distinguished between different "environments directly influencing parties" and depicted them as "arenas in which relations between parties and other organizational actors take place". These arenas are interdependent, and advantages or setbacks in one arena can heavily influence the opportunities or restrictions in another. Thus parties' activities in the various arenas can be apprehended as efforts to secure the resources necessary for existence and success overall. Among the different environments for parties, the electoral and the parliamentary arenas are arguably the most important ones (Panebianco 1988: 208). The main procedures of the parliamentary arena are clearly those relating to the creation of specific policies and obtaining the majorities required to pursue them (Strömbäck 2007: 59). As a consequence, political actors must be equipped with more pragmatism, conflict capacities, and negotiation skills in parliamentary settings than in other arenas.

In contrast to the parliamentary arena, in the electoral arena the need for negotiation and pragmatism is much more limited. This results in part from the differing degrees of public attention devoted to the different arenas; while the parliamentary arena is a permanent and thus less newsworthy locus (which consequently is covered more selectively), the electoral arena features unique conditions stemming from its pivotal importance in democracies. The electoral arena allows access to legitimate political parties regardless of their size, level of organization, or goals; it is subject to increased public attention as voters aim to meet their democratic responsibilities; it is also subject to more media attention due to parties' and candidates' campaigns and recipients' demands for information; and finally, it intensifies the confrontations between competing ideologies and interests in order to offer discernible choices to the electorate. This makes electoral competition the archetypal research environment for party politicization, especially with regard to issues such as migration and ethnic relations, which are emotionally charged, of broad social concern, and of more or less permanent relevance (Strömbäck et al. 2011: 3).

Politicization is inextricably embedded in the electoral context, since competition in the electoral arena, more than any other, places pressure on parties to stage-manage their communication in order to succeed in a battle for attention (Franck 2003). Hence electoral politicization is a meaningful indicator of the different degrees of relevance of policy issues within a certain polity and in parties' corresponding positions. In contrast to the continuous PR endeavors outside the framework of election cycles, short-term campaigns focused at critical junctures such as elections are of vastly different character (Blumler et al. 1996: 50). As Kriesi et al. (2009) emphasized, "crafting the message" has become the heart of parties' election campaigns. Yet while it is commonplace for "parties [to] face constraints in selecting campaign issues" (Nadeau et al. 2010: 369), one particular constraint resulting from the nature of electoral campaign communication lies at the center of this study. Several authors have argued that parties are restricted in their campaigns by the daily issue agenda in the public sphere, most importantly reflected in daily news, and that they are tempted to "ride the wave" of salient public issues (Ansolabhere/Iyengar 1994; Sides 2006; Hayes 2008). As a consequence, parties are unable to promote their agendas with total independence, and these short-term constraints may also result in convergence between parties and candidates on issues (Sigleman/Buell 2004). Aldrich/Griffin (2003) even argued that once they manage to receive a considerable degree of public attention, parties will prioritize the public importance of certain policy issues over their individual issue ownership. For that reason, this book argues that parties use a diverse set of channels to achieve different communicative goals, and thus different patterns of politicization are to be expected depending on the channel used.

The evolution of election campaigning and channels of communication

The vital role of election campaigns in contemporary Western democracies is widely acknowledged, although the analysis of campaign strategies of political actors has received less attention from political scientists than voter-related aspects of elections have (Kriesi et al. 2009: 345). However, though election campaigns have always been crucial for the dissemination of information by political parties and candidates to the "reasoning voter" (who is usually rather ill-informed about government activities and parties' actual work – see Popkin 1991: 70; Arceneaux 2005), their scope and the selection of channels available for communicating this information have expanded substantially in recent decades.

The literature commonly distinguishes between three different stages in the development of political campaigning (Farell 1996; Farell/Webb 2000; Norris 2000; Plasser/Plasser 2002).[15] The first period, dating back to the 19th and early 20th centuries, was characterized by the dominance of direct, interpersonal campaign communication between candidates and voters, as well as by short-term and ad-hoc planning on the part of the party leadership. Campaign organization was very localized and based on personnel-intensive mechanisms for campaigning to local communities, such as rallies, doorstep canvassing and party meetings (Norris 2000: 137), as well as printed media products (billboards, posters and newspaper advertisements). In the second period, by the middle of the 20th century, the emergence of radio and, more importantly, television as dominant mass media channels encouraged parties to push toward campaign professionalization, with this period witnessing the first uses of professional campaign advisors, independent party polling, political marketing instruments, etc. (Norris 2000: 139-40). Press releases and press conferences were products of this period, with election campaigns trying to establish permanent and differentiated information flows toward journalists and adapting to the demands of changing mass media coverage. The third advancement in the development of election campaigning occurred at the end of the 20th century and resulted from a number of new phenomena: growing electoral dealignment; the emergence of new parties and a considerable increase in fragmentation of party systems; and increasingly fragmented mass media supply both in traditional media as well as "new" (i.e. online) media. These factors demand ever more complex campaign management of today's political parties, which not only have to mobilize their electorates, but also need to convince (ever larger) groups of undecided voters. Segmented and targeted campaigns are a functional consequence of these changes, and they have led to the extensive use of new communication channels in order to appeal to these undecided voters (Gibson/Römmele 2001: 33; Wlezien 2005: 105). Although these three-stage models of campaign professionalization have become object of critique – arguing that patterns of campaign evolution are highly dependent on a country's particular political system, the specific electoral context (such as first/second-order elections) and the variability of parties' campaign goals (Tenscher 2013: 243-5) –, the increasing complexity of contemporary election campaigns is beyond doubt.

---

[15] These phases, however, are labeled differently by different authors: Farell 1996 talks about a 'premodern' period followed by a 'television revolution' and a 'telecommunications revolution', and Norris 2000 and Plasser & Plasser 2002 call them the 'premodern', 'modern', and 'postmodern' periods, whereas Farell & Webb 2000 simply label them "Stages 1 to 3".

In a nutshell, election campaigns have become more professionalized and me-
dia-oriented, leading to increasing complexity in campaign communication. The
channels employed by political parties to convey "the message" have multiplied
and grown to serve the multiple interests of campaign strategies that nowadays
are decisively shaped by political marketing (Strömbäck 2007). In order to
achieve their strategic electoral goals, political parties alternate the use of direct
and controlled channels of communication (such as pamphlets, billboards, posters, meetings, manifestos, party broadcasts, websites, direct mailing) with indirect and mediated channels which address widely dispersed potential audiences
via organized mass media (de Vreese 2010: 119). By trying to stimulate mass
media agendas and the dominant frames of public discourse, parties aim to influence the mediated public sphere to their own advantage. Thus, while indirect
channels are primarily designed to arouse mass media attention through press
conferences, press releases, interviews, and any other form of media events, the
direct dimension of campaign communication aims to address potential voters
without the intermediation of professional journalism or other forms of organized media (Schulz 2008: 308-9; Kriesi et al. 2009: 351).[16]

Of course, not all campaign outlets are equally useful for the analysis of parties'
positions and their priorities in competition. The decision to focus on specific
campaign channels implies a selection from the broad range of tools that parties
can make use of in the course of an election campaign (Budge 1987: 17). At the
same time, it is exactly this variety of materials that makes possible highly fruitful analyses of political communication, since it mirrors the diverse conditions
and settings in which political parties have to craft their messages. For the purposes of this study, i.e. identifying the longitudinal relevance of and positions on
migration and ethnic relations, a number of prerequisites must be met. First, the
material has to be of continuing and regular character, for only then can it be
regarded as reflecting the changes in a party's positioning over time. Electoral
communication, due to its regularity, has proved to be the most fruitful source of
data for such a long-term comparison. Second, the material must be recognized
as an official expression of a party line at a given point in time. This necessarily
glosses over the possible internal differences within a party; nevertheless, following standard rational choice models of party behavior, it is a tolerable reduction of complexity. Third, the material must be of a type used by all electoral
contestants, disregarding the usual variations in the degree to which different
campaign resources are utilized by different political parties.

Owing to the three prerequisites stated above, there is one particular mode of
campaign communication that has become the most commonly used source for
electoral studies in political science: programmatic communication. Analysis of

---

[16] However, in times of increasing interdependence and growing relevance of new media the
distinction between indirect and direct campaign channels is blurring, because the different
instruments are ever more often used for both intentions (Schulz 2008: 309).

party manifestos and electoral platforms has become a staple of party competition studies, not least due to the pioneering work of the Comparative Manifesto Project (CMP). However, to focus solely on the programmatic level of electoral competition is to risk missing a crucial aspect of the electoral struggle, since the actual character of competition during hot election campaigning periods and the momentum of day-to-day politicization arguably differ from the programmatic ideas that are devised in the undisturbed seclusion of party headquarters. This essential dissimilarity between the programmatic and the day-to-day politicization of political parties becomes a crucial question for this study and lies at the center of the next section.

2.3.2 Electoral politicization and campaign consistency

Content analysis of party documents has a long research tradition and brings certain advantages over other approaches. Other input sources (e.g. surveys of the electorate, interviews with party members, expert commentary, interpretations of journalist observers, etc.) suffer from the influence of third-person interpretation and themselves often refer back to the same original party materials anyway. For this reason, original party programs have occupied a central place in the analysis of party profiles and their development (Volkens 2007: 117).

Political programs: characteristics and differences

Among parties' campaign channels, programmatic documents stand out as one of the basic constitutive elements of political parties, ensuring the integrity of a party's profile and political identity (Klingemann 1989: 99). Programs in any one of their diverse forms can be seen as major carriers of party politicization. There are various types of programs which differ from each other with respect to a) the concreteness of the political goals they express, b) the applicability of their suggestions, c) the temporal scope of their concepts, d) the number of issues they address, and e) the strictness of the obligations that they represent (Klingemann 1989: 99). This has led to the distinction of three basic types of programmatic party documents (see Table 3): party platforms, (election) manifestos, and action programs (ibid.). Pelinka (1979: 8) pointed to a gradual increase in the concreteness of policy suggestions that distinguishes party platforms from election manifestos by their differing degrees of topicality. When policy positions are analyzed over time, election manifestos have some crucial advantages over other programmatic documents. While analyses of party platforms run the risk of overlooking short-term changes due to overly wide scopes and little policy concreteness, action programs represent an imperfect source for research because of the irregularity with which they are produced and their monothematic focus. Election manifestos on the other hand play a pivotal role in the development and diffusion of a party's agenda and positions, mainly because "[...] they are unique being the only authoritative party policy statement approved by an official convention or congress. Possibly because of this they stand alone in being full 'five year plans' for the development of society" (Klinge-mann et al. 2006: XVI). Thus election manifestos most reliably enable the re-searcher to make statements about long-term developments in the salience of specific issues, the stances of parties or the party spectrum as a whole, and the relation between policy formulation and policy conversion by governing parties (Klingemann 1987: 300; Ickes 2008: 16-7).

Manifestos do not derive their relevance from any direct impact on readers and supporters; in fact, few voters even read them (Budge 1987: 18). Their main im-portance comes instead from their indirect exterior function, i.e. their influence on observers and commentators in public discourse, as they "can be singled out as a uniquely representative and authoritative characterization of party policy at a given point in time" (Budge 1987: 18). It is exactly this exterior function that represents the primary reason for choosing manifestos as a base reference for party profiles. Beyond their exterior relevance, manifestos also fulfill intra-organizational functions. In post-war democracies, manifestos have long been developed and legitimized by party conventions and thus served to secure inter-nal party cohesion (Klingemann 1987: 300). Thus manifestos can be regarded as a reference of the party position for the purpose of simplifying the complex body of participants, from the leadership to individual party members, to a sin-gle monolithic body. Even though the development of electoral manifestos has become a less thoroughly deliberated process, their intra-organizational signifi-cance is still great, since they continue to serve as basic benchmarks for party members in times of increasingly diversified policy competences, fulfilling a guideline function that is of particular importance in the highly complex context of electoral competition.

Apart from their interior and exterior importance, manifestos also fulfill a third function, namely that of facilitating inter-party coordination, which, from a stra-tegic perspective, may in fact be their most important aspect for electoral com-petition. By highlighting specific issues as pre-eminently relevant, enunciating specific positions on these issues and suggesting concrete measures to convert these positions into policies, parties not only get a message across to members of their own organization, probable opinion leaders, disseminators and their poten-tial supporters; they also signal their preferences to their direct opponents, i.e. other parties competing in the same electoral arena. This is an important consid-eration, since policy choices are made in light of constant anticipation of the ri-valries, potential alliances and opportunity structures that surround a party. Thus the analysis of the policy positions expressed in party manifestos can offer dis-tinct indications of the way politicization by parties develops over time.

Day-to-day campaign communication

Programmatic communication is only one of the various communicational tools used by political parties to get their messages across. In fact, electoral cam-paigns are sustained endeavors that require parties to distribute their messages on a multitude of channels in order to secure the attention of the public. As competition over public attention has increased, influencing the mass media's agenda has become a major objective of election campaigns (Strombäck 2007). Thus the concept of agenda setting has emerged as an important theoretical foundation for analyzing strategic communication, a point substantiated by McCombs (2008: 141), who named the question of input sources as the most recent (fifth) stage of research on agenda setting. Other scholars have used terms such as "agenda-building" or "media agenda setting" to refer to this phenomenon (Brandenburg 2002; Dearing/Rogers 1996; Walters et al. 1996; Weaver et al. 2004). Its key recognition is that strategic communicators are able to influence the media agenda to their advantage by delivering continuous input to media selection processes. The tango metaphor has become a common means to describe the relation between journalists and strategic communicators. Whether the leading partner in the tango is deemed to be the political actors (Gans 1980) or the journalists (Strömbäck/Nord 2006), the connection remains a reciprocal one. On the one hand, media coverage has arguably become the main link between political parties and their electorates (Strömbäck 2010: 26), and in attempting to satisfy consumers' demands for information, journalists are increasingly dependent on an ever widening array of information sources ranging from personal ties to party staff to media services provided by party campaigns. On the other hand, the strategic communication of political actors must also become ever more diversified and sophisticated in order to have an impact on the media agenda at all. This results in a growing mediatization of parties' campaign communication, an alignment with media logic and demands in order to increase the chances of it being noticed by journalists in the first place (Semetko/Schönbach 1999).

From the viewpoint of political parties, then, "[e]lection campaigns are agenda-setting games" (Blumler et al. 1996: 51) and influencing media agendas has developed into an important capability in postmodern electoral competition.[17] These agenda-setting games have become enduring processes that not only permanently screen public opinion and media coverage, but also continuously produce new content to manipulate the media agenda as well as online public communication to parties' advantage. For the present analysis, one particular result of mediatization stands out most visibly: the accelerated pace of election campaigns. As political actors conform ever more closely to media logic, so too do their schedules align with those of the media (Haynes/Flowers 2002; Carsey et al. 2011). Whether communicating through press conferences, press releases,

---

[17] In fact, this influence is not limited to the mere transfer of issue-salience (first-level agenda setting), but can also be expanded to the transfer of salience of "attributes" (second-level agenda setting) (McCombs 2008). Thus strategic communicators may even influence the direction of public or media discourse by highlighting specific attributes of issues while downplaying or simply ignoring others.

and candidate interviews to meet the immediate needs of daily news media production or through background reports, pseudo-events, and manifestos to meet the more comprehensive needs of weekly or monthly media, political parties must coordinate their campaign services with the frequencies of the information demands of media actors. Blumler et al. (1996: 51) vividly described the daily schedule of campaign managers: "Battle commences early in the day, with the party researchers looking at first editions of the daily press and analyzing overnight television coverage. The aim is to pick up the latest stories and give them a spin or relate them to the party's chosen issue of the day. The party's position on that issue is presented by spokespersons at an early morning press conference and woven into subsequent events and interviews of the day [...] aiming to catch the midday news with material from the morning press conferences, staging leader 'walkabouts' in visually appealing settings in the afternoons for early evening news coverage, and inserting passages into leader speeches at party rallies in the evening for inclusion in the main nightly news".

Thus, with the establishment of 24-hour news cycles and the permanent circulation of information via online communication, the need for constant commentary and rapid response tools has steadily increased for strategic communicators, resulting in ever more sophisticated day-to-day campaigns (Wlezien 2005). Confronted with "real-time coverage" of electoral competition by contemporary media, parties use immediate and flexible campaign channels to quickly influence the agenda and, even more importantly, "spin" current issues of public debate. Accordingly, Haynes/Flowers (2002: 3) distinguish different "news cycles" (event cycle, campaign cycle, weekly cycle, annual cycle) that are monitored by campaign managers in order to time the release of campaign information, "issuing more press releases in periods of high demand – the beginning of the week – and fewer during news lulls – the weekend" (Haynes/Flowers 2002: 6).

Consequently, for analysis of party agendas in the course of an election campaign, referring to manifestos is hardly sufficient, as they do not reflect developments during the campaign period at all. They also give no hint whether parties are able (or willing) to promote their programmatic appeals on a daily basis. In pre-election times, a crucial task for campaign advisors is to convert the programmatic communication of issues and positions into contents of daily discourse, since it is exactly this permanence of day-to-day campaign communication that increases the likelihood of party agendas and policy preferences becoming relevant and persistent in public discourse. Thus campaign managers have to link long-term interests with short-term and highly situational demands in order to communicate those interests. For understanding whether parties translate programmatic appeals into daily campaign communication, official *press releases* have turned out to be the most useful source of data for this study. They are a vital "rapid response" tool with which parties attempt to set the agenda and respond to stimuli from opponents or the media. Hence press releases, more than any of the other traditional channels used by political parties, reflect the actual development of an election campaign and serve as an indicator of the issues and positions that dominate party competition. As explained by Burton/Shea (2010: 182-3), there is no instrument that is more important and more suitable for managing the news and "selling" the parties' own candidates and issues to the media than press releases, as they "announce candidate statements and upcoming events, attempt to spin breaking news, highlight endorsements, and provide background facts that help reporters make sense of the race. This form of communication, inexpensive in both production and distribution, plays a central role in earned media strategy" (Burton/Shea 2010: 183). With the limited amount of journalistic attention available and the mountains of releases disseminated by all the organizations of public life, press releases are designed "to make life easy for reporters". First of all, they have to be kept short in order to aggregate the most basic information for the reader into a "bite". Second, their structure follows journalistic criteria for the composition of articles by including headlines, leads and pictures, and by answering the important "W's" and reflecting "the journalist's inverted-pyramid format, with the most important information at the top and less important information farther down" (Burton/Shea 2010: 183). Thirdly, they are always designed to get a powerful message across by using simple language and third-person style, by including action verbs to strengthen their statements, and by relying as much as possible on facts (ibid.) They are produced and disseminated constantly by numerous branches of party organizations, which might produce dozens of releases in a day, some of them linked to each other in order to draw the media's attention to specific issues.

Applying the same evaluation criteria for manifestos to press releases, it becomes evident that the purposes of the latter are exactly the opposite of those of programmatic communication. Press releases are highly concrete in their proposals due to the small number of issues they address in a single edition; in fact, usually they address only a single issue. Owing to their up-to-the-minute context specificity they commonly propose short-notice implementation of policies and measures that address recent developments and that consequently are far more concrete and applied in their treatment than the general suggestions made in manifestos. This finally means that press releases bring relatively strict obligation for measures suggested in them (Table 3).

Table 3:   Characteristics of political programs and press releases

	Party platform	Election manifesto	Action program	Press releases
Degree of concreteness	Low	Medium	High	Very high
Applicability of suggestions	Low	Medium	High	High
Temporal scope addressed	Wide	Medium/Tight	Tight	Very tight
Number of issues addressed	High	High/Medium	Low	Very low
Strictness of obligation	Low	Medium	High	High

Source: Based on Klingemann 1989: 99.

These characteristics make press releases the ideal material for comparing parties' day-to-day election campaign strategies with the programmatic roadmaps outlined at the beginning of these campaigns. For the longitudinal design of the present study, press releases have another major advantage over other channels, especially those emerging in the third stage of campaign communication (i.e. new media): They have been in use by political parties for a long time already and thus allow comparison throughout the whole examination period (Hopmann et al. 2010).

Campaign consistency and the role of party types

A central question with regard to the different channels of campaign communication is their degree of consistency. From a normative perspective, "cohesion of the communication campaign" is a crucial task for campaign management (Maarek 1995: 197). In order to present a cohesive profile to voters, the media and the public in general, campaign communication has to retain a high degree of consistency between its programmatic and day-to-day channels. Clear and consistent messages are a key element for campaign managers, who are expected to promote the same selection of issues and positions across all of their different campaign channels (Blumler et al. 1996: 56).

However, the capacity to sustain this consistency varies significantly between different types of parties (Adams et al. 2006; Helbling 2013). Because mainstream parties target a broader spectrum of voters than niche parties, they need to satisfy a more diverse range of interests, which is why they attempt to address a much wider palette of issues in their election campaigns (Krouwel 2006: 21). As a consequence, they are characterized "[...] by their pursuit of votes at the expense of ideology, by their centrist and often inconsistent platforms designed to appeal to ever wider audiences", and by their comparatively large size in terms of vote share (Williams 2009: 539).

In contrast to mainstream parties, a rising number of niche parties such as ethno-territorial parties, left-libertarian and Green parties, and new right-wing populist parties (Mudde 1999; Meguid 2008) have emerged to challenge the established actors and lines of conflict. Although there is scholarly debate on exactly how to determine the "nicheness" of a party (Adams et al. 2006; Meguid 2008; Ezrow 2010; Wagner 2012; Meyer/Miller 2013), there is some agreement that a decisive indicator is neither its size nor its position on a traditional left-right axis, but rather the degree to which it "carve[s] out a particular 'niche' for [itself]" (Wagner 2012: 7). Niche parties can be described as opportunistically exploiting a set of issues that appear promising for competition (Ignazi 2003), although their choice is limited to those issues that are linked somehow to their core values (Mudde 1999) and that have not been claimed by traditional mainstream parties (Crotty 2006). Thus niche parties have a much narrower range of 'attractive' issues available to them than their mainstream counterparts do, and their politicization is expected to show greater consistency between campaign channels than mainstream parties' (Williams 2009: 539). In part this is probably a result of the greater consistency in the issues chosen by niche parties. This prediction is supported by the findings of Adams et al. (2006), who demonstrated that niche parties rarely shift their fringe positions to more moderate ones, and that when they do so, they tend to lose votes. Conversely, mainstream parties have been shown to shift their issue positions more regularly in pursuit of public opinion – without being punished for it at the ballot box (ibid.). Their need to address a broader range of issues together with their greater maneuvering room with regard to emerging issues that cut across established cleavages thus most likely materializes in more diversity of issue subtopics and positions addressed across campaign channels.[18]

Besides these electoral orientation aspects, differences are also to be expected on the basis of parties' organizational natures, since campaign strategies are constrained both in terms of "intensity of the mobilization and its direction [...] by the amount of resources available" (Kriesi et al. 2009: 347). The high costs of campaign communication are generally more easily borne by mainstream parties, which is why they can make use of a broader variety of campaign channels (Gibson/Römmele 2001: 33) than niche parties, which are obliged to spend their electoral budgets more judiciously. Moreover, mainstream parties are often bound by the responsibility of a governing party to synchronize its messages with governmental and ministerial communication, a constraint that applies less often to niche parties.

Gathering these differing characteristics of mainstream and niche parties, the present study states the following hypotheses to guide its analysis of parties' campaign consistency in both issue (subtopic) selection and policy positions (frames):

In their choice of subtopics, mainstream parties are less consistent between programmatic and day-to-day campaign communication than niche parties (H1).

In their choice of policy positions, mainstream parties are less consistent between programmatic and day-to-day campaign communication than niche parties (H2).

---

[18] Niche parties, of course, are subject to change. Thus a party's initial status as a niche party may change over time, most commonly due to success and growth. However, authors such as Mair (1991) maintain their categorizations of parties even when they begin to transform into another type (such as a medium or major mainstream party). This book adopts this strategy, because Austrian "niche" parties – though they cross the conceptual borders now and then – for the most part can be described by the niche party concept (as will be demonstrated more precisely in Chapter 3).

Synopsis

This chapter outlined the theoretical framework of this book. Its first goal was to identify parties' underlying motives in competition, separating ideology and policy-based motives from vote-seeking and office-seeking motives. It argued that differing motives would result in different politicization strategies in the competition of parties over particular issues. In order to develop an approach capable of identifying these differences, the chapter briefly introduced standard spatial perspectives of party competition as well as its extensions by directional and salience theory. By linking these concepts to recent literature on competition between mainstream and niche parties, an integrated model of politicization was developed that will be able to capture both the competitive dimension of salience as well as the role of policy positions in the discourse on migration and ethnic relations.

Using the framework of this model, the chapter moved on to describe the current state of research on party competition on migration and ethnic relations in European democracies, extracting a set of assertions describing the politicization strategies of different party families. It argued that, unlike established mainstream parties, niche parties would seek to exploit new issues in the context of electoral competition as long as they do not get severly punished in terms of votes or coalition potential. Moreover it concluded that among mainstream parties, conditions for center-right parties differ from those of center-left parties when it comes to dealing with niche party pressure in the context of migration and ethnic relations. These assertions will be developed into complete hypotheses in the next chapter as part of an introduction of the Austrian case.

In addition to developing these statements describing party politicization of migration and ethnic relations, the chapter also highlighted the peculiarities of the electoral arena as a setting for party competition. It argued that the increasing diversification of election campaigns and the rising number of available politicization channels challenge political parties to produce consistent campaign communication, especially when comparing the programmatic with the day-to-day sphere of competition, an aspect mostly ignored by current research on electoral competition. In order to remedy this deficit, and to compare different moments in the election campaign process, electoral manifestos and daily press releases were selected as the best sources for the purposes of this study.

The chapter concluded with two hypotheses about the behavior of mainstream and niche parties. With the theoretical framework completed, this study will proceed with a discussion of the specific case chosen for its focus. Hence the next chapter will introduce the particular context and conditions of Austrian party competition on migration and ethnic relations.

3. Migration and ethnic relations in Austria: Opportunities and constraints in electoral politicization

Political parties have been characterized as prototypical agents of interest aggregation. Nevertheless, they must make do with limited resources and attention for their attempts to politicize particular issues. As Ian Budge (2006: 422) put it, "[t]he number of potential issues which might be taken up in a given society is vast – notionally the number of individuals living in it multiplied by the number of their concerns". Consequently, prioritizing certain issues over others is imperative for any party competing for voter and media attention, though scholarly discussion has suggested various approaches to explain the development of parties' agendas.

Above all, *societal problems* are obviously key factors influencing political agendas. Parties will barely emphasize non-existent problems and without refugees or immigrants there will hardly be political debate. From such a societal perspective, external factors are thus considered to be fundamental drivers of party competition, and "[v]ariation in the magnitude of societal problems may thus explain variation in the amount of attention paid by political parties to an issue" (Green-Pedersen/Krogstrup 2008: 612). Although this argument is far from conclusive, the importance of societal inputs to party competition must be taken into consideration in any analysis of party agendas (van de Wardt 2011). Along with empirically observable developments in the corresponding policy field (such as growing numbers of migrants or foreign residents), societal influences also emerge from *public opinion* and demands made by the electorate, which implies that parties will tend to reflect voters' perceptions and preferences on an issue. As a result, changes in the distribution of voter preferences will force parties to respond by aligning their policy strategies to these changes (Adams et al. 2004). Thus, the policy strategies of political parties are largely constrained by the policy preferences of the electorate and party strategists align their strategies to these patterns (Adams 2012: 405). On the whole, since potential societal inputs are diverse and originate on many different levels, their relevance is far from clear and generally accepted.

In contrast to these societal perspectives, large parts of the literature on issue evolution and party competition instead focus on the dynamics of party competition and the incentives and constraints that arise from specific party system constellations (Green-Pedersen 2007a), as was already discussed in the previous chapter. The focus is placed on parties' strategic objective of finding winning formulas, although 'success' may be defined in different terms by different parties. According to this party competition perspective, these considerations result in parties' selective emphasis of potential winning issues (Budge/Farlie 1983) as well as their strategic evaluation of individual issue ownership (Carmines/Stimson 1993; Ansolabehere/Iyengar 1994; Petrocik 1996), based on their assessment of *party ideology*. Furthermore, these strategic considerations are obviously tied to the competitive patterns in the given party system, which create opportunities and constraints for individual parties' strategic positioning and circumscribe their strategic maneuvering room (Strøm 1990; Müller/Strøm 1999; Wolinetz 2002; Adams et al. 2004). Among these framework conditions are the *number and strength* of the political parties, which, together with their assessment of previous successes and failures, are assumed to influence their competitive behavior. In addition, due to the conditions in a multi-party system, with its greater need for coalition building, the evaluation of *coalition scenarios* is deemed another decisive factor that must be taken into consideration.

The sections that follow will reflect on these explanatory traditions and generate concrete assertions about the politicization strategies of Austrian parties in regard to migration and ethnic relations. Chapter 3.1 will sketch the context of societal inputs that might have driven Austrian party competition on migration and ethnic relations since the late 1960s, including a discussion of actual immigration numbers, the role of asylum, and the constitution of an ethnically heterogeneous society (3.1.1), before examining values and attitudes on migration and ethnic relations amidst the Austrian population (3.1.2). Following the description of the societal context, the subsequent sections will then focus on the internal factors of the party system crucial to explaining politicization of migration and ethnic relations, i.e. the ideological spectrum of Austrian parties (3.2.1), the evolution of competitive patterns in the Austrian party spectrum (3.2.2), and the probable role of coalition considerations (3.2.3). The chapter will conclude with hypotheses for each of these internal explanatory variables.

3.1   Societal inputs for party competition. Empirical evidence from a reluctant country of immigration

The present analysis starts from the assumption that, from the perspective of political parties, there are factors and conditions that constitute the environment for their actions. These conditions differ in nature, of course: While some are located outside of what is called the 'political system', quite a few are part of it and a smaller number are actually constitutive of the party system itself. This section focuses on certain conditions that, analytically speaking, are external to the party system and competition, but that nonetheless can exert influence on parties' behavior and strategies.

The societal environment of party competition

Politics and political debate are clearly linked to what is termed *social reality*, an assertion common among scientific as well as mundane observers of political life. Clearly, the political debate itself constitutes a vital part of social reality, though we tend to presume there are certain non-discursive foundations that political debate is grounded on. If we suppose such an empirical foundation of political discourse, i.e. if we assume that what political parties do is discursively related to a social reality beyond, then we have to take a close look at how this reality can be characterized in the first place. With that said, literature review reveals that a number of authors have expressed, or at least implied, a theoretical link between empirical indicators of migration and their interaction with public awareness, media attention, political debate, and even specific policy outcomes (Lewis-Beck/Mitchell 1993; Betz 1994; Freeman 1995; Knigge 1998; Givens 2002; Lahav 2004; Givens/Luedtke 2005; Green-Pedersen/Krogstrup 2008).

Empirical findings, however, appear to be diverse. Among authors offering evidence for links, Gibson (2002) pointed out the interaction between empirically observable conditions and public opinion, with a growing number of foreigners leading to more success for anti-immigrant parties. Similarly, Knigge (1998) commented that "[...] real changes in the composition of the national population, as captured by the annual national immigration statistics, are related to support for extreme right-wing parties" (Knigge 1998: 270), which would likely lead to the politicization of immigration, at least by radical right parties.[19] Golder (2003: 457) reinforced the argument by highlighting the relevance of the electoral system and stating that the effect of real-world immigration increases the more proportional the electoral system becomes (which is why, in majority-voting systems focused on mainstream parties and their issues, radical right parties face greater difficulties in promoting "their" issues). The effect on media attention paid to immigration has been examined in several previous studies. In a study of news magazines in seven countries, Esser (2000) revealed correlation between the magnitude of immigration and the public media debate and in the case of the Netherlands in the early 1990s Lubbers et al. (1998: 420) found similar evidence that the media attention paid to ethnic minorities correlates with the pattern of residence permits.

Other studies, however, have cast doubt upon the validity of such generalizations by detecting that socio-economic factors fail to explain media attention, voter behavior and party responsiveness with regard to immigration. Focusing on media reception, Vliegenthaart (2007: 83) concluded that from 1990 until 2002, "[r]eal world developments in immigration and asylum applications do not have a great impact on the attention for immigration and integration"; instead, he stressed the relevance of certain key events whose impacts vary in nature and degree (Vliegenthaart 2007: 86-7). Considering the role of public attention, van der Brug et al. (2005) and Arzheimer/Carter (2006) found no interaction of the empirical indicators for immigration/asylum and anti-immigrant party support. Taking a longer period of time into consideration, Boomgarden/Vliegenthaart (2007: 414) discovered only tenuous evidence for interaction between immigration and support for anti-immigration parties. Kitschelt/McGann (1997) criticized approaches that reduce anti-immigrant party behavior and success to mere responses to the societal conditions surrounding

---

[19] However, it must be pointed out that relying on annual national immigration statistics does not account for clandestine immigration, which may lead to actual numbers being substantially different from those reported in countries like Greece, Italy or Spain.

immigration. Instead they urged taking into account the strategic dimension of issue attention: "Strategic political entrepreneurs skilfully bring together long-term and short-term opportunities to mobilize voter coalitions" (Kitschelt/McGann 1997: 3). McDonald et al. (2004) provided evidence that the issue selection of political parties is linked to their ideologies rather than to public opinion or empirical indicators of current problems. Givens/Luedtke (2005) even tried to test for the interaction of growing immigration levels with more restrictive policy outcomes in Germany and France in the 1990s, but they found no empirical evidence for their assumption. In sum, the existence of a coupling between immigration as an empirically observable phenomenon and immigration as an issue of public and, more specifically, political debate or action is far from proven. As a consequence, in order to avoid coming to false conclusions, the present study will consider key data on immigration only as necessary initial indicators (Green-Pedersen/Krogstrup 2008) of the opportunities and constraints in political parties' competition on the issues of migration and ethnic diversity.

3.1.1 Immigration and ethnic diversity: numerical evidence

Even if it remains contested whether the impact of real world events relating to immigration on its relevance in public and political debate is immediate or more complex, these events nonetheless remain an important context for party politicization in a society. Even if their influence is indirect, they can at least give clues to those aspects likely to become objects of political contest. For this reason, this section will look at key data on immigration, integration and asylum in Austria since the 1960s.

Data availability in Austria

In attempting to examine empirical data on migration and ethnic diversity in Austria, an important remark concerning data availability needs to be made. Prior to the 1990s, statistical data on non-nationals and residents of immigrant origin in Austria was collected unsystematically and therefore is only partially complete (for detailed discussion see Reeger 2008; Kraler et al. 2009; Kraler/Reichel 2010; Peintinger 2011). The Austrian population census was carried out regularly from 1951 on; however, considering that the definition of resident population was adjusted between different censuses and that the variable of residents' country of birth was not included in 1981 and 1991, the census is an imperfect source of longitudinal immigration data (Kraler et al. 2009: 10-1). Moreover, as the census is limited to considering resident population, it neglects other types of migration such as seasonal migration or transnational mobility (Reeger 2008: 114). What was conducted regularly, on the other hand, was the constant adjustment of resident population statistics. Quarterly extrapolation from the population statistics using data gathered from regular statistics on birth, death, naturalization and net migration (Kytir et al. 2005: 203) offers at least basic and continuous data on net migration, which is presented in Figure 1.[20] A further basic constraint in the assessment of immigrant population is the comparatively late consideration of indicators for second-generation immigrants (such as "country of parents' birth"), which were included only in recent years (Peintinger 2011). For non-nationals, another source of data is available from the Central Population Register (POPREG, or the Central Register of Residents prior to 2002), which quarterly releases systematic data on households and offers information on nationality for registered population in Austria (Figure 2).[21]

If the prospects for acquiring general longitudinal data on immigration seem dim, the situation is all the more dire for indicators reflecting the integration of non-nationals and ethnic minorities. As Reeger (2008: 128) quite bluntly put it: "For 40 years up until the 2001 Census, Austrian migration-related statistics only used citizenship to describe the resident immigrant population. As a consequence, there was no information on naturalized immigrants, since they could not be identified in any statistical source. This is more than a subtle hint that policymakers were not really interested in these new Austrian citizens, their social situation and housing or their performance on the labor market." Thus only a few parameters are on hand when considering developments since the 1960s. One such indicator lies in information maintained by provincial governments and municipalities, such as statistics on naturalizations, as well as births and deaths of non-national residents (Figure 4). Taken together, though, these indicators still offer an incomplete picture and hence are insufficient for capturing the complexity of integration throughout the examination period.

Finally, a third source area that is somewhat disconnectedly relevant to politicization and political legislature surrounds the question of asylum. Here the institutional interest in statistical data capture has been more intense, though the actual availability of historical data still remains quite low. A centralized source of information was established only in 1983, the "Asylum Seekers Information System" (AIS), which was followed by the "Information System on Federal Care of Asylum Seekers" (BIS), established in the 1990s (Kraler et al. 2009: 14). Nevertheless, statistical yearbooks had recorded basic information on the number of asylum applications in previous decades, which allows at least for an

---

[20] Another potential source for the assessment of immigrant population in Austria is the micro-census, a quarterly survey of a representative sample of Austrian households that also includes information about immigrant origin of the sampled population. However, the micro-census is not considered a reliable source prior to the mid 1990s because of inconsistencies in sampling and question selections (Kraler et al. 2009: 6).

[21] Irregular migration is documented only from the establishment of the Alien Register in 1993 on, leaving the situation in earlier decades obscure.

approximate comparison of different time periods (Figure 3).[22] In sum, the data sources inventoried above are sufficient to draw a rough picture of developments in the sectors of immigration and asylum and to discuss major periods and transformations in Austrian immigration history since the 1960s.[23]

Migration and asylum in Austria since the 1960s

In the beginning of the 1960s, the extensive migrations of the immediate postwar period (characterized by the emigration of Austrian citizens and a net migration total of 129,000 between 1951 and 1961 [Münz et al. 2003: 20]) had come to an end. A comparatively large number of non-national residents populating Austria in the immediate aftermath of World War II had decreased over the course of the 1950s to only 1.4% of the total population in 1960 (Lebhart/Marik-Lebeck 2007: 166). Due to parallel patterns of immigration and emigration balancing the net migration, this level remained quite stable during the early 1960s (Figure 1). While emigration among the Austrian workforce remained steady in the early 1960s, the increased need for human labor in Austria was offset by early agreements for guest worker recruitment with Spain in 1962, with Turkey in 1964, and with Yugoslavia in 1966 (Matuschek 1985: 160; Münz et al. 2003: 21), even though much of the labor migration was not actually organized by recruitment offices, but rather was stimulated by chain-migration starting from labor migrants already working in Austria (Kraler 2007: 6; Gächter 2000: 69). Consequent to the growing demand and the increasing use of alternative immigration channels to overcome the labor shortage, the annual number of foreigners immigrating to Austria grew continually until the early 1970s, while the number of Austrian emigrants remained steady during this period. Accordingly, the number of foreign laborers increased dramatically from only 16,200 in 1961 to a record high of 226,000 at the climax of the guest worker period from 1970 to 1973 (Butschek 1992 as cited in Weigl 2009: 39).

---

[22] Though, as Stadler (1995) emphasized, the fall of the Iron Curtain marked a turning point for the concept of asylum in Austria. Following the political upheavals of 1989, a new conception of refugees excluded people formerly considered refugees on two basic premises. Firstly, a number of "political" immigrants were excluded from being treated as asylum seekers under the Geneva Convention, while secondly and more specifically, refugees from Bosnia and Croatia were administrated under a separate regime dealing with "de facto" refugees (and were not included in the annual asylum statistics). Thus the statistical number of "refugees" as published by the Ministry of the Interior relates to two distinctly different populations prior to and since the 1990s (Stadler 1995: 241). These conceptual changes were manifested in the asylum law of 1992 (AsylG 1992).

[23] For a synoptic analysis of the Austrian immigration tradition in the 19th and early 20th century, see John & Lichtblau 1993; Faßmann & Münz 1995; Heiss & Rathkolb 1995; Bauböck 1996; Kraler 2007; Perchinig 2009.

Figure 1:   Immigration to and emigration from Austria, 1961-2012

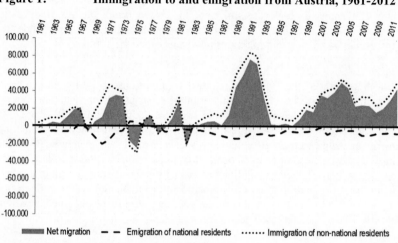

▬▬▬ Net migration   — — Emigration of national residents   ······· Immigration of non-national residents

Source: Statistics Austria, 2013.

Note: Numbers based on inter-census population estimates (until 1995) and on a newer database on migration movements after 1996. Results for the year 2001 were estimated and revised. International migration is defined here as the change of residence across national borders.

This development came to an abrupt halt in 1974, mainly as a consequence of the recruitment freeze imposed by the Austrian government that was intended to reduce immigrant labor in favor of remigrating Austrian employees (Münz et al. 2003: 23). In tandem with a new law on immigrant labor (*Ausländerbeschäftigungsgesetz*, AbG) in 1975, the recruitment freeze led to a sharp decrease in immigration that lasted almost the entire decade and turned the trend in net migration slightly negative. However, decreasing immigration was not attended by emigrating patterns among guest workers (except in 1974/75). Instead, many guest workers stayed in Austria, fearing they would lose the option of coming back if they left the country (Bauböck 1996: 13). As a consequence, the remaining guest workers and their relatives – who joined them by means of family reunification processes – compensated for the number of non-nationals who had returned to their home countries (Münz et al. 2003: 23). Thus what originally had been designed as a temporary arrangement then turned into a structural condition (Lebhart/Marik-Lebeck 2007: 166). Accordingly, the period after 1973 has been characterized as the "heyday of family reunification with parallel cutback of labor" (Weigl 2009: 43) in which the absolute number of non-national residents stayed relatively stable (see Figure 2).

Figure 2:   **Non-national residents in Austria, 1961-2012[24]**

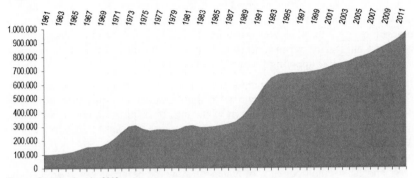

Source: Statistics Austria, 2013.

Note: Population statistics based on inter-census population estimates (until 1995) and, after 1996, from a newly established database on migration movements.

In the aftermath of this influential stimulus to permanent migratory influx during the guest-worker period from the early 1960s until the mid-1970s, the development of immigration to Austria remained at a comparatively low level, in a time that has thus been described as an "unspectacular period between return and settlement of former guest-workers" (Münz et al. 2003: 23-4). Along with the slight increase in labor migration from Turkey and Yugoslavia starting in the mid-1980s, and due to the exit facilitation for citizens of Eastern European countries established by the end of the 1970s, the question of asylum began to take on greater significance (Reeger 2008: 112; Münz et al. 2003: 24). The granting of asylum had become a vital part of the Austrian identity in the postwar era. Two refugee flows most notably marked milestones in the history of Austrian self-perception: The Hungarian Uprising in 1956, which caused between 180,000 and 194,000 Hungarian refugees to seek asylum in Austria, and the Prague Spring of 1968, in the course of which about 162,000 Czechoslovakian refugees fled to Austria. In both cases the Austrian government immediately signaled support and tried to foster the country's image as a bridge be-

---

[24] To speak of the origins of immigrants to Austria, census history shows the emigration countries of its non-national population (see Appendix 2): While Germany has always been a common country of origin of foreign residents in Austria, the Balkan region started to become another common region of origin during the guest-worker period in the 1960s, and immigrants from the Balkans have remained the largest group if all those from successor states of former Yugoslavia are counted together. Turkish citizens grew to represent a significant proportion of foreign residents only later, during the 1970s, and for almost three decades they exceeded even the number of German citizens. Due to naturalization processes this hierarchy has changed in the last decade, however, and Germany has again become the most common single country of origin of foreign residents in Austria.

tween East and West. However, it was able to do so only because these transitory refugee flows were characterized by little permanence: Only 25,000 Hungarian refugees finally settled in Austria, while the others returned home or, in most cases, moved on to other Western countries. Among the Czechoslovakian refugees, the number of permanent asylum seekers was even lower, with no more than 12,000 people applying for permanent asylum (Weigl 2009: 32-3).

In the 1980s Austrian self-perception was put to the test again: A sudden eruption of applications for asylum in 1980 that came as a result of the Solidarity crisis in Poland kicked off a pattern of the entire decade, throughout which the number of applications remained elevated compared to prior decades (see Figure 3). Nonetheless, despite the growing number of applications for asylum, predominantly from Eastern European citizens (85% of all applications between 1982 and 1986), the frequency of instances in which permission was granted did not increase. While the transitory character of the refugee flows into Austria remained, e.g. with regard to the Polish refugees,[25] the more restrictive approach of the Austrian authorities, which demanded stricter examination of Eastern European citizens who formerly had been granted asylum automatically, had an impact (Münz et al. 2003: 24). Due to the lower rate of recognition, asylum thus did not significantly affect the number of legalized foreign residents until the end of the 1980s.

Figure 3:   **Applications for asylum in Austria, 1961-2012**

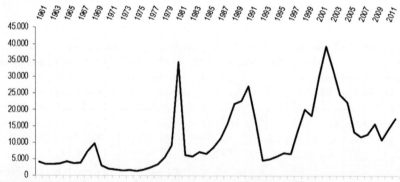

Source: Statistical Handbook of the Republic of Austria (1960-2000); after 2000, Statistics Austria.

Note: De facto refugees from former Yugoslavian territories – about 108.000 refugees from Croatia, Bosnia & Kosovo arriving between 1991 and 1999 – are not included in the official statistics on asylum requests (Fassmann/Fenzl (2003).

---

[25] While between 120,000 and 150,000 refugees came to Austria in 1981, only about 33,000 applied for permanent asylum; see Weigl (2009: 33).

Yet the peak in the number of applications at the end of the decade marked the beginning of a new period of Austrian immigration patterns that was driven both by developments in the number of refugees and by changing conditions in labor migration and the associated channels of immigration. Thus around the turn of the decade, a sharp increase in foreign national influx boosted the number of foreign-national residents by about 80% in four years, from 390,000 in 1989 to 690,000 in 1993 (Münz et al. 2003: 25). This increase was largely owed to the concurrence of three developments: Firstly, the fall of the Iron Curtain set the scene for migration flows of Eastern European citizens, many of whom used Austria as a backdoor entrance to Western Europe without any intention of settling. Secondly, the emerging crisis in Yugoslavia culminated in a decade of wars in the Balkans and led to an increase in refugees, with Austria being one of the foremost destinations due to its geographic proximity (Bauböck 1996: 20). At the beginning of the decade, refugees from the civil wars in Croatia (1991) and Bosnia-Herzegovina (1992/93) were treated as "de facto" refugees and consequently granted a preliminary residence permit. While a majority of the 13,000 Croatian refugees remigrated after the war, around two thirds of the 95,000 Bosnian refugees settled permanently in Austria, unlike the refugee groups of the previous decades (Münz et al. 2003: 25-6). Thirdly, but unrelatedly to the refugee situation, the booming economic conditions at the turn of the decade exacerbated the need for immigrant labor. While this demand was met partially by the regularization of 30,000 illegal foreigners (Weigl 2009: 45) as well as by the refugees from the aftermath of the Yugoslavian crisis, emigration from Turkey turned out to be a major channel for actual labor immigration (Bauböck 1996: 20; Münz et al. 2003: 26). Thus, as Fassmann/Münz (2000) documented, the majority of incoming foreigners during the period from 1989 to 1993 were not of Eastern European origin, as had been predicted by critics, but were rather immigrants from Turkey (the traditional source country of labor migration to Austria) and the successor states of former Yugoslavia due to the violent conflicts (Münz et al. 2003: 25).

The Austrian government responded to these developments at the beginning of the 1990s with a number of legislative reforms. The passage in quick succession of the Asylum Act (AsylG 1991), Residence Act (AufG 1992), and Aliens Act (FrG 1992) imposed a tighter regime of migrant entrance and asylum criteria. These events coincided with the end of the refugee flows from the Balkans, and accordingly the influx of non-nationals decreased dramatically from 1994 onwards. More legislative reforms reduced immigration in 1997: a revision of the Aliens Act (FrG 1997) that curtailed family reunifications (Antalovsky/Wolffhardt 2002: 164-5), and an amendment to the Asylum Act (AsylG 1997) that included further restrictions on asylum, allowing rejections based on Dublin agreements and secure third country rules, and of evidently groundless requests. Thus in the course of the 1990s legal measures for stricter regulation of migration and asylum were instituted by the grand coalition government; only toward the end of the decade did a renewed increase take place, both in asylum requests as well as in regular migration (Lebhart/Marik-Lebeck 2007: 167). In sum, however, by the end of the decade, these developments together with the other sources of immigration led to an immigrant population twice as large as it was prior to the 1990s (1988: 4,4%, 1999: 8,7%), though this trend was further strengthened by EU foreigners moving to Austria who did not need to apply for residence. After the country's EU accession in 1994, Austria was urged to apply EU standards in questions of labor access and family reunification for EU members as well as for third-country nationals (Weigl 2009: 46).

Besides the resulting increase in family reunifications, the modes of migration within the EU also played an important role in shaping immigration during the early years of the 2000s. Continuing the trends of the late 1990s and accompanied by a slight annual increase in immigrant residence, the number of non-national residents grew further over the course of the decade. What characterized this period was the growing relevance of immigration from "old European countries", from neighboring Germany in particular (Weigl 2009: 47). These shifts in migrant origins contributed to rising net totals of migration, even though the legislation of the decade consisted of further restrictions (imposed by a center-right/radical-right government coalition): An amendment to the Alien Act (FrG 2002) strengthened restrictions on labor migration to allow only "key workers" (*Schlüsselkräfte*), but more importantly, it reinforced cultural pressure toward migrant integration by introducing a mandatory "Integration Agreement" (Mourão Permoser/Rosenberger 2012: 47-8).[26] An amendment to the Asylum Act (Asyl-G-Novelle 2003) aimed at massively accelerating asylum procedures by introducing an admissions procedure prior to the actual asylum procedure, by weakening rights to appeal, and by accelerating expulsion in cases of procedural rejection; the amendment was heavily criticized for its disregard for fundamental human rights and the principle of refuge (Vogl 2007: 24-5). In response to the newly issued EU directives[27] of the European Council and Parliament, in 2005 the governing parties (ÖVP/BZÖ) succeeded with the support of the SPÖ in

---

[26] The Integration Agreement was introduced as a set of mandatory tasks for third-country nationals (nationals of other EU members are excluded), although asylum seekers, "highly qualified workers" (*Schlüsselkräfte*), "important executive personnel" (*besondere Führungskräfte*), and graduates of Austrian school education were exempted. The "Agreement" obliged signatories to attend language/country courses as well as exams (for detailed discussion of the Integration Agreement and its implementation, see Mourão Permoser 2010).

[27] Council Directive 2003/86/EC (right to family reunification); Council Directive 2003/109/EC (status of third-country nationals who are long-term residents); Council Directive 2003/9/EC (minimum standards for the reception of asylum seekers); Directive 2004/38/ECof the European Parliament and of the Council (right of citizens of the Union and their family members to move and reside freely within the territory of the Member States).

passing a whole new Alien Legislation Package (Fremdenrechtspaket 2005), which included a new Asylum Act (AsylG 2005), Settlement and Residence Act (NAG 2005), Aliens Police Act (FPG 2005), and several amendments to existing laws (Bruckner 2006: 5). Implementing the framework of the directives, the new legislation brought improvements, especially for long-term residents. However, as Perchinig (2009: 245) qualified it, the implementation of the standards of the directives was not unreserved: Rights were granted to family members only to a limited extent, family reunification rights were linked to the use of EU rights of free movement and to high income requirements, protections of native third-country children from expulsion were dismantled, permanent residence rights were restricted to highly qualified workers and their family members, and the integration agreement was made more strict (with more obligatory class hours and deductibles of up to 50%). Despite these legislative measures, the number of foreigners immigrating to Austria increased considerably during the first half of the decade, though this increase was accompanied by a growing number of naturalizations and thus only slightly increased the total number of foreign residents (Lebhart/Marik-Lebeck 2007: 167). In fact, naturalizations reached their highest level in decades, revealing their decisive role in the management of immigration.

Figure 4: **Naturalization of non-national residents in Austria, 1961-2012**

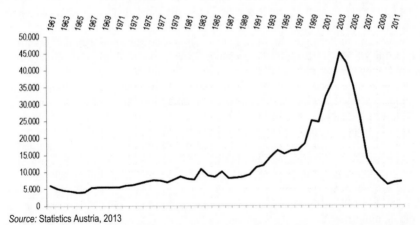

Source: Statistics Austria, 2013

Note: Results are based on information from the databases on conferral of citizenship submitted by the provincial governments. Included in this naturalization statistic are only cases of conferral in consequence to a declared intent by the applicant (StbG 1985, idF Novelle 2009 [§§ 10 to 17 and 58c]) and other modes (such as automatic acquisition by birth or by regularization of children born out of wedlock).

Figure 4 documents the different practices of naturalization when comparing the pre-1989 with the post-1989 period: What had been a quite stable pattern from the 1960s to the 1980s came to an end with a distinct increase in naturalizations in the late 1980s. These developments went hand in hand with continual reforms of the 1965 Nationality Act (StbG 1965) and with citizenship historically having been based on *ius sanguinis* rather than *ius soli*; thus all of the amendments (1973, 1983, 1985, 1993, 1999) were inspired by a logic that viewed naturalization as the end goal of successful integration (Davy/Çinar 2001: 645-6). Throughout the decades, the period of permanent residence required for the acquisition of citizenship has remained at ten years (Mourão Permoser/Rosenberger 2012: 51). However, due to many guest workers taking up permanent residence, some provinces, especially Vienna, demonstrated a more inclusive approach during the late 1980s and early 1990s, increasingly granting citizenship on the grounds of "particular noteworthy reasons" after permanent residence of four years, and thus contributing to the increase in naturalizations (Davy/Çinar 2001: 646). The sudden increase in immigration also manifested in the rising number of naturalizations from the 1990s onwards, which peaked around the turn of the millennium at almost 45,000 naturalizations in 2003 (as migrants were granted citizenship after ten years of permanent residence). Since then, however, the number has sharply declined, returning to levels similar to those of the 1960s and 1970s.

Obviously, naturalization practices have a considerable impact on statistics measuring the presence of foreign nationals in Austria. While the low rate of naturalization until the late 1980s had only marginal distorting effects on the statistics of foreign residents in Austria, since the 1990s the numbers have been obscured by the rising naturalization rate. These circumstances beg the statistical question of how to capture the presence of second and third-generation immigrants who are commonly labelled as having "immigrant backgrounds". Existing data on immigration and asylum fails to consider the central question of what in public discourse is closely linked to the "immigration issue": the question of integration. The integration of ethnic minorities – regardless of whether they possess Austrian citizenship or not – has not been captured by any data on immigration and asylum until recently. As explained above, continuing, undiminished naturalization rates, together with family reunifications, have led to the presence of a significant number of second and third-generation immigrants, many of whom hold Austrian citizenship and thus enjoy certain social and political rights, but still suffer from the same social exclusions typically experienced by ethnic minorities.

Unfortunately, statistical evaluation in Austria has only recently started to observe this group, making historical analysis difficult. As Figure 4 shows, naturalization has been constantly increasing since the 1960s, especially in the last decade. Yet while nowadays about 1.578 million (or 18.9% of) Austrian citizens have "immigrant backgrounds", with more than a million of them having been born abroad and about 412,000 of them being descendants of foreign-born parents,[28] such statistics cannot be adduced for earlier decades. Few longitudinal indicators are available that help us to understand the ethnic diversity of the Austrian population over time. The number of Austrian citizens who spoke a colloquial language other than German rose from 1.16% (1971) to 1.56% (1981), 2.35% (1991), and finally to 4.52% (2001).[29] Assessing the different countries of origin of naturalized residents reveals that during the 1960s and until the 1980s, German citizens were by far the largest national group naturalized by the Austrian state. As is also true of the second-largest group during that period, Hungarian citizens, this proportion has steadily decreased ever since. While during the 1980s and early 1990s Poland and Romania were the main origins of newly naturalized citizens, since then the Balkan region and Turkey have emerged as the most common countries of origin. However, none of this provides any further information about the actual integration of ethnic minorities. The only conclusion that can be inferred from such knowledge is that the question of integration may have grown in importance during this period, but there is no clear-cut indication as to how and when politicization may have influenced the developments recounted above. Due to this lack of differentiated data on integration, this study refrains from specific statements about the link between socio-structural indicators and party politicization of integration.

Expected influence on politicization

What conclusions can be drawn then regarding the politicization of migration and ethnic relations? Positing a direct association between empirically observable conditions and political engagement, the study's conceptual hypothesis regarding the policy fields of migration and ethnic relations is that *an observable increase of immigration/asylum will increase the systemic salience of these issue dimensions in the political debate (H3)*. This assumption still needs to be specified further with regard to certain issue dimensions. Primarily, it can be hypothesized that in times of dramatic increase in immigration the political debate will be more intense than in periods of lower relevance. To reformulate this in operational terms:

---

[28] *Source:* Statistics Austria. Data based on inter-census population estimates. Download: http://www.statistik.at/web_de/statistiken/bevoelkerung/bevoelkerungsstruktur/bevoelkeru ng_nach_migrationshintergrund/index.html, Download 11. Nov. 2013.
Migration background is defined as cases of native Austrians whose parents both were born abroad.

[29] *Source:* Statistics Austria. Data based on census of population; results include cases with combination of German and foreign colloquial language. Of course, colloquial language is an inaccurate indicator for immigrant population, since it does not reflect the divergences between allochtonous and autochtonous minorities. Download: http://www.statistik.at/web_de/statistiken/bevoelkerung/volkszaehlungen_registerzaehlung en/bevoelkerung_nach_demographischen_merkmalen/022886.html, Download 11. Nov. 2013.

The greater the net total immigration has been in the legislative period prior to an election, the more strongly the issue dimension "immigration" will be electorally politicized (H3a).

As already shown above, the highest peaks in net migration to Austria can be dated to certain periods: the late 1960s (1969 to 1974), the late 1980s (1989 to 1993) and the beginning of the 21st century (2000 to 2005). According to the hypothesis, elections within these periods should show the strongest increases in the salience of the immigration dimension (1971, 1990, 2002, 2006). A different hypothesis needs to be advanced concerning the question of asylum, since its relevance emerges independently of other issues such as general labor migration or family reunification, though the structure of the assumption remains the same:

The greater the number of applications for asylum (including applicants for de-facto contingents) has been in the legislative period prior to an election, the more strongly the issue dimension "asylum" will be electorally politicized (H3b).

Based on this hypothesis, the real world developments in asylum would suggest increasing relevance at the advent and in the second half of the 1980s, a peak during the early 1990s (due to the special contingents for de facto refugees from Croatia and Bosnia), and an increase in applications for asylum in the first half of the first post-millennial decade. Nonetheless, as mentioned previously, there are other important external factors that constitute the environment of party competition, among them public opinion.

3.1.2 Public opinion on migration and ethnic relations

Linking societal indicators that influence the public and, more specifically, the political debate is a difficult endeavor. What might be seen by one actor to be a highly significant development might be completely disregarded by another. However, if parties are organizations that try to satisfy their constituencies in the long run, it stands to reason that the values and preferences of these constituencies can be considered fairly influential on party strategies. Thus scholars of party competition have argued that it is less the empirically observable environment of a policy field that animates a party's decision to politicize it than the perceptions and attitudes of the electorate (for an overview, see Adams 2012). The general relevance of public opinion to the electoral strategies of political parties is a natural assumption, particularly among authors in the tradition of Downs, who argue that parties' policy choices are responsive to public opinion. Only by seeking to assess the public's policy preferences are parties able to derive reference values of positions in a given policy dimension. Therefore, obvious shifts in public opinion might be expected to be a central issue to party strategy. However, empirical observations have not clearly indicated this. For example, in their comparison of nine Western democracies, McDonald et al. (2004) found no evidence whatsoever for any significant relationship between "electoral concerns and party policy", which leads them to conclude that "parties choose policy positions independently of public sentiments at the time of the election" (McDonald et al. 2004: 854). Conversely, Adams et al. (2004: 590) demonstrated that parties' ideological orientations and their politicization strategies do indeed shift in response to changes in public opinion (though only when public opinion takes a different direction from a party's policy position). So it seems to be a vital task for parties to determine the preferences of their constituencies and the current trends of public opinion. As a consequence, this study is obliged to uncover the perceptions and attitudes that Austrian voters have expressed over the course of recent decades. Unfortunately, while any ex post reconstruction of knowledge about public preferences in recent decades poses a challenge, it is even more difficult when focusing on the role of migration and ethnic relations, as very little survey data is available that might give a longitudinal indication of either their relevance or the positions predominating in Austrian public opinion. Comparative data is available only starting in the 1990s, which drastically limits our prospects for analyzing the role of public opinion. In order to offer at least a rough impression of the available information on public opinion, some selected previous findings shall be discussed.

In a comparative study, Lebhart/Münz (2003) contrasted surveys conducted independently between 1992 and 2001 that investigated various indicators of hostile attitudes toward foreigners among the Austrian population (see Table 4). The comparison reveals conflicting tendencies in the indicator pool: On the one hand, indicators of cultural rejection as well as political exclusion of foreigners have increased over the decades. Demographic rejections show the same pattern, whereas exclusionist arguments based on labor displacement declined up until 2001. Taking these indicators together, it appears that attitudes were slightly more averse in the early 1990s, while around the turn of the millennium the tendency shifted slightly toward more open attitudes, most visibly in 2001.

Table 4:   Agreement with the item … (in %)

	1992	1998	2001
… foreigners deprive Austrians of their jobs	44	42	25
… foreigners contribute to cultural gain	30	35	44
… foreigners should obtain municipal voting rights after five years of residence	22	29	39
… immigration is necessary to stop decrease in population	32	27	40

Source: Holzer/Münz (1994) and Lebhart/Münz (1999) as cited in Lebhart/Münz (2003)

Friesl et al. (2009) offered a more extensive comparison, combining survey results from 1994 (Solidaritätsstudie, "Solidarity Study") with findings from the dataset of the European Values Survey (EVS) from 1999 and 2008 (Table 5). Based on similar questions to those of Lebhart/Münz (2003), they devised an index to measure the hostility of Austrian attitudes toward foreigners. Their findings somewhat contradict the results from Lebhart/Münz, indicating an increase in antipathy toward foreigners from the early to the late 1990s and a stabilization of predominantly hostile attitudes in 2008 (with 55% of respondents agreeing with restrictive items). In spite of that, the results of 1994 must be interpreted with caution, since they were conducted by different researchers and they examine a time period in which the heated debate over the "Austria first" petition of the FPÖ and the counter-demonstrations ("Lichtermeer") may have contributed to elevated approval of "solidarity" items. Thus, due to survey heterogeneity and the data points selected, the assumption of an increase between the early and late 1990s needs to be qualified.

Table 5:   Index "hostility to foreigners" (in %)

	1994	1999	2008
Agreement	45	54	55
Neither/nor	27	25	30
Rejection	18	17	13
Missing	10	3	2

Source: Holzer/Münz (1994) and Lebhart/Münz (1999) as cited in Lebhart/Münz (2003)

Rosenberger/Seeber (2011) tried to overcome both deficits (time frame and survey heterogeneity) by using the EVS dataset in order to quantify antipathy toward foreigners based on the survey question of which groups would be less tolerable as neighbors by the respondents (Table 6).

Table 6:   Index of antipathy toward immigrants

	1990	1999	2008
Austria	.142	.119	.232
Belgium	.213	.165	.087
Denmark	.113	.114	.069
Finland	.131	.145	.155
France	.132	.124	.051
Germany	.159	.087	.128
Ireland	.081	.130	.132
Italy	.133	.164	.171
Netherlands	.101	.074	.148
Portugal	.155	.056	.114
Spain	.089	.102	.069
Sweden	.108	.049	.092
United Kingdom	.118	.128	.110
Average	*.129*	*.112*	*.120*

Source: Rosenberger/Seeber (2010), 180-6, indices based on European Value Surveys 1990, 1999, 2008.

Note: Antipathy is calculated based on attitudes toward unwelcome neighbors. "Migrants" in this survey denotes people of a different skin color, Muslims, and immigrant or guest workers. The index is calculated by the number of unwelcome neighbors indicated by a respondent, and ranges from 1 (every group being rejected) to 0 (no groups rejected). Country results are based on the average value of all respondents from that country.

The changes in the index over nine-year intervals (1990, 1999, 2008) confirm the fluctuating attitudes among Austrian respondents and thus the data gathered by Lebhart/Münz showing weaker antipathy around the end of the 1990s than during the contentious period of 1990. Most importantly, it highlights the great increase in antipathy of recent years, with Austria in 2008 having the highest index value of any country at any time point sampled (0.232). Thus while Austria already ranked among the most antipathetic countries in 1990, it set a new benchmark for hostile attitudes in 2008.

A similar verdict on attitudes toward migrants and minorities was reached by the Eurobarometer in 2005, which compared the old EU-15 on their degree of "resistance to multicultural society". Austria is one of only four countries to consistently feature resistance scores that are above the average of all 15 countries, and is topped only by Belgium, Germany and Greece (Table 7).

Table 7:   'Resistance to multicultural society' in each Member State, Old EU-15, mean scores

	1997	2000	2003
Austria	.404	.405	.391
Belgium	.552	.490	.480
Denmark	.412	.318	.301
Finland	.270	.355	.322
France	.301	.320	.317
Germany East	.458	.458	.487
Germany West	.450	.474	.443
Great Britain	.233	.311	.305
Greece	.604	.673	.698
Ireland	.223	.374	.257
Italy	.412	.374	.370
Luxembourg	.251	.370	.274
Netherlands	.286	.307	.334
Northern Ireland	.266	.255	.261
Portugal	.263	.294	.324
Spain	.236	.270	.263
Sweden	.314	.330	.288
EU (country average)	*.355*	*.381*	*.366*

Source: EUMC 2005, scores based on 1997, 2000 and 2003 Eurobarometer

Note: Based on a bipolar scale from 0 (no resitance) to 1 (absolute resistance).

All together, these selective indications show a considerable prevalence of antipathetic attitudes amidst the Austrian population, at least for the last two decades. These patterns make Austria rank among the most averse European countries in terms of public opinion on people of immigrant origin. This tendency seems even to have increased in recent years, although – or perhaps because – two decades of intensified public debate and political action have shaped the perception of the issue. However, it remains difficult to glean impressions of the same kind for the period prior to 1990. There are only a few rather intuitive indications that there may have been less public awareness and skepticism with regard to migration and ethnic relations. For example, Zuser (1996) and Plasser/Ulram (1991b) suggested that what they labeled the "foreigner question" (*Ausländerfrage*) dates back to the year 1990. The latter even present as evidence data from a survey that was conducted among Viennese and Lower Austrian citizens in December 1989, after the Austrian border to Czechoslovakia had been opened. At that time, respondents expressed positive attitudes toward the border opening, and even the long-term impact of these developments was seen optimistically (Plasser/Ulram 1991b: 313). Negative associations with the issue, according to the authors, arose only in spring of 1990 due to a variety of circumstances including the continuous overcrowding at the refugee camp in Traiskirchen, the "Causa Kaisersteinbruch"[30], increasing black-market activities, petty crime, clandestine labor and, last but not least, an aggressive anti-foreigner campaign by the foremost Austrian tabloid paper, Neue Kronen Zeitung (Plasser/Ulram 1991b: 312-4). Thus the importance of the issue and its negative associations increased over the course of the year, and, for the first time, negative campaigning against migration and ethnic relations became politically fertile ground. In the course of 1990 nearly every party jumped on this bandwagon (Plasser/Ulram 1991b: 316-7).

Unfortunately, no such survey (with a particular focus on migration and ethnic relations) was conducted for other elections. As a consequence, despite the findings outlined above, it is not possible to make more detailed conjectures on the interaction of public opinion and electoral politicization from a longitudinal perspective. Firstly, there is no reliable information about the attitudes of the Austrian population concerning migration and ethnic relations during or prior to the 1980s, rendering it impossible to determine the role of public opinion during the period of party system transformation in the mid-1980s, and to chart public attitudes in the 1960s/70s (i.e. the guest-worker period). Secondly, even the data since the 1990s reveals only gross patterns of development, because the time intervals between the surveys were considerable and because many of the surveys were structured differently, which raises the difficulty of comparing their findings. As a consequence, this study is limited to rather general conjectures regarding the influence of public opinion, such as that the comparatively high prevalence of anti-immigrant sentiment among the Austrian population may favor parties representing restrictive rather than liberal positions. However, this majority view might be a less decisive factor for Austrian niche parties' strategic evaluations, since they are less obliged to align their stances to majority views for two reasons: Not only are they ideologically linked to particular fringe posi-

---

[30] In March 1990, the Austrian government aimed to shelter about 800 Romanian refugees in a former military barracks located in the village of Kaisersteinbruch, which had no more than 250 residents. After continual demonstrations and road blockades organized by the resident population, the government's plan was abandoned.

tions on migration and ethnic relations (see section 3.2.1), but their specific electorates also predominantly promote either liberal or restrictive stances (see Table 8).[31]

Table 8:   **Voting decisions based on niche parties' stance on migration and ethnic relations, 1986-2008**

		1986	1990	1994	1999	2002	2006	2008
FPÖ	% of voters naming party's "immigration-stance" as voting motive	2	39	49	47	52	56	-[2)
Greens	% of voters naming party's "immigration-stance" as voting motive	-[1)	-[1)	48	58	47	58	10

Sources: Plasser/Ulram 1987; Plasser et al. 1991a; Plasser et al. 1995; Plasser et al. 2000; Plasser et al. 2002; Plasser et al. 2007; Ulram 2008

Note: Results are based on exit polls.
1) Survey reports do not indicate whether "foreigner policies" were excluded from the questionnaire or were in fact unimportant for Green voters.
2) Multiple items related to migration and ethnic relations prevent calculation of a single valid result.

While the general tendencies of public opinion are of lesser importance for niche parties' considerations, the majority opinion may be of much greater importance for Austrian mainstream parties' considerations. Mainstream parties, which target a broader spectrum of voters and are more flexible in choosing their positions on new issues orthogonal to traditional cleavages, naturally react more sensitively to overall public opinion than do niche parties. As a consequence, Austrian *mainstream parties are expected to respond more visibly to antipathetic prevalence in Austrian public opinion by favoring restrictive stances over liberal ones (H4),* for example in the early 1990s and after the millennium.

In a nutshell, what has become apparent is the difficulty of isolating available data for examining societal inputs to party politicization of migration and ethnic relations. Although theoretically these factors merit considerable attention, the absence of data limits the actual possibilities for assessing them empirically. Nonetheless some indicators and their possible interactions with politicization have been discussed, at least, in order to take them into consideration as explanatory clues. However, the main argument of this book takes a different direction: Based on the theoretical debate presented in chapter 2, it assumes instead that parties align their strategies much more strongly to opportunities and constraints that emerge from within the system of party competition.

---

[31] The most surprising aspect of these findings is the very low relevance the question of immigration had for FPÖ voters in 1986 immediately after Jörg Haider took over the party leadership. While about two thirds of FPÖ voters named the person of Jörg Haider as their voting motive, the party's success in 1986 was only marginally a "national, right-wing conservative phenomenon" (Plasser/Ulram 1987: 70).

3.2   Influencing party competition from within: The Austrian party system as a framework for party behavior

The socio-structural and attitudinal conditions discussed in the previous section constitute a common environment of opportunities and constraints that is shared by all parties. If parties were merely troubleshooters purposing to tackle existing social problems, changes in real world conditions would raise concerns across all parties alike. Obviously, such a static characterization hardly accurately describes the political world, as it disregards how real world conditions might be perceived, interpreted and addressed differently by different parties. What might be evaluated as being highly significant or problematic by one actor might be completely disregarded or treated affirmatively by another. These differences in approaching the empirically observable world, however, are impossible to explain by factors external to the party system. On the contrary, they result from characteristics that constitute the individual parties themselves as well as their interrelations in the party system. As a consequence, this book is searching for conceptual explanations originating within the competitive framework itself. It is the core argument of this study that party behavior in regard to migration and ethnic relations can be well understood only by focusing on the strategic considerations of parties in striving for success in competition with their opponents.

The first step is to focus on the individual characteristics of parties, prefacing it with an investigation of the major political cleavages in the Austrian party system in order to develop ideology-based conjectures about party behavior regarding the politicization of migration and ethnic relations. Besides the static influence of ideology, intra-party dynamics of the party system itself are also considered as a vital factor influencing both the positions occupied and the amount of emphasis placed by political parties on these policy fields. Thus the number and strengths of parties in the Austrian party system, the pressures they exert on each other, and the coalition options between parties resulting from these numerical patterns serve as essential explanations for the behavior of individual parties vis-à-vis their opponents.

3.2.1   Political cleavages and party ideology

The socio-structural inputs discussed in the previous section may be crucial factors for party politicization; however, in order to comply with the constructivist view that conceptions of reality may diverge among observers with different ideological backgrounds, certainly party ideology needs to be considered as much as socio-structural inputs if politicization strategies linked to migration and ethnic relations are to be accurately predicted. Like individuals, parties and politicians alike see the world through different lenses. Thus what might be defined as a problematic condition by one actor might very well be portrayed as a positive circumstance by another, and accordingly lead to different ways of dealing with the phenomenon. These different ways of approaching the world and defining its patterns, problems, and norms are bundled in what we term "ideology", which has been proven to be an even more important factor in explaining politicization than current problems or public opinion (McDonald et al. 2004).

Cleavage theory and party families

In fact, such a perspective is inherent to the cleavage theory of party competition, one of the most influential approaches for explaining the development and transformations of party competition in Western democracies. To understand parties as genuine translators of basic conflicts in a society, both the social cleavages as well as party ideologies need to be examined in greater detail. Using the basic distinction offered by Lipset/Rokkan (1967: 14-5), four traditional cleavages have been identified in the 19th and early 20th centuries: *dominant vs. subject culture (administrative and cultural level), church(es) vs. government, primary vs. secondary economy, and workers vs. employers&owners.* These four lines of conflict have dominated European democracies since their establishment and, with regional variations, generally led to the establishment of a set of parties that are differentiable using the notion of ideology.

The distinction between "ideological families" of political parties results from the fact that they translate social divisions and conflicts into a mode of competition that is settled through voting instead of violence (Lipset/Rokkan 1967: 5). Although the criteria for constructing typologies of party families can vary significantly (Mair/Mudde 1998), Vasallo/Wilcox (2006: 413) distinguished at least seven major families of parties that are common today in the majority of studies of party politics: Communist parties, Socialist parties, Left-Libertarian parties, Green parties, Liberal parties, Christian Democratic parties and new (radical) right parties. The rise of each of these different party families has been linked to particular cleavage conflicts. For example, Communist and Socialist parties derive their primary ideological structure from the support of mass labor protest and the struggle for the extension of rights against the interests of owners and employers, though the strategies they have proposed have differed in the course of centuries (which has created new lines of conflict, i.e. a "Communism/Socialism cleavage" – see Caramani 2007: 324). Although Christian Democratic and Conservative parties obviously have addressed conflicts of capital and labor, too (promoting the interests of employers and owners), their primary source of identification originally emanated from a conflict with liberalist perspectives (i.e. the defense of traditional privileges of church and monarchy versus liberal attempts to advance the autonomy of the nation state and to promote liberal values, as well as the protection of agricultural interests in the periphery versus liberal efforts to establish a free market in the industrialized urban parts of the countries (Caramani 2007: 323). These traditionalist tenets have been reflected in conservative economic concepts and efforts to promote law and order in times of crisis (Vasallo/Wilcox 2006: 419). On the other side of these cleavages, liberal parties historically emerged as the voice of middle-class interests against the old aristocratic elites, pressing for the autonomy of the nation-state as part of the state-church cleavage, and thereby came to represent the interests of employers and owners on the capital-labor cleavage as well as on the urban-rural cleavage, which led them into conflict with conservative, agrarian/peasant and regionalist parties (Caramani 2007: 320-2). The last parties in particular pressed for cultural, religious, or linguistic autonomy against the attempts toward cultural standardization of the nation state (such as in Scotland, Ireland or Spain) and thus addressed a special element of the center-periphery conflict, namely the cultural dimension (Caramani 2007: 320-1).

These 19th and early 20th-century cleavages and their respective party proponents have continued to shape European democracies up to the present day, although many of the traditional lines of conflict have blurred during the last few decades and been overshadowed by new divisions addressed by new types of parties. The most influential cross-regional transformations have developed as a consequence of what Bell (1973) labeled the "post-industrial revolution" of the 1960s and 1970s. In the emerging conflict over "post-materialistic values" like peace, participation, equality, and environmental issues (Caramani 2007: 325), a number of new social movements have arrived on the political scene, though they rarely evolve into political parties. The major exception, of course, is the environmental movement, which, little by little starting in the 1970s, has established political parties as its institutional outlets all over Europe (and in the process has often included proponents of other "post-materialistic" social movements who have helped it to diversify its single-issue foundations [Inglehart 1990]).

A second important cleavage arising in the post-industrial revolution period is linked to the conflict over the negative consequences of globalization, which especially concern those who suffer the greatest disadvantages as a result, such as blue-collar workers, small and medium-sized businesses, and peasant farmers. The growing controversies over the effects of globalization have facilitated the emergence of new (or in some cases renewed) radical right protest parties promoting protectionist policies and "locals first" attitudes that often were and still are linked to "cultural, anti-immigration and xenophobic prejudice stressing religious and national values against multi-ethnic society and cosmopolitanism" (Caramani 2007: 325). Even though some of them focused on no other issue (Mudde 1999; Gibson 2002: 8), many of these radical right parties either always had or gradually developed somewhat broader agendas, including aspects such as criticism of the welfare state, appeals for greater economic liberalism, and calls for strict law & order regimes (Vasallo/Wilcox 2006: 420).

The evolution of Austrian political cleavages

Historically, the Austrian party spectrum can, for the most part, be explained by reference to the ideologies of these classic party families and the main cleavages defined by Lipset/Rokkan. The dominant actors of Austrian party politics – despite experiencing internal shifts of varying magnitude – have maintained their presence since their origins in the 1880s. In the closing decades of the 19th century, three traditional "camps", mainly from the German-speaking regions of the Austro-Hungarian Monarchy (Luther 1999: 119), became fertile ground for political parties. These early parties were rooted ideologically in certain cleavage positions that appealed to their support bases in the electorate. The largest of them, the anti-clerical Social Democratic Workers Party (*Sozialdemokratische Arbeiterpartei*, SDAP), first and foremost represented working-class interests in socio-economic conflicts, explicitly emphasizing this position in its name (Plasser/Ulram 2006: 352).[32] The Christian Social Party (*Christlichsoziale Partei*, CS) represented the second large camp in Austrian society, which was predominantly of Catholic faith and anti-capitalist orientation and occupied itself with a religious or denominational conflict embedded in the state-church cleavage. Its primary goal was to combat the ousting of the Catholic Church and traditional Catholic values and customs by secular or liberal state hegemony (Pelinka/Rosenberger 2000: 21). These two parties thus represented prototypically divergent electorates and occupied opposing positions on both of their characteristic cleavages (capital-labor, state-church).

Yet these dominant camps shared a common line of conflict against the third important camp in 19th-century Austria, the significantly smaller pan-German camp, which was represented by a group of smaller parties rather than a single established party (Pelinka/Rosenberger 2000: 21).[33] Though they differed in their anti-clerical and anti-socialist orientations, these parties were unified by the assertion of a pan-German identity in the face of ethnic conflict in the multiethnic Austrian Habsburg Empire and the subsequent First Austrian Republic (1918-1933). This cultural conflict over the core and limits of a national identity, pan-German vs. Austrian (Plasser/Ulram 2006: 352), has been identified as the cultural component of the center-periphery cleavage, as in the model of Lipset/Rokkan (Pelinka 1998: 74). By the time of the fall of the monarchy and the end of the First World War, the cultural cleavage in Austria had become a crunch question in a country that had shrivelled to a microstate and a party system that was built on shaky ground. Consequently, past conflict lines other than the cultural were exacerbated, resulting in increasingly intense conflicts during the 1920s that eventually culminated in a brief period of civil war in 1934, followed by a single-party regime installed by the victorious CS (critically labelled "Austro-Fascism"), which itself was supplanted by the "Anschluss" to Hitler's Germany in 1938 (Luther 1999: 120-1).

---

[32] Supported by mainly urban proletariat, the advancement of (industrial) labour interests by the SDAP conflicted with the interests of both the Christian conservative camp (representing vast parts of the rural peasantry and landowners) and the German National camp (representing above all white-collar workers and members of the state bureaucracy) (Luther 1999: 119-20).

[33] Many of these German National parties persisted only briefly or merged with the more important German National Workers' Party or the Greater German People's Party, founded in 1918.

The reconstruction of a functioning Austrian party system after World War II reflected not only the pre-war cleavages, but also the inter-war experiences and the trauma of the National Socialist regime, as, after 1945, the political elites had developed an awareness of the need to redress the atrocities of those decades (Plasser 1999). Even though conditions largely resembled those of 1918 (a starving economic situation, a residual microstate, and continuity of political camps, political parties and even political personnel), some decisive factors had changed, such as the widespread discrediting of the pan-German ideology, open support of the Western Allies, and the experience of the Allied occupation (1945-1955), which fostered a sense of Austrian nationality and a desire for sovereignty (Luther 1999: 121). Thus the relevance of the cultural cleavage had decreased in comparison to the inter-war period, since pan-German claims had largely lost their appeal and support in society by the 1950s (Plasser/Ulram 2006: 353). Together with the anti-communist and anti-fascist consensus of the Western allies, this effectively bounded the party system's ideological spectrum (Luther 1999: 121).

As a matter of fact, the radical right segment of the electorate had shrunk dramatically, which is why even after the end of prohibition of such parties, the League of Independents (VDU), renamed the Freedom Party of Austria (FPÖ) in 1956, failed to effectively re-establish a cultural cleavage and would not gain more than a minor share of the federal votes for another three decades. On the other hand, due to the country's orientation to the Western model, the far-left Austrian Communist Party (KPÖ) also failed to establish a permanent base of support, and since 1959 it has never surpassed the 4% parliamentary threshold, which has left an open flank for center-left social democrats and has had major consequences in the development of the Austrian party spectrum.

The two Austrian mainstream parties, too, witnessed characteristic transformations that were mirrored in the adaptations of their names to "Austrian People's Party" (ÖVP) and "Socialist Party of Austria" in 1945 and then "Social Democratic Party of Austria" (SPÖ) from 1991 onwards, changes which were aimed at facilitating their development into catch-all parties (Pelinka 1998; Pelinka/Rosenberger 2000: 133). Due to the absence of niche parties, both Austrian mainstream parties were guided by an "essentially accommodative culture" (Luther 1999: 124), as a result of which the ideological spectrum of the Austrian party system only ever shifted slightly for almost 25 years. Reinforced by a "proportional electoral system" that supported mainstream parties at the expense of niche parties (Müller 2006: 287),[34] three players (SPÖ, ÖVP, FPÖ) remained in what had effectively become a two-and-a-half party system and one of the most stable of all Western democracies (Siaroff 2000: 179).

---

[34] This condition was slightly mitigated by the 1970 reform of the electoral system (a concession made by the Social Democrats in exchange for the FPÖ's support of a minority government) but restored by the electoral reform in 1992.

It was only by the (late) 1970s that an erosion of these ideological patterns began to set in. A period of single-party governments (1966-1983) brought an end to the historical post-war compromise and catalyzed the transformation of the FPÖ from a "backward-looking party, emphasizing protest and German-nationalism, toward gradual liberalization, albeit of a distinctly conservative variety" (Luther 1999: 129). Elsewhere in the party spectrum, the influence of "Green" parties had been increasing since the late 1970s as a result of their promotion first of environmental issues and later of post-materialistic values in general. From the 1980s on, the decreasing though not vanishing significance of traditional cleavages was met by the emergence of new conflict grounds, such as post-materialistic and libertarian demands in addition to monocultural vs. multicultural and cosmopolitan vs. national perspectives on society (Inglehart 1991; Dolezal 2005; Kriesi et al. 2006). In 1986 these shifting cleavage patterns materialized in the emergence of new niche parties that founded their success on these new divisions within the Austrian population (Plasser/Ulram 1987). While the dominant cleavage issue for the "Green Alternative" was obviously the post-materialistic question of environmentalism together with demands for more extensive minority rights (such as gender rights, ethnic minority rights, etc.), the dominant lines of conflict for the FPÖ lay in attacking the "old regime" and in advancing a welfare chauvinist and nationalist ideology that claimed to speak for the losers of globalization and manifested itself as a populist anti-system, anti-immigration platform. Thus the traditional pan-German sympathies in regard to the cultural aspect of the cleavage between center and periphery were reconstituted as a more general struggle between nationalism and cosmopolitanism and thus grew to be compatible with a more easily tolerated Austrian patriotism in place of the discredited German Nationalism (Pelinka 1998: 74; Fröhlich-Steffen 2004).

Developments ever since have clearly confirmed these transformations; both the Greens and the FPÖ have established themselves as forces to be reckoned within the Austrian party environment, albeit with varying degrees of success (see section 3.2.2). A fifth party entered the parliamentary arena in 1994: the "Liberal Forum" (LIF). A splinter party of the FPÖ, the LIF aimed to fill another vacant spot in the Austrian party spectrum by addressing traditional liberal issues such as the market economy, libertarian values, etc., and by having a popular party leader in the widely respected Heide Schmidt. Nevertheless, it failed to establish itself as a permanent presence and dropped out of Parliament in 1999. It became obvious that the conditions were not conducive to the continuing presence of a liberal party. Rather, there now appeared to be room for a second populist radical right party, the "Alliance for the Future of Austria" (BZÖ), another FPÖ splinter party that was founded in 2005 by Jörg Haider as a consequence of internal FPÖ controversies and the party's collapse in the 2002 election. Though both populist right parties addressed similar sections of the Austrian electorate, they did so with differing degrees of success. While the FPÖ re-established

strength under its new leader Heinz-Christian Strache, the BZÖ has been bat-
tling for its existence, especially since being deprived of its leading figure by
Haider's death in 2008, and finally dropped out of Parliament in the 2013 elections after having gradually reoriented its profile toward a center-right economic
liberalist position. This, however, was no indication that there was no further
electoral potential in the bourgeois segment of the electorate, since in 2013 two
newcomers capitalized on different sorts of dissatisfied voters: On the one hand,
"Team Stronach", a party patched together by the charismatic Austro-Canadian
billionaire Frank Stronach, succeeded with a center-right populist, heavily lead-
er-oriented campaign. However, the party's longevity was cast into doubt immediately after the election by internal conflict and the partial retreat of the party's founder. On the other hand, the second party to enter Parliament in 2013
was the newly founded "NEOS", which in fact represented a grassroots movement that collaborated with the remains of the LIF and thus occupied a similarly
liberal position in the party spectrum. Though it remains to be seen whether
these parties will manage to establish themselves more permanently, the increased turnover rate of parties since 1986 has demonstrated that what for decades was known as one of the most stable ideological party spectrums has become much more fluid and attractive for new niche parties capitalizing on vacant spots in the electoral spectrum.

To classify Austrian parties using the mainstream/niche party typology, because
of their ideology and their importance in the Austrian party system, both the
SPÖ and the ÖVP represent prototypical mainstream parties with catch-all platforms (Safran 2009). Furthermore, it is rather straightforward to identify the
FPÖ, Greens and BZÖ as examples of Austrian niche parties, with all of them
belonging to party families that show characteristics of the niche party group
(Adams et al. 2006, Meguid 2008). Classifying the three remaining post-1970
parliamentary parties, i.e. the LIF and the recent newcomers Team Stronach and
the NEOS, is a more difficult task (Deegan-Krause 2011). Since it has been dis-
puted among scholars whether a party's position on an overall left-right scale
(including economic issues) is adequate to identify it as a niche party (Adams et
al. 2006; Ezrow 2010) or whether the niche party concept by definition excludes
parties that compete on traditional economic issues (Meguid 2008; Wagner
2012), Meyer/Miller (2013: 2) suggested instead calculating a party's
"nicheness" based on the values of all its issue dimensions combined. Hence
they arrive at a minimalist description of niche parties, defining them as parties
that stress different political issues from their established opponents, and that
show similar organizational characteristics (such as a lack of mass organizational resources, atypical internal decision-making rules, and the role of public party
funding for their activities) that distinguish them from mainstream parties. According to this argument, a niche party can only be classified by its role within
the overall competitive structure, its focus on specific issues, and the organizational differences between itself and established mainstream parties. By this to-

ken, the LIF much more strongly resembled other niche parties, such as the Greens or the FPÖ, than it did the Austrian catch-all parties in the mainstream of the party spectrum. Thus, although the LIF occupied a centrist position on a left-right scale, its fringe position on a *green/alternative/liberal* vs. *traditional/authoritarian/nationalist* scale was as extreme as that of the Greens (see Table 9). This, along with the party's organizational structure and topical focus (which is effectively the same as that of its successor party, the NEOS), made it markedly resemble other niche parties in the Austrian party spectrum. Something similar might be said of the more recent newcomer parties, the NEOS and Team Stronach, since both promote a comparatively narrow electoral platform and address a small segment of the electorate. For this reason, in this study all three parties will be assigned to the niche party group in the evaluation (a decision that is borne out by the study's findings, as will be shown in Chapter 6).

Table 9:   Austrian party positions according to Chapel-Hill-expert survey

	1999		2002		2006		2010	
	left/right	gal/tan	left/right	gal/tan	left/right	gal/tan	left/right	gal/tan
SPÖ	4.00	4.00	3.75	3.38	3.38	3.50	3.36	3.93
ÖVP	6.20	6.50	7.00	8.25	7.00	7.67	7.07	7.21
FPÖ	7.90	7.10	8.63	9.00	9.67	9.67	8.93	8.71
Greens	2.90	2.00	2.83	1.38	2.17	0.83	2.29	1.50
LIF	4.60	1.80	4.60	2.40	4.60	1.40	-	-
BZÖ	-	-	-	-	8.83	8.83	8.29	7.79

Source: Chapel Hill Expert Survey (CHES)

Note: Scales range from 0 (extreme left/gal) to 10 (extreme right/tan), where "gal/tan" signifies a scale from green/alternative/libertarian to traditional/authoritarian/nationalist values.

Austrian cleavages relating to migration and ethnic relations

The general ideological foundations of Austrian parties permit predictions about how they will politicize the issues of migration and ethnic relations. This study expects that the strongest politicization will come from those parties whose predominant cleavage positions are linked to these issues, i.e. which have "issue ownership". Despite their historical associations and origins, migration and ethnic relations have been identified as comparatively new issues (at least in any form that represents a permanently divisive issue for societies), and are situated orthogonally to traditional cleavages such as socio-economic and religious conflicts (which are "owned" by the Austrian mainstream parties). Instead, they run parallel to the emerging post-materialistic cleavage (predominantly addressed by libertarian and green parties) and also correspond to a nationalistic cultural cleavage (politicized mainly by new radical right parties that usually explicitly position themselves as "anti-immigrant parties" [Bale et al. 2010: 412]). This should inform the expectations regarding the relevance of migration and ethnic relations to the various Austrian political parties:

Since questions of ethnicity have been a vital part of the cultural aspect of the center-periphery cleavage and a basic element of nationalist identity for the "third camp" ever since, the FPÖ will likely be the most assertive actor as far as the politicization of migration and ethnic relations is concerned, especially after the change in leadership from the liberal Norbert Steger to the nationalist, populist Jörg Haider in 1986. Given the party's explicitly anti-immigrant principles, its issue position is expected to be of a more restrictive nature. On the opposite side of the spectrum, too, ethnicity represents a constitutive element of a post-materialistic set of values promoted by the left-libertarian Greens. This party's guiding principle of supporting minority rights, together with its comparatively high proportion of party members of immigrant or minority background, makes the Austrian Greens another party that can be expected to actively politicize migration and ethnic relations issues. Its issue position is the opposite stance to that of the radical right, and it promotes liberal causes, particularly in regard to migration and ethnic relations. With the FPÖ and the Greens marking the opposing ends of the ideological spectrum on migration and ethnic relations, the remaining parties can be located between them. The liberal LIF, along with its successor, the NEOS, characteristically addresses issues according to its basic liberalist values (such as religious freedom and ensuring basic individual rights), but with close ties to the entrepreneurial interests present in facilitated regimes of labor migration. Their position thus might be expected to tend in a liberal direction, arguing for facilitated regulations of labor migration and the maintenance of cultural and religious liberties. Conversely, the BZÖ – being the result of a schism in the FPÖ and trying to carry on the heritage of its founding figure, Jörg Haider – might adopt positions closer to those of the radical right FPÖ, albeit in a more moderate tone. Following the party's overall shift toward a center-right profile after Haider's death, its restrictive but moderated stances on migration and ethnic relations are expected to somewhat resemble those of the center-right populist Team Stronach.

Making predictions concerning Austrian mainstream parties, however, is a more difficult task. As has already been discussed, both party families, Social Democrats as well as Conservatives, formed around traditional cleavages and have been colonizing the Austrian electorate for centuries according to these basic divides. With the issues of migration and ethnic relations cutting across their traditional cleavages and issue ownerships, the behavior expected of mainstream parties is one of depoliticization, though it seems highly likely that their issue positions will fit into the classic left-right divide as follows: The center-right ÖVP is likely to take more restrictive stances in accordance with its conservative values and law & order background, which, in political contexts, usually clearly prevail over Christian calls for tolerance and compassion. The center-left SPÖ, on the other hand, is expected to adopt a somewhat more liberal position in line with its socialist core values of solidarity and equality, which tend to eclipse the equally characteristic calls for protectionism, even with regard to immigrant labor.

Thus, while the conceptual hypothesis regarding the intensity of politicization conjectures that the more strongly an issue is linked to a cleavage owned by a party, the more strongly the issue will be politicized by that party (H5), the operational hypothesis for the Austrian case reads as follows:

> Radical right (FPÖ, BZÖ), left-libertarian (Greens) and liberal parties (LIF, NEOS) will be the most dominant actors politicizing the issues of migration and ethnic relations (H5a).

> Center-left (SPÖ) and center-right parties (ÖVP, Team Stronach) will be the actors least actively politicizing migration and ethnic relations (H5b).

These hypotheses must be supplemented with conjectures regarding the issue positions of the political parties on migration and ethnic relations. Here the conceptual hypothesis asserts that *issue positions of Austrian political parties on a liberal-restrictive axis of migration and ethnic relations are based on the ideological characteristics of their party families (H6)*. This results in the following operational hypotheses:

> Radical right parties (FPÖ, BZÖ) will take the most restrictive positions on the issues of migration and ethnic relations (H6a).

> Left-libertarian (Greens) and liberal parties (LIF, NEOS) will take the most liberal positions on the issues of migration and ethnic relations (H6b).

> Center-left parties (SPÖ) will take balanced positions on the issues of migration and ethnic relations, but lean toward the liberal side of the spectrum (H6c).

> Center-right parties (ÖVP, Team Stronach) will take balanced positions on the issues of migration and ethnic relations, but lean toward the restrictive side of the spectrum (H6d).

As previously discussed, prior research on party positions in general has indicated political parties to be quite insistent on their ideologies and associated political issues within party competition. However, under conditions characterized by party system transformation, increasing voter realignment, and growing pressure from niche parties, some measure of ideological purity might be sacrificed for strategic considerations, even by mainstream parties. It is this alternative perspective on party behavior that pushes research toward analysis of party competition in terms of rational choices made by the actors involved. These models offer effective tools for explaining changes in party behavior and thus add further prognostic power to that of purely ideological explanations, although obviously a party is hardly driven by a single motive alone, but rather implements different strategies under different conditions. The conditions of the party system are to be perceived as important structural constraints that influence party behavior in general as well as specifically in electoral competition over migration and ethnic relations. In order to get a better understanding of how the shape and the power structures of the party spectrum itself may have become a vital influence on both the salience and the positioning of Austrian parties, two key elements of party competition in particular will be examined – the number and strength of the parties that have constituted the competitive framework of the Austrian party system, and the fluctuating opportunities for them to participate in government coalitions.

3.2.2 On success and failure: The party system in numerical terms

As was already mentioned in the previous section, for a long time the Austrian party system was one of the most stable in Western Europe, which resulted from the tight spectrum of its two-and-a-half-party system. This pattern has since faded, and the system has undergone considerable changes that introduced new ideological players (as discussed above) and effectively changed the balance of power in simple numerical terms.

Table 10:   Vote share in Austrian national elections (in %) / Fragmentation indices, 1945-2013

Sartori's typology	Moderate Pluralism							Two Party System with predominant party					Moderate Pluralism								
Election	'45	'49	'53	'56	'59	'62	'66	'70	'71	'75	'79	'83	'86	'90	'94	'95	'99	'02	'06	'08	'13
Vote share																					
SPÖ	44.6	38.7	42.1	43.0	44.8	44.0	42.6	48.4	50.0	50.4	51.0	47.6	43.1	42.8	34.9	38.1	33.2	36.5	35.3	29.3	26.8
ÖVP	49.8	44.0	41.3	46.0	44.2	45.4	48.4	44.7	43.1	42.9	41.9	43.2	41.3	32.1	27.7	28.3	26.9	42.3	34.3	26.0	24.0
KPÖ	5.4	5.1	5.3	4.4	3.3	3.0	0.4	1.0	1.4	1.2	1.0	0.7	0.7	0.6	0.3	0.3	0.5	0.6	1.0	0.8	1.0
Vdu/FPÖ		11.7	10.9	6.5	7.7	7.0	5.4	5.5	5.5	5.4	6.1	5.0	9.7	16.6	22.5	22.0	26.9	10.0	11.0	17.5	20.5
Greens													4.8	4.8	7.3	4.8	7.4	9.5	11.1	10.4	12.4
LIF															6.0	5.5	3.7	1.0		2.9	
BZÖ																			4.1	10.7	3.5
Stronach																					5.7
NEOS																					5.0
Fragmentation																					
Molinar	1.9	2.1	2.2	2.0	2.1	2.0	1.9	2.0	1.9	1.9	1.9	2.0	2.3	2.3	3.0	2.7	2.9	2.3	2.8	3.5	4.3
Laakso/ Taagepera	2.1	2.6	2.5	2.2	2.2	2.2	2.1	2.1	2.2	2.2	2.2	2.3	2.6	3.0	3.7	3.5	3.4	2.9	3.4	4.3	5.2
Sartori r.P.	3	3	3	3	3	3	3	3	3	3	3	3	4	4	5	5	4	4	5	5	6

Source: Calculations are based on data from electoral documentation of the Federal Ministry of Interior (BMI).

Note: Only parties relevant in at least one election were considered. Parliamentary representation in the Austrian electoral system requires parties to surpass a threshold of 4% (of valid votes on the federal level) or obtain a regional direct mandate (Grundmandat).

As Table 10 illustrates, both indicators for party system fragmentation show the evolution in the late 1950s of a narrow and stable party system that lasted into the mid-1980s, when a distinct transformation began that has pertained into the present. Sartori's count of relevant parties (r.p.) demonstrates in simple terms that the number of parties influencing party competition was stagnant until 1986[35] and, except for a brief interruption, has been increasing ever since. The Laakso/Taagepera index also indicates the intensity of competition and reflects the long-standing predominance of the two mainstream parties (SPÖ and ÖVP), and consequently indicates a low number of "effective parties". It clearly reveals the shape of the Austrian party system during the 1960s and 1970s with three parliamentary parties, one of which (FPÖ) had only minor relevance, which made Austria a prototype for the so-called "limping two-party" or two-and-a-half-party system (Pelinka/Rosenberger 2000: 135). The Molinar Index reflects these power relations even more starkly by emphasizing the importance of the single most powerful party, deviating from Laakso-Taagepera as the difference between the strongest party and the remaining parties decreases (from 1990 onwards). In sum, all the numerical indicators signify a transformation of the Austrian party system that started in the mid-1980s, with an increasing number of niche parties entering the system and gathering considerable strength. The indicators peak in 1994 (after the entrance of a fifth niche party, the LIF), in 2008 (due to the BZÖ's assertiveness), and finally in 2013 (with two newcomer parties, Team Stronach and NEOS, resulting in the greatest number of parliamentary parties in the whole post-war period). These new appearances came at the expense of the two traditional mainstream parties, who have been steadily losing ground to these emerging niche parties, culminating in the 1999 election in which the ÖVP was for the first time surpassed by the FPÖ. After a brief recovery period for the two mainstream parties in 2002 and 2006 (due to the collapse of the FPÖ), the declining trend was aggravated in 2008 and 2013, with the mainstream parties achieving their worst results ever and effectively being reduced to medium-sized parties.

However, Sartori (1976) rightly stressed the fact that the numerical criterion does not provide information about the mechanics of a party system, i.e. the patterns of inter-party competition. In distinguishing between different types of two-party systems (i.e. those with a single hegemonic party, with a predominant party, and with a bipolar balance) and multi-party systems (i.e. moderate pluralism and polarized pluralism), Sartori accorded an important role to the mechanics of conflict, allowing for more precise description of party systems in flux. Characterizing the Austrian system according to his typology, three different periods of development after the reestablishment of democracy in 1945 become apparent.

---

[35] The Communist Party KPÖ lost its relevance in the Sartorian sense in 1949 as a result of the Cold War and the anti-communist compromise of the Austrian mainstream parties.

The first stage, classifiable according to Sartori as *moderate pluralism*, was initiated by the end of World War II and was marked by the necessities of rebuilding. Although the immediate relevance of the Communist party in 1945 successively diminished in the following elections, its continuous parliamentary presence until 1959 together with that of a fledgling VdU/FPÖ, created an early form of pluralistic party system. However, a number of factors maintained tight restrictions on ideological polarization: The civil-war experience of the First Republic, the bans on any form of National Socialist activities, and Soviet pressure from without led to a declaration of solidarity between the two big camps and the creation of Austrian consociationalism (which brought arranged proportional representation, strong integration of the mainstream parties and their social partners, and mainstream parties' commitment to a grand coalition). Moreover, the vote share of the two mainstream parties hovering around 90% of the valid votes[36] and an electorate closely attached to and organized by those parties prevented any third party from achieving significant strength (Pelinka 1998: 76).

The crisis of the grand coalition in the early 1960s gave rise to a slight change in the competitive patterns. Although the ÖVP had almost achieved an absolute majority before (in fact, the party only missed it by one mandate in 1956 and in 1962), it was explicitly named as a goal for the first time in the run-up to the 1966 elections (Müller 1998: 200). Following the ÖVP's victory and the formation of the first single-party government of the Second Republic, the Austrian party system moved into the second stage, that of a *two-party system*, with the ÖVP and SPÖ taking turns in forming single-party governments. After a short period of SPÖ-led minority government from 1970 to 1971, the elections of 1971 heralded the beginning of an era of absolute majority for the SPÖ (1971, 1975, 1979), which formed a single-party government under Chancellor Bruno Kreisky. This period lasted until 1983 and resembles Sartori's definition of a *two-party system with predominant party*.

The loss of the SPÖ's absolute majority in the 1983 elections and the formation of an SPÖ-FPÖ coalition under Chancellor Fred Sinowatz marked the *third stage* after 1945, i.e. the return to a system of *moderate pluralism*, although under somewhat different circumstances from those of the immediate post-war period. Firstly, for the first time in the Second Republic, a third party was included in a government coalition in place of one of the two mainstream parties, strengthening the position of third parties thereafter (Müller 2000: 284). Secondly, after 1983 the number of parliamentary parties steadily increased to four, then to five, and finally to six parties in 2013. Thirdly, the combined power of the traditional mainstream parties fell from 93% of the total vote share in 1983 to only 50.8% in 2013 as they conceded a great number of votes to the emerging and reforming niche parties; as voter transition analysis has documented, both

---

[36] The only exceptions to this were in 1949 and 1953 (Müller 1997: 224).

mainstream parties conceded the most votes to the radical right, though in different waves.[37] Fourthly, after 1986 the mainstream parties' commitment to a renewed grand coalition was clearly weaker than in the post-war period, although it nevertheless persisted for another 14 years. As a consequence, competition in the post-1986 system has been much fiercer, and the question remains whether the system has turned into what Sartori describes as "polarized pluralism". Despite some aspects that favor this conclusion, Müller (1997: 227) argued that they are not sufficient to indicate a change from moderate pluralism.

However, it has been pointed out repeatedly that the qualitative changes in the Austrian party system are not covered by Sartori's indicators. As Müller (2000: 284-5) summarized, after the 1999 elections, a new period appeared to have set in, with a) three parties competing for the majority position, b) the logic of coalition building becoming important even in minority constellations (in the absence of any absolute majority party), c) elections and the coalition preferences of voters losing importance in the process of government formation (which is now shaped by parties' operational coalition considerations instead), and d) with the pivotal position of a party and the size principle becoming increasingly relevant, after a minimum-winning coalition had been formed for the first time. Even though in 2006 the "familiar" Austrian pattern of a grand coalition between the mainstream parties returned, as Table 10 shows, the size of this coalition has reached an all-time low, while the number and the combined strength of the opposition parties has increased even more since then, peaking in 2013 with four parties scoring a combined total of 43.6% of the vote share in opposition to a slim mainstream party majority of 50.8%, which indicates that the label of pluralism applies even more clearly today. In fact, today the patterns of the Austrian party system do not just resemble but in fact even surpass the pluralism of the late 1990s, with an all-time high of six parliamentary parties joining the competition, with three medium-sized parties of similar strength, with niche parties winning at the expense of mainstream parties that are "forced" into grand coalitions, with ideological dispersion increasing, and with a centrist government facing multipolar opposition from different fringes – all of which are factors indicative of Sartori's concept of polarized pluralism.

Linking these patterns of fragmentation to the ideological perspective examined in the previous section, this study asserts that the change in the balance of power since 1986, i.e. the increasingly great challenge to mainstream parties emanating from emerging niche parties, vitally stimulates adaptive strategies for politicizing the issues of migration and ethnic relations, the effects of which will likely take some time to materialize. Since most of the relevant parties that have emerged during the second period of moderate pluralism have a stronger ideo-

---

[37] See Gehmacher et al. 1988; Ogris 1991; Hofinger & Ogris 1996; Hofinger et al. 2000; Hofinger et al. 2003; Picker et al. 2004; Hofinger et al. 2007; Filzmaier et al. 2009.

logical affinity for migration and ethnic relations issues than do the traditional mainstream parties, and bearing in mind that these issues are orthogonal to mainstream parties' traditional issue ownerships, these transformations are expected to contribute to an increase in both the relevance as well as the divisiveness of the issues of migration and ethnic relations.

Expectations for individual party politicization

Unlike party ideologies, which are more or less stable, the balance of power, being dependent on voting results, is highly subject to change, creating an ever-shifting context for the success and failure of the individual parties and thus necessitating constant reconsideration of their politicization strategies. Longitudinally speaking, from a vote-seeking perspective, parties will likely prioritize those strategies which have previously proven to help them gain votes, and therefore will stick to them as long as they continue to pay electoral dividends. Conversely, parties will adapt their strategies if they consistently lose large shares of votes to other parties. Therefore, this study assumes that *the more successful a party has been in the previous election, the more strongly it will stick to its previous strategies of politicization (H7)*.

Recalling the theoretical discussion in Chapter 2, the hypotheses regarding party behavior in competitive contexts can be applied to and evaluated for each individual party. As mentioned previously, within the time frame of the study's examination, three distinct periods have constituted substantially different contexts for party behavior in Austrian electoral politics; what follows is a characterization of the assumed politicization strategies employed in each of those periods.

1970-1986. Prior to the turning point election of 1986, the Austrian party system's "limping two-party" shape was its dominant characteristic. The mainstream parties faced little if any pressure from niche party opponents and their strength remained more or less stable. Accordingly, there were few incentives for them to abandon their orientation toward mainstream party competition. Considering their roots in traditional ideological cleavages, this study conjectures that, during that period, both mainstream parties will largely depoliticize the issues of migration and ethnic relations due to their lack of issue ownership and the lack of any vote-seeking incentive of deserting voters. Thus the only actor interested in politicizing the issues more strongly in order to gain votes was the FPÖ, despite its liberal interlude under the leadership of Norbert Steger.

1986-1999: With the election of 1986 and the subsequent transformation of the party system, the first considerable change in politicization of migration and ethnic relations is to be expected. From 1986 onwards, both niche parties (the FPÖ and the Greens) followed explicitly non-centrist tendencies and continuously increased their vote shares until 1999;[38] therefore it can be assumed that they will not only try to establish issue ownership of migration and ethnic relations by pursuing ideological emphasis but continue to do so in the light of electoral success. Conversely, it is reasonable to expect changes in the behavior of the Austrian mainstream parties in order to gain back votes. In the light of increasing niche party success and voter defection, both the SPÖ and the ÖVP were under pressure to respond to niche parties' issue campaigns.[39] However, according to the arguments of Downs (2001), Meguid (2008) and Bale et al. (2010), two constraints on mainstream parties' politicization strategies need to be considered. Firstly, it has been noted that mainstream parties adapt their strategies only when niche parties manage to successfully politicize a new issue continuously, i.e. only if the "threat" is of permanent character. This indicates that the initial response of mainstream parties, a strategy of depoliticization, should persist as long as niche party pressure remains limited. Only once significant pressure (in terms of opposing vote share and voter defection) has been applied will mainstream parties start to abandon their dismissive approach and engage in direct competition with their niche party opponents. Secondly, it has been observed that the first mainstream parties to alter their strategies are the ideological neighbors of those niche parties that most successfully politicize migration and ethnic relations (e.g. Schain 1987; Eatwell 2000; Downs 2001; Norris 2005). The pressure exerted by niche parties manifested differently for the two Austrian mainstream parties, since the success of the radical right FPÖ surpassed that of the leftist Greens (and LIF) by far; hence the center-right ÖVP, being the ideological neighbor of the FPÖ, was the first mainstream party to lose large shares of its voters to the radical right (Picker et al. 2004: 264). Accordingly, the center-right ÖVP is likely to respond to the pressure from its radical right opponent by adopting an accommodative strategy at an earlier stage than the SPÖ, which will remain dismissive for much longer (Meguid 2008; Bale et al. 2010).

2002-2013: In the post-millennial period, vote share results should solidify politicization strategies, most of all among the Austrian niche parties. The Greens are expected to continue their issue emphasis (considering their increasing success in terms of vote share) and the FPÖ is also assumed to continue its strong politicization of the issue, especially since the parts of it that remained after the party's schism were more radical and vote-oriented than Haider's FPÖ was (Luther 2008: 1005). Additionally, the FPÖ needed to compete with a second right-wing party (BZÖ) from 2005 on, and by the same token the BZÖ is expected to have competed for anti-immigrant voters. As regards the recent newcomers in 2013, due to the lack of any historical information it is difficult to make predictions

---

[38] The snap elections of 1995 were the only exception due to a monothematic election campaign period and singular focus on the race between the two major mainstream parties.

[39] Pressure in this context has to be defined as both "increasing niche-party vote share" as well as "increasing voter movement from mainstream to niche parties" (Meguid 2008: 16).

based on mere vote-seeking considerations. As for the mainstream parties, the center-left SPÖ is expected to give up its dismissive stance and take a more accommodative position than the radical right's stance on migration and ethnic relations in an attempt to regain votes previously lost to the right (the need for which was sharpened by the party's opposition status until 2006). The center-right ÖVP, having lost even more voters to the FPÖ before 1999, should intensify its previous accommodative strategy in order to attack the radical right's issue ownership more overtly (Downs 2001; Bale 2003; Bale et al. 2010; van Spanje 2010).[40] In a nutshell, both the expectation of vote-seeking behavior and the widespread literature on contagion in mainstream parties of radical right parties' politicization make likely not only an overall increase in the average salience of migration and ethnic relations, but also a shift toward restrictiveness as more parties engage in competition for the anti-immigrant vote. Of course, pure vote-seeking considerations may be insufficient to explain party behavior in multi-party constellations, as successful vote-seeking strategies may interfere with parties' office-seeking considerations by limiting their coalition options. In order to take these constraints into account, it is essential to expand the explanation to address the role of coalition considerations.

3.2.3 The need to share power: Coalition perspectives

Electoral competition intrinsically shapes the relations between the relevant parties. While gains from and losses to other competitors constitute the most central criterion for parties' decisions, the allocation of votes on its own becomes insufficient when the electoral setting incorporates a need for coalition building that influences parties' campaign strategies, such as in most electoral systems based on proportional representation. It has been noted that mainstream parties will adapt their strategies regarding migration and ethnic relations only when niche parties succeed in politicizing the issue. While success was defined above from a vote-seeking perspective as an increasing party vote share, from an office-seeking perspective the definition focuses instead on the coalition potential of a party and its corresponding influence on other parties' coalition considerations. For this reason the next section discusses developments in the coalition options among Austrian political parties, and argues that new opportunities arising from changes in the situation have heavily influenced the strategies employed by Austrian parties in recent decades.

---

[40] According to van Spanje (2010), even far-left parties can be expected to shift towards more restrictive stances in the light of continuous radical right party success. Although he offers some evidence from communist and even some Green parties, the argument remains questionable. If far-left parties were to suffer from a contagion effect, we (in line with Meguid's POS model) would expect far-left parties to lower their issue-emphasis rather than give up their previous issue-positions (as this would be costly).

Coalition-building in Austria: The crucial role of the pariah

In order to condense the coalition scenarios in the Austrian party system, Figure 5 gives an overview of the majority relations in the Austrian parliament since 1945. It lists the coalition alternatives (minimal/minimum winning coalitions) resulting from each election and sketches the composition of the government cabinet that was formed for that period.

Figure 5: **Parliamentary seats / Government coalitions / Coalition options in Austria, 1945-2013**

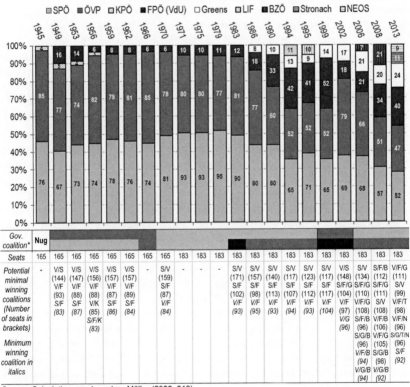

Source: Calculations are based on Müller (2008: 313).

Note: After an electoral reform, the number of parliamentary seats increased in 1971 from 165 to 183.
"Minimal winning coalitions" include no more parties than necessary to achieve a parliamentary majority.
"Minimum winning coalitions" (printed in italics in this figure) are minimal winning coalitions that obtain the smallest parliamentary majority (Riker 1962).
* Government coalition after that election
NUG=national unity government, S=SPÖ, V=ÖVP, K=KPÖ, F=FPÖ(VdU), G=Greens, L=LIF, B=BZÖ, T=Team Stronach, N=NEOS

There is a visible disparity between coalition practice and coalition options in Austrian post-war history. With the long-standing importance of grand coalitions, Austria became an exception to the European rule of minimum winning coalitions (Pelinka/Rosenberger 2000: 61). Consociational democracy and the strong role of social partnership contributed to a continuous relevance of the grand coalition, with the years between 1945 and 1983 seeing only grand coalitions and single-party governments in power. Coalitions of a large party with a small one or of medium-sized parties have resulted from only three out of twenty elections since 1945: for the first time in 1983 (SPÖ&FPÖ), and more recently with the right-bloc coalitions built after the elections of 1999 (ÖVP&FPÖ) and 2002 (ÖVP&FPÖ/BZÖ). Although the grand coalition has remained the familiar choice until the present (Müller 2006), the declining dominance together with the greater mobility in coalition-building of the mainstream parties demands a more detailed evaluation of the possible coalitions in the Austrian party system during the examination period covered by this study. While during the period of bipartisanism potential coalition options were hardly a significant factor in the mainstream parties' calculations, the need to consider coalition options has sharpened ever since the decline in the party concentration of voters, although the number of majority constellations nevertheless remained comparatively small until 1999.

The grand coalition continued to be the strongest coalition option, even offering a comfortable two-thirds majority, which is particularly important as it allows for the passing of constitutional amendments.[41] These considerations may have influenced the Austrian mainstream parties to some degree in maintaining their coalition until 1999 despite their mounting losses and the growing success of their niche party competitors. More importantly, however, this decision may be attributed to the circumstance that all other possible minimal winning coalitions since 1986 would have included the FPÖ, a party that, at least until the mid-1990s, was treated as a pariah by the mainstream parties. In the entire examination period there was never the option of a left-bloc majority (disregarding the SPÖ's absolute majorities between 1971 and 1983), and, up until 1999, both the Greens and the LIF never succeeded in becoming more than "surplus parties" possessing no capacity to help constitute minimal winning coalitions (Müller 2000: 290). Hence the only alternatives to a grand coalition were a renewed SPÖ-FPÖ coalition or a center-right/radical-right coalition between the ÖVP and the FPÖ.[42] After the millennium the balance of power shifted and the num-

---

[41] The grand coalition's two-thirds majority in parliament was lost only during the period between 1994 and 1995.

[42] There was only one exception, in 2002: After the landslide victory of the conservative ÖVP, for the first time since 1986, a mainstream party had the chance to build a minimal winning coalition with the Greens. However, although coalition talks were conducted between the two parties, the ÖVP eventually decided to continue its coalition with the FPÖ.

ber of potential minimal winning coalitions increased, though many of the combinations were impossible for ideological reasons, but even so, none of them would have represented a pure left-bloc majority. While the ÖVP still had the option after 2006, at least theoretically, of a right-bloc coalition (which was made practically impossible, however, by the fierce resentment between the ranks of the FPÖ and BZÖ), the options of the SPÖ, ruling out any government cooperation with the FPÖ, were reduced to that of continuing the grand coalition, even after the entrance of two newcomer parties in 2013 (one of which, Team Stronach, presented itself as anything but a reliable coalition option anyway).

As for the government coalitions that were actually formed, after the period of single-party governments and the short interregnum of a centrist SPÖ-FPÖ government from 1983 to 1986, the grand coalition was the natural response to the early stage of party system transformation after 1986. Though this bulwark was far from unbroken on a regional level, on the federal level both mainstream parties adopted a strategy of radical right exclusion, making it clear that neither considered the often anti-system FPÖ a potential coalition partner (Minkenberg 2001; Art 2006). The FPÖ's strategic pressure had differing effects on the two mainstream parties; the ÖVP, being its ideological neighbor, appeared to suffer earlier and more acutely from the pressure exerted by the radical right than did its mainstream party opponent, the SPÖ. Moreover, since 1970 the ÖVP had been stuck with the role of the perennial runner-up behind the SPÖ and thus was never really given the opportunity to open up talks about government formation itself. Stuck in the role of the junior partner in the grand coalition, the party not only lost votes with each election, but consistently failed to promote itself as the number one choice and subsequently remained unable to challenge the SPÖ in the battle for chancellorship. But what appeared to be a disadvantage from one angle turned out to be a boon from another. Being the ideological neighbor of an increasingly victorious FPÖ in fact improved the ÖVP's options once it had finally abandoned its exclusionary posture toward the radical right neighbor. By the same token, the ÖVP's new strategic option automatically increased pressure on the center-left SPÖ, which had always much more emphatically refused to cooperate with the radical right FPÖ and has continued to do so since. Therefore it was logical for the SPÖ, lacking an alternative, left-of-center coalition option and in danger of losing its traditional coalition partner, the ÖVP, to respond strategically.

After the watershed of 1999, especially, coalition considerations grew to be of increasingly vital importance. For the first time in Austrian post-war history, a government had been formed by a right-bloc coalition (incidentally, the first minimum winning coalition ever to assume government duties). The ÖVP-FPÖ coalition put an end to a number of other constants of Austrian post-war politics as well: It forced the SPÖ, despite being the strongest party, into an opposition role for the first time since 1970; it divested consociational forces ("social part-

nership") of some of their power, and most importantly, it brought an end to bi-
lateral opposition pressure toward a centrist government. All of these factors
severely intensified a bipolar pattern of left-right competition between the two
blocs manifested in government coalition and opposition. Thus tendencies toward an actual "bipolar multiparty system" (Ray 2004: 183), with a right-bloc
government versus a left-bloc opposition, became obvious (Pelinka et al. 2000:
440; Müller/Fallend 2004: 818). According to the classic portrayal of Sartori's
typology, this pattern suggests centripetal logic, i.e. parties moving toward the
center; however, such behavior was highly improbable in the case of the Austrian party system during the transition period after 1999. First of all, ideological
polarization of party competition had been increasing since the 1990s, and parties had already begun shifting toward the poles of the spectrum (Pelinka et al.
2000: 449-52). As a consequence, "the distances between the parties within each
of the 'blocs' decreased, while those between them and the parties of the 'other'
'bloc' increased" (Müller/Fallend 2004: 818). Moreover, before 1999, and increasingly again since 2006, the system became tripolar, with three parties of
similar strength (Plasser/Ulram 2000: 169). Consequently, Pelinka et al. (2000:
444) predicted that party competition in the new millennium would resemble
neither a muted kind of competition (as is typical for consociational democracies) nor the typically conflicted but – due to their center-orientation – centripetal forms of competitive democracy described by Sartori's model. Instead, they
expected centrifugal competition similar to that of the Austrian First Republic.

Taking into consideration all these patterns in Austrian party competition since
1999, it would be rather counterintuitive to expect the tendency toward polarization to suddenly reverse after the formation of a right-bloc government. From an
office-seeking behavioral perspective, the continuation of the governing coalition was the logical and more attractive option for both the ÖVP and the FPÖ,
while the SPÖ plainly aimed for a left-bloc alliance with the Greens (Müller
2000: 305). It is not by chance that every party has used the scenario of an oppo-
site-bloc coalition as a mobilizing threat in its electoral campaigns since 1999.
Beyond that, parties' parliamentary behavior also indicated preference for intra-
bloc coalitions and subsequently led to a perception of bipolarism as being without an alternative, at least in the first years of the decade.[43] Thus, with the gov-
ernment/opposition dichotomy becoming "strictly competitive in the electoral
arena" (Müller/Fallend 2004: 832) and coinciding with the left-bloc/right-bloc

---

[43] Initially, the SPÖ remained somewhat reluctant to force a bloc confrontation, a large part
of the SPÖ's ranks preferring a return to a grand coalition with different ÖVP personnel
prior to the 2002 election (Müller/Fallend 2004). However, after the prolongation of the
ÖVP-FPÖ (BZÖ) coalition from 2002 to 2006, the SPÖ's preferences clearly shifted toward a coalition with the Greens, which was made impossible only by the re-election of the
BZÖ (Luther 2008: 1011).

dichotomy, centrifugal tendencies in the politicization of Austrian parties is most likely in the aftermath of 1999.

However, the return of a grand coalition in 2007 may have put an end to these centrifugal tendencies, since both mainstream parties were deprived of or shied away from cooperation with the radical right and other coalition options were basically unviable for ideological reasons (not to mention the reluctance toward coalitions of three or more parties in a country whose history has been dominated by two-party coalitions). Consequently, the mainstream parties agreed to two further editions of the grand coalition (2006/2008) and, despite suffering severe losses in the 2008 and 2013 elections (depriving them of their "grandness"), have decided to continue for yet another legislation period. As a consequence, the centrifugal patterns of the early post-millennial period had presumably been interrupted by the end of the decade, which will likely be reflected in both parties' electoral strategies.

Expected influence on politicization

How do these coalition scenarios relate to the electoral politicization of migration and ethnic relations? As mentioned above, while there is little intuitive need from an ideological perspective for mainstream parties in the center to shift their positions, the incentives seem much stronger from an office-seeking perspective that considers the possible coalition options. Consequently, the hypothesis based on a coalition perspective also includes a temporal consideration, and states that *if new niche parties on the fringes establish themselves as potential minimal winning coalition partners, mainstream parties will turn toward centrifugal behavior (H8a).*

With bipolarism and centrifugal tendencies growing after the millennium (Müller/Fallend 2004: 818), and given the absence of a mediating party at the center of the spectrum (Hazan 1997), mainstream parties are expected to use the issues of migration and ethnic relations to benefit their coalition considerations. Hence, from the coalition perspective, the center-right ÖVP most likely will join its radical right coalition partner, the FPÖ, in a more restrictive stance, trying to satisfy its coalition partner with respect to one of its central issues (Minkenberg 2001). However, as far as the center-left SPÖ is concerned, the opposite behavior is more likely. As Givens (2007: 76) has pointed out, "conservative parties are the only parties that have gone into coalitions with radical right parties," while center-left parties have shied away from sharing office with radical right parties and from taking overly restrictive stances on migration and ethnic relations. In the Austrian case a similar pattern can be expected: Due to the colonization of the restrictive end of the discourse spectrum by the right-bloc majority, the SPÖ is expected to actively challenge the governing coalition by increasing the salience of liberal perspectives. However, the longer a mainstream party is deprived of serious coalition alternatives, the more reduced its centrifugal tendencies will be – in its politicization of migration and ethnic relations, as well.

In recent literature, rational considerations of political parties regarding migration and ethnic relations have been used most prominently to explain mainstream parties' responses to niche party success, mostly because mainstream parties have a wider range of ideological mobility as concerns these issues. With regard to niche parties however, Meguid's POS model (2008) shows more explanatory potential, as it isolates salience as a separate tool of party strategy. This is of particular importance for analyzing the behavior of both radical right as well as leftist parties. Given their location on the fringes of the ideological spectrum, it appears unlikely that these parties will shift their issue positions significantly; instead, niche parties will most likely alter the salience of their positions rather than change them entirely. From a coalition perspective, therefore, this study expects that *niche parties will reduce their issue emphasis over time in order to become and remain prospective coalition partners when migration and ethnic relations is a conflictive issue with potential coalition partners (H8b)*.

In the Austrian case, only two out of the four niche parties in the examination period have been present on a lasting basis (the FPÖ and the Greens), so the operational hypotheses have to be limited to those two. However, the hypotheses will diverge when accounting for the differing degrees of success of these two parties. Both the FPÖ and the Greens (re)emerged on the federal scene in 1986 and gained parliamentary strength until 1999, although only the FPÖ achieved coalition size and was finally included in a government coalition. Thus, though coalition considerations are expected to play less of a role prior to 1999, after that both parties are likely to adapt their behavior. While the FPÖ's achievement of government participation is likely to be accompanied by a reduction of salience to prove itself a viable coalition partner, at least for as long as it is in power (Müller/Fallend 2004: 818), the Greens should weaken their emphasis from 1999 onwards in order to become a viable coalition partner at all. After the FPÖ's split during its period as a government party in 2005, the tempering effect of coalition responsibility is expected to primarily influence the second radical right party, the BZÖ (which inherited all of the party's remaining government positions), while the remainder of the FPÖ is less likely to tie its politicization to coalition considerations and will focus instead on its internal and ideological recovery.

3.2.4 Synopsis

To condense the conjectures developed in this chapter, the three lines of driving motives identified above shall be recapitulated. Over the course of the examination period, this study expects the issue of migration and ethnic relations as well as the approaches to politicization of the different parties constituting the Austrian party system to develop rather than maintain a uniform pattern of competition. Parties will gradually adapt their approaches and strategically rearrange their patterns of politicization within their party family's ideological framework. Hence party politicization of migration and ethnic relations is expected to be initially driven primarily by Austrian niche parties (Greens, FPÖ, LIF, BZÖ) with strong issue ownership in accordance with their ideological characteristics, whereas mainstream parties (SPÖ, ÖVP) will likely depoliticize these issues since they lack ownership.

However, as the issues develop and become established as part of the competitive structure, parties are pressured to adapt their behavior in the light of a changing balance of power. As outlined in the book's conceptual chapter (see Table 2), both mainstream and niche parties are expected to change their strategies, though their choices will vary depending on the parties' prioritization of vote-maximization and coalition considerations.

Niche parties are predicted to increase their emphasis as long as it has paid off in previous elections, while from a coalition standpoint they will instead temper their issue emphasis as participation in a government coalition becomes more likely (if migration and ethnic relations are deemed potentially divisive issues). Since both Greens and FPÖ have continually increased their vote share after 1986 (except of the FPÖ's setback in 2002 being part of a coalition government), from a vote-seeking incentive there is little reason to change their approach of ideological emphasis (similar patterns can be expected for the two more short-lived niche parties, the LIF and the BZÖ). From a coalition perspective, however, especially after the turn of the millennium Austrian niche parties find growing incentives to cut their emphasis in order to become (Greens) or to remain (FPÖ, BZÖ) a viable coalition partner.

As regards mainstream parties' approaches, a purely vote-seeking orientation would suggest a rather accommodative strategy of politicization vis-à-vis the radical right aimed at regaining the large number of anti-immigrant voters that both parties have lost to the radical right (though the center-right ÖVP is expected to respond sooner than its center-left counterpart, the SPÖ). From a coalition standpoint, theory would predict instead more centrifugal behavior. Thus, especially after millennium, the center-left in particular would have more incentives to adopt an adversarial strategy vis-à-vis the radical right in order to counter the pressure from a right-bloc majority, while the center-right is expected to look to foster this majority through a strategy of accommodative politicization.

This book evaluates the validity of these predictions in the Austrian case by linking them to an analysis of Austrian parties' electoral politicization. Accordingly, the next chapter discusses the methodological approach developed to identify the different aspects of parties' politicization strategies in the policy fields of migration and ethnic relations, with particular regard to the diversity of channels in election campaign communication.

4. Study design: Data and methods

This chapter summarizes the methodological framework of the empirical analysis conducted in this study. To this end, first it describes the strategies of data collection used, which differ according to the various types of materials included in this study (4.1). Secondly, the chapter aims to explain the content analysis tools that were applied in the course of the examination. The study differentiates between several steps of analysis used to distinguish between a) salience as a general concept of politicization, b) issue dimensions and subtopics addressing different topical segments in parties' campaigns, and c) policy frames as a tool for transferring preferred interpretations of a political issue. For each of these analytical steps, a conceptual discussion is linked to an explanation of the codes and coding procedures applied (4.2).

4.1 Data selection and implementation of the study

As discussed in chapter 4, this study is based on the premise that different election campaign channels will lead to different outcomes for party politicization, and that parties will not be equally successful in promoting coherent campaigns. Consequently, programmatic communication was contrasted with day-to-day communication, for which purpose two different data corpora were compiled.

The former – programmatic – dimension of campaign communication was analyzed using the election manifestos of political parties for each election, with the sampling unit thus being the manifesto of each political party for each general election in the Austrian national assembly. Only parliamentary parties, i.e. parties with parliamentary seats prior to or after that particular election, were taken into consideration, whereas minor parties that failed to surpass the election threshold were disregarded. The selection included only general election manifestos containing a cross section of parties' topical preferences, while (mono-thematic) action programs and the like were not considered. In order to ensure the comparability of the results, the selection of manifestos was aligned to that of the Comparative Manifesto Project (Budge et al. 2001; Klingemann et al. 2006). Thus, for the time period between 1971 and 2002, manifestos were obtained directly from the Leibniz Institute for the Social Sciences (GESIS), while for the remaining elections manifestos were collected manually from party archives and the Austrian National Library.

The other, day-to-day dimension of campaign communication was analyzed on the basis of press releases, which are produced on a daily basis. The study focused on the hot pre-election period as the primary time frame for the sampling process, collecting all press releases within six weeks prior to the election day. Only press releases that were explicitly forwarded by the federal party headquarters were considered in the data corpus. Up to the year 1986, press releases were extracted from parties' daily press portfolios, while from 1990 onwards the press releases were collected from the database of the Austrian Press Agency (APA).[44] Each press release was identified by both the APA token and the contact details of the originator.

Every national election between 1971 and 2013 was included in the data corpus except the snap election of 1995 (which was declared only shortly after the regular election in 1994 and which, due to the monothematic election campaign focus on budget and horse-race questions, sharply deviated from the other elections in the examination period).[45] In sum, this led to a total of 50 election manifestos and 14486 press releases constituting the basis of the empirical analysis (Table 11).

Table 11: Data selected for empirical analysis

	1971	1975	1979	1983	1986[a]	1990	1994	1999	2002	2006	2008	2013	**Sum**
Manifestos	3	3	3	3	4	4	5	5	4	5	5	6	**50**
Press releases	539	742	878	773	1038	1367	1228	1624	1684	1603	1704	1306	**14486**

Note: The numbers count sampling units, i.e. individual party manifestos or parties' total press releases.
a) Due to the lack of availability data for the election of 1986, no press releases for the Greens were considered.

The manual coding of the material was done entirely by the author, while intracoder reliability was tested between two points of the coding process in order to prevent distortion of the coding during the examination period. In a comparison of about 40% of the manifesto material, Cohen's Kappa scores confirmed an acceptable consistency between the two points of observation both for the coding of subtopics (0.92) as well as the coding of policy frames (0.94). The coding of parties' manifestos and press releases was conducted using the software Atlas.ti, guiding the qualitative development of policy frames as discussed in

---

[44] The compilation of the press releases was conducted in accordance with the FWF project "Continuity and Change in Campaign Communication in Austria since 1966" (http://www.oeaw.ac.at/cmc/en/131625en.php), of the Commission for Comparative Media and Communication Studies at the Austrian Academy of Sciences. For the opportunities and support, my sincerest thanks go to the project leaders DDr. Gabriele Melischek and Dr. Josef Seethaler.

[45] The decision to consider only elections since the 1970s results from data limitations: The availability of material drastically decreases for elections prior to the 1970s as a) there are no press releases archived for any of the three parties relevant back then and b) only the SPÖ and ÖVP have published documents even remotely similar to what is conceived as an election manifesto today (in fact they were "election announcements" rather than real election manifestos/platforms) while the FPÖ had no actual electoral documents expressing their goals at all. Taken together, these factors led to the decision not to include elections prior to the 1970s, especially since salience of migration and ethnic relations among the SPÖ's and ÖVP's election announcements is in line with this study's findings for the 1970s (1962: 1% and 0%; 1966: 0,7% and 1,1%) – as documented in Chapter 6.

Chapter 5. In a second step, word count tables of the codings were exported to an SPSS dataset which served as the foundation for the quantitative analysis of campaign patterns that is documented in Chapter 6.[46]

The following sections will discuss the steps of analysis applied to both data corpora described above. For each of the two campaign levels, three aspects of the competitive strategies of political parties were examined, each of which represents a different means available to a party of politicizing issues in their campaigns. Firstly, the study assumed that a party's emphasis of an issue in comparison to other policy fields might be taken as a first essential clue to the importance the issue is accorded within a party's overall agenda. Thus the first level of analysis examines the general salience that parties grant to migration and ethnic relations (4.2.1). After that, the analysis digs deeper into strategies of politicization by discussing the use of spatial concepts for the analysis of party competition (4.2.2). This is followed by a discussion of how to measure different subtopical nuances of the debate. Given the cross-sectional character of the issues of migration and ethnic relations, it is of vital importance to distinguish between the different facets that parties carve out in their campaigns (4.2.3). Finally, the chapter discusses how parties' positions on migration and ethnic relations can be identified adequately in order to contrast the different policy perspectives by which parties can be distinguished from each other (4.2.4).

4.2   Measuring party politicization

4.2.1   The concept and measurement of salience

As noted in Chapter 2, salience theory, or the assumption that parties will put the most emphasis on those issues that are the most relevant for them at a given point in time, lies at the heart of this study. Based on this assumption, this study's data examination procedure was developed around measuring the salience of specific aspects of electoral party competition. Obviously the concept of salience has various meanings within a number of different scientific disciplines; however, in political science it has been used most prominently with regard to public opinion, as in the common application of the "most important problem" question (for an overview see Wlezien 2005). Linked to the questions of salience in public opinion, the perspective has also been applied to texts, most prominently in the agenda-setting approach, since the 1970s (McCombs 2008).

---

[46] Although inferential statistics are usually omitted in the analysis of complete samples, some authors argue that even in complete samples stochastic elements play a role if the data should be explained and not only described (see Broscheid/Gschwend 2005; Broscheid 2009). Moreover, given that the description of Austrian campaign material covers only one of many potential realizations of country campaign patterns, this study included complementary statistical inference to offer some assessment of the observed differences' general probability (see Berk et al 1995; Broscheid/Gschwend 2003; Behnke 2005; Köhler 2008).

Issue salience has been commonly applied in such inquiries by examining the quantitative share of some specific content item in comparison to others. Additional indicators (such as the size of the coding unit, its position within a greater text, visual emphasis of the coding unit, etc.) have been suggested as viable criteria for determining the prominence of an item (Behr/Iyengar 1985, Epstein/Segal 2000). Yet salience measurements were not limited to the salience of issues, per se, but rather developed as a separate concept that proved viable for several kinds of textual attributes (McCombs 2008). Thus they provide a useful tool for this study and help to operationalize the importance of different aspects of politicization, i.e. the general issues, subtopics, and policy positions promoted by political parties.

Confronted with different campaign channels, however, it was crucial to the development of a sound methodological design to find a coding unit suitable for comparing these two channels. In the end, word count prevailed as the best measurement quantity for comparing politicization on both campaign channels (Laver et al. 2003; Klemmensen et al. 2007). Accordingly, for each of the coding dimensions, absolute salience was defined as the proportion of words contained in a particular coding unit in relation to the total word count of the sampling unit (i.e. the individual manifesto or all of the press releases of that party in that election).[47] For both campaign channels, the coding unit was defined as a single sentence or fragment to which both a specific subtopic (see section 4.2.3.) and a policy position (identified by policy frames, see Chapter 5) could be assigned. Of course, consistent references to a subtopic or a policy position quite often extend beyond a single sentence and sometimes cover whole passages. Consequently, the coding procedure linked sentences that continuously addressed the same subtopic and the same policy position to form one coherent unit of evaluation. Thus, the end of each coding unit was marked by either the beginning of a reference to a new subtopic or policy frame or the beginning of a reference unrelated to migration and ethnic relations. In the case of lists, each list item was treated as a separate unit. Coding units were bounded as conservatively as possible, meaning that only those sentences and fragments were taken into consideration that were strictly necessary for the comprehension of a statement on migration and ethnic relations. However, if a sentence contained references to migration and ethnic relations, the whole sentence (including its headers) was coded, notwithstanding the possible presence of other references (Früh 2007: 88-90). This same coding procedure was applied in each of the three dimensions of analysis.

47

$$S_n = W_n \left(\frac{1}{W_N}\right)$$ with S denoting the salience of all relevant coding units n in relation to the total size of the sampling units N at a given data point (a single manifesto or sum of all press releases of that party in that election), and W denoting the word count of those units.

The most overarching dimension – the general prominence of migration and ethnic relations – was measured by the total sum of words of the relevant coding units without regard to the specific subtopics or policy positions addressed. This accumulation led to the separation of migration and ethnic relations from the other contents of electoral discourse and thus made it possible to determine the prominence of these policy fields at any given data point. For the purposes of this study, the conceptual definition of migration and ethnic relations was based on a broad definition that included all references to cross-national border movements and evaluation of access or residence rights (including asylum), all explicit remarks on the inclusion or exclusion of ethnic minorities of any administrative status, and all general expressions about societal concepts of coexistence in ethnically diverse societies. This conceptual definition will be explained in more detail later on, when the more specific aspects of topical and policy analysis are discussed, because subtopics and frames enable to grasp the multitude of meanings represented in the discourse on migration and ethnic relations.

4.2.2 Spatial positions and distance measurements of politicization

The very notion of 'competition' implies the interrelation of multiple competitors. An analysis of party politicization in electoral competition thus needs to document the patterns of relations between the individual parties. Simple qualifications such as "A and B are closer together on this question than are A and C" are commonly applied in scholarly and everyday political commentary alike and lie at the heart of our understanding of political competition. Similarly, qualitative approaches to discourse analysis identify "discourse coalitions", each of which is a set of actors sharing a discursive construct, or more specifically, "the ensemble of a set of story lines, the actors that utter these story lines, and the practices that conform to these story lines, all organized around a discourse" (Hajer 1993: 45). Though these patterns of convergence can only be described in relative rather than absolute terms, they are useful indicators nonetheless by which actors can be grouped together within some area of discursive space.

However, in quantitative studies, formal calculation of discursive coalitions is by no means a trivial task. The question of proximity of or distance between actors on a specific matter implies a number of concepts, most prominently a *space* in which they can be described (Benoit/Laver 2006). Distances between party strategies acquire meaning only through the comparison of two or more coordinates, i.e. by the quantification of their locations in a finite space of activity. It is because of this "relativity" of spatial maps of political competition that they can vary significantly in design between approaches. Concerned mostly with analysis of party stances on specific issues, Budge (2006: 431) distinguishes various ways of creating such spatial frameworks. Firstly, models can assume a "pure a priori policy space" that is designed on theoretical principles by the researcher, who then locates actors (parties, voters, etc.) on this a priori defined scale (this approach is closely linked to Downsian spaces). Secondly, an approach can instead posit a "party-dominated pure policy space", meaning that scales are theoretically derived from party ideology as it is known to the researcher – an approach that is most notably linked to the Manifesto Research Group's work (Budge et al. 2001; Klingemann et al. 2006). Thirdly, using factor analysis of policy texts or issue questions, an "inductive policy space" can be generated that underlies the issues under consideration and that may be constrained to a single dimension (generally a spectrum from left to right), though often further dimensions are then detected (e.g. Gabel/Huber 2000). Fourthly, an approach may discard the idea of an absolute scale ranging between "absolute" policy points (like "absolute left" or "absolute right") and instead draw up a "party-defined space" by taking "absolute" party positions as the boundaries of the ideological spectrum, which enables it to define empirical party positions by their distance from these constructed boundaries (e.g. Budge/Farlie 1977).

This wealth of previously used approaches clearly demonstrates the need for any spatial analysis to specify a number of premises in advance. The first step is to identify the relational content, since actors can be compared to each other on any aspect of their behavior. Among scholars of party politics, distance measurements have been used most commonly to describe the policy stances of political actors (Enelow/Hinich 1984; Laver/Hunt 1992; Hinich/Munger 1997; Laver/Garry 2000). However, spatial concepts are by no means limited to policy positions; they are equally viable as a means for examining other aspects of competition. Hence this study's research framework evaluates two aspects of party politicization: topical preferences and policy positions. Each aspect represents a strategic instrument of party politicization and can be evaluated in spatial terms. Thus the present study marries the concept of party-defined space with a salience theory-based model. Party strategies are identified by the salience they grant to different subtopics and policy positions, and their proximity is evaluated by comparing their emphasis. Since subtopics and policy positions differ in the categories they contain, the present study proposes two different analytical approaches:

For comparing parties' emphasis of subtopics, a nominal set of codes with random ordering was applied. The selection of subtopic codes was conducted on a purely deductive basis, by determining a priori the set of subtopics (see the next section, 4.2.3). In the coding process these topical codes were linked to the salience granted to each subtopic by each party (in relation to the total emphasis of all subtopics addressed by each party).[48] By arranging these categories in one

---

[48]

$$S_i = W_i \left(\frac{1}{W_n} \right)$$ with S denoting the salience of the individual subtopic i in relation to the number of relevant coding units n at a given data point (a single manifesto or the sum of all press releases of that party in that election), and with W denoting the wordcount of these units

dimension, the precise topical preferences of each party could be determined for any given election.

The approach applied in the identification of parties' policy positions differed both in the development of codes as well as in their scaling. Since the construction of policy categories is a more complex task than the mere identification of subtopics, a simple deductive approach proved insufficient to adequately capture the diversity of discourse. Instead, codes were generated through a process that combined deductive and inductive frame development. Chapter 5 is entirely devoted to the introduction and discussion of this qualitative analysis, which was conducted prior to the quantitative coding and which, through its use of inductive as well as deductive methods, developed a set of substantial policy frames on migration and ethnic relations. For the coding categories, the nominal set of policy codes presented in Chapter 5 was plotted on a bipolar axis, distinguishing between restrictive and liberal positions on migration and ethnic relations (and arranging liberal and restrictive positions along a single tendency measure). Again, each code was linked to the salience granted to the associated policy position by each party (in relation to the total emphasis of all policy positions addressed by that party).

In order to quantify the dis/similarity of parties' politicization patterns, this study applied distance measures for spatial comparison. As Benoit/Laver (2006) have shown, the correct choice among the variety of approaches for distance measurement depends on the objectives of the analysis as well as on the number of dimensions constituting the spatial framework. Since the categories of subtopics and positions are nominal variables tied to metric salience scores in unidimensional spaces, the analysis is limited to the use of city block distance (d), also known as "Manhattan" distance (Mooi/Sarstedt 2011). City block distance[49] calculates the sum of absolute difference in all categories between two actors, although this study bisected the measure for ease of interpretation. Bisected city block distance between two actors expresses the distance between them using a scale from 0 and 100 – with 100 expressing total difference and 0 expressing total congruence. In sum, calculation of city block distance expresses the relationship between each pair of parties and consequently enables identification of which parties are clustered around similar topical and policy emphasis, i.e. which are most similar in their strategies of politicization.

---

[49]

$$d\,(A,B) = \sum_{i=1}^{n} |\,A_{S_i} - B_{S_i}\,|$$

with S denoting the salience of a subtopic/policy-frame i for each actor A, B at a given data point (a single manifesto or the sum of all press releases of that party in that election), and n representing the number of subtopics/policy-frames

4.2.3 Parties' topical preferences: Issue dimensions and subtopics

Migration and ethnic relations differ from traditional policy fields in that – characteristically for all types of diversity politics – they represent a cross-sectional subject that projects into a number of other policy areas (Borkert/Penninx 2011). Thus, when different political actors discuss migration, they do not necessarily address the same set of aspects. For researchers of political discourse, this necessitates an analytical framework that is able to distinguish between these aspects and to identify the topical building blocks of the debate, though there are various possible levels of abstraction. Donati (2001: 153) helped solve the puzzle by arguing that discourse is not constructed around macro-level issues (such as economy, environment, immigration, etc.) but in fact revolves around specific objects (micro-level issues) that are linked to overall policy fields only analytically. As a consequence, the task for the researcher is "to find the right object-key for the set of arguments through which an issue is communicated and defined" (Donati 2001: 153). These objects may be labeled explicitly as being migration or ethnic relations issues in the macro-level sense, but they can be part of discourse on other macro-issues and at the same time related to the question of migration (e.g., the regulation of labor market access for non-nationals falls under the umbrellas of both labor market policy and immigration policy). Consequently, in order to capture the whole range of discourse, any passage addressing migration and ethnic relations needed to be considered regardless of whether they represent the main issue or just a secondary aspect of a main issue from a different macro-level policy field. Furthermore, this study broke down migration and ethnic relations into more specific contextual categories by distinguishing between various *issue dimensions* and *subtopics*. This allowed to disentangle the complexity of parties' electoral politicization of migration and ethnic relations even as it shifts over time. In order to focus on the relevant part of discourse, the selection of source material was limited to only those passages in which migration and ethnic relations were explicitly mentioned.

Previous examples of categorization

Since migration and ethnic relations are cross-sectional issues that are intertwined with a variety of other policy fields, this study aimed to consider the different nuances of these broad issues in order to discern the diverse topical strategies applied by parties. Upon examining the coding instruments of previous content analyses of migration and ethnic relations, it becomes clear that previous methods of defining topical categories differ substantially. For example, media content analysis as conducted by Signer et al. (2011) generally distinguishes news contexts of migration from journalistic categories such as "politics", "crime", "court hearings/decisions", "society", "economy", "sports" and the like. Distinctions like these, however, are of limited use for strategic policy documents, which relate to political contexts rather than to news departments. Bonfadelli (2008: 41) addressed this need in his news media analysis by distinguishing between particularly migration-related subtopics such as "immigration politics", "crime", "integration", "religion", "racism", etc. Similarly, in their content analysis of political PR and news coverage, Froehlich/Rüdiger (2006) looked for what they call "thematic frames", distinguishing between a general category of "immigration" and more concrete subtopics such as "migration of labor", "refugees/asylum seekers", "integration of immigrants", "family reunions", "ethnic German immigrants" and "illegal immigrants". Although their set of issue categories does not seem sufficiently comprehensive to register all aspects of the migration debate in Austria (especially for conducting a time-series analysis),[50] their distinction between general and specific aspects of the discourse is a helpful guideline for the present study.

In a more schematic approach, the comparative project "Support and Opposition to Migration – SOM" suggested a two-level matrix for the topical classification of discourse, distinguishing between immigration and civic integration on the one dimension and four broad policy categories ("security&crime", "economy&welfare-state", "politics&institutions" and "society&culture") on the other (Berkhout/Sudulich 2011: 11-2). Within this matrix, sub-categories are listed for each of the eight cells, generating a set of more specific subtopics (such as "international crime", "illegal migration", "refugee support", "guest-workers", etc.). Although the principles of the SOM approach on topical coding are a helpful guideline for this study, the list of subtopics is sometimes insufficiently discriminating. To consult studies beyond the realm of content analysis, research projects on migration and integration policies such as the Migrant Integration Policy Index (MIPEX) offer some additional hints to the codes for the present analysis of political discourse. The MIPEX framework, for example, distinguishes between seven policy areas, i.e. "labor market mobility", "family reunification", "education", "political participation", "long-term residence", "access to nationality" and "anti-discrimination", a set of categories that obviously is not exhaustive when applied to the complexity of political discourse. Lynch/Simon (2003) headed in a different direction by distinguishing more specific facets of immigration policy: "admit policy", "admit practice", "naturalization policy", "naturalization rate", "control policy", "administration discretion", "public integration efforts" and "illegal immigration". Their advantage is a highly specific focus on particular aspects of immigration policy; however, they again do not offer the necessary range for longitudinal analysis of electoral debate.

A viable source of orientation is offered by Koopmans et al. (2005: 89), who suggest a set of issue codes for their analysis of national political contests over citizenship. For this reason they distinguish between three pillars, one focusing on the regulation of different forms of cross-national mobility ("Immigration, asylum, alien politics"), one dedicated to the various political questions concern-

---

[50] In fact, their analysis was limited to the time period between the years 2000 and 2002, which might explain the narrowness of the issue categories (Froehlich & Rüdiger 2006).

ing the inclusion of ethnic/religious minorities ("Minority integration politics") and a third pillar focusing on questions related to the political regulation of diversity ("Antiracism, xenophobia, and interethnic conflicts"). Although the subcodes subsumed under these pillars are not comprehensive enough for the goals of this study,[51] the threefold distinction of issue pillars is a fruitful basis for the design of this study's coding instrument.

Informed by these heterogeneous examples, the present study attempted to merge these approaches into one coding instrument that a) reflects the peculiarities of strategic political discourse, b) applies to the particular challenge of conducting a time-series analysis (which creates the need for a much broader instrument than do short-period studies), and c) is sensitive to the specifics of the discourse on migration and ethnic relations. Accordingly, two dimensions of topical analysis suggested themselves: firstly, a broad representation of the key issue dimensions that constitute migration and ethnic relations, and secondly, more specific subtopics aimed at capturing the topical contexts to which the politicization of migration and ethnic relations is linked.

Issue dimensions

In a first step, and inspired by the distinction of Koopmans et al. (2005), the study coarsely distinguishes between four general issue dimensions, which together comprise the basic pillars of what is subsumed under the common label of "Fremdenpolitik" ("foreigner issues") in Austrian political discourse, namely *immigration, integration, asylum* and *diversity* (Hammar 1985; Green-Pedersen/Krogstrup 2008: 611; van Kersbergen/Krouwel 2008: 398). These issue dimensions are more abstract than the specific subtopics of the debate; still, their distinction is of vital importance, since subtopics can be linked to more than one of these issue dimensions (e.g. labor aspects can equally be addressed within the context of immigration, asylum or integration). In order to discern the particular relevance for the discourse on migration and ethnic relations of each of these issue dimensions, they needed to be identified separately. In this study, *immigration* issues were defined as those relating to cross-border movements, the control of such movements, and the regulation of access to the country for non-nationals (Borkert/Penninx 2011). The coding of *integration* was reserved for explicit remarks on policies specifically designed to promote the permanent inclusion or exclusion of migrant populations and ethnic minorities of any administrative status (Bijl/Verweil 2012) except for refugees. Asylum seekers and all references to the process of asylum were separately coded under the issue dimension of *asylum* (Nickels 2007). Finally, the issue dimension *diversity* in-

---

[51] For example, the authors distinguish only three codes for the pillar of immigration politics ("residence rights", "entry and exit", "institutional framework") which are arguably to broad if one aims to cover the various modes of immigration, different political parties might address for strategical reasons in their electoral politicization.

cludes all remarks on the organization of society as a whole, comments about the social coexistence of majority and minorities (including both allochthonous and autochthonous ethnic minorities alike), and positive or negative evaluations of social homogeneity or heterogeneity (Zapata-Barrero/Triandafyllidou 2012).

Subtopics

The second step descended to a more concrete level of topical coding that allowed for a straightforward coding instrument. This study developed topical categories based on traditional policy fields that provide a policy context for questions of migration and ethnic relations. Based on the notion of "subtopics" as commonly applied in discourse analysis (van Dijk 1989 and 1991; Wodak 2008; Jäger/Maier 2009), in this study, the politicization of migration and ethnic relations is broken down into various topical components, each of which links to other discourse strands. The subtopics of electoral discourse are differentiated into two types of categories. On the one hand, if connections to other policy fields such as "labor policy", "educational policy", "foreign relations", "crime&border-control", "social&family policy", "science policy" etc. were made explicit, then the coding unit was subsumed under those policy contexts – each of them being an autonomous government department in the Austrian polity structure. These, then, were grouped under the category of *policy-specific subtopics*. On the other hand, *generalist references* to immigration, integration, asylum or societal models that were not explicitly linked to any specific policy dimension were subsumed under corresponding generalist issue categories. Thus, by distinguishing policy-specific from generalist subtopics, this study reveals the concreteness of the electoral debate and its dominant topical contexts.

Table 12 collects the codes for both types of topical categories. Each coding unit was coded according to this scheme, which identifies both its *issue dimension* as well as its *subtopic*. While some policy contexts are intrinsically connected to a particular issue dimension in that they address it directly rather than addressing more specific issues and topics, others are independent and could in fact be linked to any of the four issue dimensions considered. The analysis of issue dimensions and subtopics allows identification of the dominant subtopics of Austrian electoral politicization on migration and ethnic relations, and it helps not only to unravel which parties adopt similar types of issue emphasis to approximate topical coalitions, but also to detect changes in parties' topical emphasis.

Table 12:   Issue dimensions and subtopics of analysis

Issue Dimensions		Subtopics			
	Asylum		Asylum general	Gender relations	Religion
	Immigration		Asylum procedures	Housing&Settlement	Science
	Integration		Citizenship&Voting	Immigration general	Social&Family
	Diversity		Crime&Border Control	Integration general	Societal Model
			Education	International Migration	Xenophobia
			Foreign relations	Labor	

4.2.4 Issue positions: Policy stances of political parties

That emphasis is put on certain topical aspects at the cost of others is only one descriptor of party politicization. Most commonly, research on party competition has dealt with the role of policy positions, meaning the specific stances of political actors on particular issues. For this reason, these two descriptors of politicization were observed independently in this study. Working toward a basic definition of what constitutes a policy position, it might broadly be defined as the set of proposals advanced by an actor for collectively binding measures for the treatment of a specific social condition (Laver/Garry 2000). As a consequence, these positions are always issue-specific and can vary in their degree of abstraction (from micro-political to macro-political positions). As a common denominator for policy position analyses, the term might refer to the systematic process of reducing a complex text into smaller and reliable coding units (Laver/Garry 2000: 622).[52] These very general tasks of attempts at content analysis need to be better specified, however, according to the research being conducted.

Multi-topical approaches, as encouraged by the Manifesto Research Group (MRG) (Budge et al. 2001; Klingemann et al. 2006) and the Party Change Project (PCP) (Janda et al. 1995; Harmel et al. 1995), have traditionally applied quantitative techniques with subtly differentiated and hierarchically structured coding schemes, because they seemed to be the only feasible way of coding multiple issues over time and space. Conversely, a vast number of single-issue studies have applied softer, qualitative coding methods (eg. Reisigl/Wodak 2001; Triandafyllidou 2002; Nickels 2007; van Gorp 2007). The great number of publications on discourse analysis indicates the undiminished importance of such perspectives in the identification of policy positions of political actors. The MRG and PCP approaches, however, have been of pioneering character for comparative designs (time series as well as cross-sectional), since they established a research design that could well be applied to policy analysis in other democratic countries and other historical time periods. The MRG codebook, for example, codes 56 categories which were grouped into seven major policy fields (Budge et al. 2001), with many (though not all) of them designed as valence categories (positive or negative). Using quasi-sentences as coding units, the project computed a total number of quasi-sentences for every document. By relating the

---

[52] The analysis of political positions has been a core task of political research ever since. Still, the development of different modes of analysis has been debated up to a certain point. While some authors have argued that expert surveys would be the best instrument to identify parties' policy positions and locate them in policy spaces (Benoit & Laver 2007; Ray 2007), these perspectives have also been contested, for the reason that expert surveys themselves can show weak reliability if the number of experts is too small (Volkens 2007). Content analysis of party materials is able to avoid some of the disadvantages inherent to expert surveys due to the originality of the source and the reduction of interpreting devices (since expert surveys in fact only reproduce experts' interpretations of devices not available to the researcher) (ibid.).

number of quasi-sentences in each category to the total number, the MRG generated levels of salience for various categories. A similar technique was used in the present study, although the basis of measurement was not the quasi-sentence. Using quasi-sentences as the counting device incurs the major disadvantage of obscuring the actual size of coding units, since some quasi-sentences are much longer and more elaborate than others. For this reason, the present study also used quasi-sentences as a coding unit, but chose a different measurement device, i.e. calculating the word count for each coding unit.

More importantly, however, MRG and PCP have made their mark on party-oriented content analysis with their use of spatial perspective. As outlined in Chapter 2, spatial approaches, i.e. attempts to describe parties' positions in policy spaces, have become the main tool for analyzing party competition in either issue-specific or general contexts (Enelow/Hinich 1984; Laver/Hunt 1992; Hinich/Munger 1997; Laver/Garry 2000). In this regard, the MRG's method is exemplary to this study, since it suggests a simple and straightforward way of assigning spatial positions to political parties. It predefines valence issues (i.e. issues that, by definition, are either positive or negative) by opposing traditionally leftist and traditionally rightist issues, calculating "(…) the left–right score of a given party (…) by summing up the percentages of all the sentences in the left category, and subtracting their total from the sum of the percentages of the sentences in the right category of that party's electoral programme" (Pelizzo 2003: 69). This computing technique served as a model for this study, although the categories are not different (valence) policy issues, but rather absolute positions on one particular policy field. Hence, this study also posited a bipolar liberal-to-restrictive axis on which to locate parties (Lahav 2004). With this approach, the changing positions of parties were made comparable over the whole examination period, enabling analysis of the changes in inter-party proximity.

Developing codes for policy positions: Policy frames

Still, the development of codes for policy positions used to capture party competition on migration and ethnic relations is somewhat more complex than developing codes for describing topical preferences in politicization. Given the broad range of positions in this policy field that could not possibly be identified a priori, a focus on deductive coding proved to be insufficient. Confronted with this deficit, the present study opted for a combination of inductive and deductive development of codes for policy positions, allowing it to advance the findings of a qualitative analysis toward the goal of quantifying the patterns of politicization.

Identifying political positions, however, is far from straightforward, as the vast amount of literature and the diversity of analytical approaches indicate. Political discourses can develop on very different semantic levels, any of which can be the subject of analysis (van Gorp 2007). For the longitudinal purposes of this study frame analysis proved to be the most effective approach. In recent years, analysis of discursive frames has become one of the most intensively used approaches in the study of political communication, the study of the complex interactions of various public actors engaged in a struggle for hegemony over the power of definition. Although its fragmented modes of application have been something of an obstacle to its universal adoption, frame analysis has established itself as one of the primary methods of analysis, evaluation and interpretation of political discourses (Entman 1993; Koenig 2005).

Beyond the general applicability of frame analysis, its usefulness to investigations of the specific questions of migration and ethnic relations has been further verified (e.g. by Lakoff/Ferguson 2006; Larsen et al. 2009; Scholten 2011; and Helbling 2013). However, as it is concerned with the development of narrow, elaborated frames that constitute the interpretive spectrum of these issues, the full potential of frame analysis in this context has not been used yet. While there have been a number of scholarly attempts in this direction, so far they have been related to one another only loosely and have usually focused on specific segments of the debate. While some authors have addressed the question of asylum (van Gorp 2005; Nickels 2007), few broadened their scope to include immigration and ethnic diversity as a whole, with the majority focusing on narrow analytical categories (Fröhlich/Rüdiger 2006) or broad descriptions of frames (Vliegenthaart 2007) and usually considering isolated national cases. Few attempts have been made to generalize frames on immigration in cross-country studies such as by Helbling (2013) or by the comparative SOM-project (Berkhout/Sudulich 2011). What fundamentally hinders the synthesis of these approaches, though, is the diversity of frames they generate and/or apply. This diversity may result from their differing concepts of frames, from the particular attributes of the discussions they trace, or, last but not least, from considering different communication channels.

Confronted with this fragmented state of the art, this study was compelled to develop its own concept to describe the framing of migration and ethnic relations in order to conduct this analysis. The next chapter aims to sketch the procedures and findings of an analysis of policy positions based on a triangulated frame analysis. By combining existing concepts from previous research with an inductive approach to frame identification based on new data, this chapter offers an important new contribution to this research field. It introduces a framework of analysis for migration and ethnic relations that offers the basis for a quantitative study (the findings of which will be presented in the subsequent section). Moreover, though grounded on the Austrian case, through linking the frames developed in the following section to previous findings discussed in the literature they should be a viable instrument for studying political discourse in other national contexts as well.

5. Framing migration and ethnic relations: A qualitative exploration of discursive strategies

Migration and ethnic relations are no average political issues. They touch the cornerstones of individual and collective identities and therefore magnify societies' fundamental questions of their own self-perception and self-regulation. The discourse on migration and ethnic relations draws boundaries of ingroup- and outgroup-constructs, of "them" and "us", and therefore poses a vital field for parties to mobilize voter sentiments and support. In the context of such emotionally charged policy issues, steering discourse into specific directions is even more important than in the context of technical debates on policy regulations. What successful political parties need to achieve, is to establish dominant lines of interpretation that allow to structure the perception of the issue, thus its main underlying problems as well as the fundamental suggestions of how to overcome them. The scholarly concept of "framing" is dedicated to the study of these construction processes and, thanks to its applicability in different political communication contexts, it has gained increasing relevance among scholars of political communication. The following chapter aims to utilize the concept for the study of parties' policy positions on migration and ethnic relations. Accordingly, it introduces the core principles of the framing concept as well as the key elements for the frame analysis of political discourse conducted in the present study (5.1), before turning to the study's qualitative findings by describing the policy frames on migration and ethnic relations in Austrian electoral discourse (5.2).

5.1 Framing and frame analysis: A general introduction

Framing is a transdisciplinary concept that has gained importance in disciplines as varied as psychology, sociology, communication studies, linguistics, cybernetics, and, not least, political science. Prior to the discussion of the frames of immigration, migrant integration, and ethnic diversity, a short introduction to the concept of framing is necessary in order to delimit the study's approach to this complex – and at times controversial – field of research.

5.1.1 Roots and characteristics of the framing concept

Scholarly activity in recent decades has yielded a range of psychological and sociological attempts to define frames. Traditionally, such attempts start with a reference to Erving Goffman's book "Frame Analysis", which introduced the concept of framing in a broader sociological context (although Goffman himself based his work on concepts developed previously by Gregory Bateson and William James). Consequently, frames are most commonly defined as "schemes of interpretation" or as "organizing principles for events (…) through which we build definitions of a situation" (Goffman 1977: 31, 19). This situational dimension is one of the characteristic elements of Goffman's approach, which investigates how individuals interpret the mass of experiences they are confronted with every day. It implies that a person's understanding of a situation depends upon the type of frames that they adopt in structuring the individual elements of the situation to produce a meaningful whole. This concept of frames as structuring devices for the production of meaning accords with several other concepts developed in psychology as well as research on artificial intelligence, and shows parallels to the concept of *scheme* or *script* (Triandafyllidou/Fotiou 1998). These concepts result from the conclusion that interpretation processes consist of more than just the re-identification of explicit contents and thus require productive processing into a greater complex of meaning. Even in artificial intelligence research, interpretation of texts is impossible if it is based solely on the information available within a text; instead, it requires a priori patterns of meaning into which individual units of information can be placed (Donati 2001: 149).

Kahneman/Tversky (1981) delivered early psychological verification of the framing concept by experimentally demonstrating that different formulations of choice problems produce differing preferences in test subjects; thus different framing of one and the same situation leads to a different understanding and consequently a different decision on how to act (Kahneman/Tversky 1981: 457). According to the framing model, individuals use frames as interpretive devices to integrate new information into a coherent whole. In this process, they rely on their previous knowledge and thus reproduce interpretive frames that they have acquired previously in a process of socialization and acculturation (Triandafyllidou/Fotiou 1998, Matthes 2007). However, socialization and acculturation processes tie individual cognitive processes to the production of larger frames in a public sphere. Thus, as Scheufele/Tewksbury (2007: 12) put it, the framing concept links the macro-level and the micro-level in that it relates the individual process of interpreting isolated pieces of information using a broader framework of interpretation (micro-level) to the modes of presentation employed by public communicators to transfer information based on common knowledge (macrolevel). Recognizing this, Rein/Schön's (1993: 146) definition of the framing process made it equally viable for both producers as well as recipients of communication units: "Framing is a way of selecting, organizing, interpreting and making sense of a complex reality to provide guideposts for knowing, analyzing, persuading and acting. A frame is a perspective from which an amorphous, illdefined, problematic situation can be made sense of and acted on".

Subsequent framing approaches have been scattered across numerous disciplinary perspectives, and in consequence, various "species" of frames have been conceived. Even in the narrow context of political communication research, according to Nelson/Willey (2003: 246), "[t]here is more than one kind of frame swimming in the political information stream. The politically most relevant species are *collective action frames* (Gamson 1992; Snow et al., 1986); *decision frames* (Kahneman/Tversky, 1984); *news frames* (Iyengar, 1991; Price/Tewksbury, 1997); and our favourite, *issue frames* (Nelson/Oxlea, 1999)".

These different types of frames are loosely linked to different disciplines; as the "collective action frame" is linked to sociology, so are "decision frames" linked to behavioral management studies and "news frames" to journalism and media studies. Consequently, these differing approaches address different aspects of the framing process, which are located either on the individual micro-level of interpretation (such as the decision frames; Kahneman/Tversky 1981) or on the organizational meso-level of strategic communication (collective action frames; Benford/Snow 2000), or are concerned with the journalistic meta-perspective of public life (news frames) (D'Angelo 2002). Within these particular disciplines, they may be differentiated even further, e.g., by distinguishing "generic news frames" (issue-independent patterns in journalistic descriptions of reality) from "issue-specific news frames" (interpretations that can only be applied to specific thematic boundaries of a news issue) in journalism and media studies (de Vreese 2005).

In a political science context, most studies are focused on the analysis either of frames promoted by strategic communicators (such as social movements, interest groups, political parties, governments, etc.) or those propagated by news media covering political competition and debates. Since the present study deals with the supply side of political communication, its major interest is in framing as it is employed by strategic communicators aiming to convey meaning to particular, intended audiences. Owing to the effects of media exposure on politics (Mazzoleni/Schulz 1999; Strömbäck 2008), it has become increasingly challenging for strategic communicators to steer public discourse in their preferred direction. Thus managing public communication has become one of the most important tasks in the expanding public spheres of (post-)modern societies. This holds true especially for political actors in liberal democracies, who not only strive for legitimacy for their policies but are also highly dependent on accumulating mass support for their political activities. Hence, political actors in mediatized democracies are under pressure to condense their political preferences and activities in such a way as to make them accessible and appealing to a larger public – and that is where the concept of framing inevitably comes in. Policy frames are, obviously, simplifications of the actual complexities of both the policy-making process itself as well as the discourse on it. They represent overarching patterns of interpretation which is exactly what makes them such a useful instrument of political communication: They resemble the structure of our thought and the way citizens approach political issues more strongly than any other discursive level of abstraction (Nelson/Willey 2003: 255-8). It is for this reason that frames are also an analytical tool that is uniquely suited to the purposes of the present study: On the one hand, they express sufficient variety to depict the cornerstones of conflict and competition over a specific issue, while on the other hand, they abstract to such an extent that they remain longitudinally viable instruments for the analysis of political discourse.

Thus, for political communication research, the process of constructing social meaning using policy frames is of vital relevance and "[t]he central question, then, for interpretive policy analysts is, How is the policy issue being framed by the various parties to the debate?" (Yanow 2006: 11). With this question being the foundation for this study's approach to framing analysis, the competition of political parties can be characterized as the strategic use of policy frames in order to distribute messages and to persuade potential supporters – or as Pan and Kosicki put it (2003: 40): "Framing an issue is therefore a strategic means to attract more supporters, to mobilize collective actions, to expand actors' realm of influences, and to increase their chances of winning". Political communicators are obliged to "frame"[53] their topics in such a way as to further their interests (Rein/Schön 1996; Triandafyllidou/Fotiou 1998). Unsurprisingly, these rationales are often not articulated in a clear and manifest way, but rather seem to be embedded in a semantic network of metaphors, idioms, and other figures of speech (Gamson/Modigliani 1987; van Gorp 2005). Thus the primary challenge in frame analysis is extracting from these linguistic devices the persistent overarching narratives that the communication units express. The question remains, however: what are discursive frames composed of?

5.1.2 Frame components in strategic political communication

Any systematic analysis of frames needs to clarify the fundamental building blocks from which individual frames are constructed, as well as the rules of their assembly into a coherent interpretation. As a first hint that helps to narrow down the characteristics of discursive frames, Reese (2003: 11) suggested that "[f]rames are *organizing principles* that are socially *shared* and *persistent* over time, that work *symbolically* to meaningfully *structure* the social world." Frames organize smaller units of information into more abstract patterns of interpretation which are not manifest in the text itself. Beyond that, frames reference commonly shared knowledge that is established in the permanent cultural heritage and thereby structure the social world into symbolic forms of expression and

---

[53] Additionally it has to be pointed out that, from a methodological point of view, it is also important to differentiate between the use of the term *frame* as a noun and its use as a verb, as this has consequences for the design of the adapted approach. The use of *frame* or *framing* as a noun refers to temporarily fixed structures that delimit the content of a communication, structures which can be observed and compared to structures in other communicative units. Conversely, the use of *frame/framing* as a verb denotes the action of producing such a structure, which can be conducted either unconsciously or – as is mainly the case in the context of political communication – strategically, thus challenging the researcher to explain the factors influencing this process (Yanow 2006: 13). This project considers each mode of use: First the frame analysis aims to identify traceable frame-structures (*frame* as a noun) of different political actors and over an extended period of time. The step following the analysis tries to determine a set of factors that might explain the rationale behind the specific structures identified.

interpretation (Reese 2003: 11-2). More precisely, Yanow (2006: 11) specified that "[f]rames direct attention toward some elements while simultaneously diverting attention from other elements. They highlight and contain at the same time that they exclude". Similarly, Gamson (1989: 157) underlined that individual facts need to be "embedded in a frame or story line that organizes them and gives them coherence, selecting certain ones to emphasize while ignoring others". Thus an analysis of the framing strategies of political actors needs to identify the main elements highlighted in each communication unit (such as a text document, a speech, etc.) and to merge them into an underlying line of interpretation. Still, this does not explain which sort of elements a frame is based on.

In addition to these preliminary hints, more specific suggestions have been made within the particular context of social movement research. In that context, the concept of framing has been in use since the 1980s for analyzing the political communication of strategic actors (Snow et al. 1986; Benford/Snow 1988 and 1992; Gamson/Modigliani 1989; Tarrow 1992; Benford 1993). Their core objective was to understand how successful social movements manage to mobilize supporters (stimulate collective action) by (re)constructing discursive interpretations of socially relevant issues. In this context, framing was conceived as a discursive tool to construct and promote particular schemes of interpretation for specific problems. Consequently, Benford/Snow (1988: 136) described "collective action frames" as the product of a strategic and "active, process-derived phenomenon that implies agency and contention at the level of reality construction". They identified three main functions of a collective action frame. Firstly, a frame serves as a means for actors to "punctuate or single out some existing social condition or aspect of life and define it as unjust, intolerable, and deserving of corrective action" (Benford/Snow 1988: 137). Secondly, a frame needs to serve an attributional function of allocating actors' responsibilities; that is, it is used to "attribute blame for some problematic condition by identifying culpable agents, be they individuals or collective processes or structures", as well as to suggest "both a general line of action for ameliorating the problem and the assignment of responsibility for carrying out that action" (Benford/Snow 1988: 137). Thirdly, according to the authors, frames perform an articulation function in that they "enable activists to articulate and align a vast array of events and experiences so that they hang together in a relatively unified and meaningful fashion" (Benford/Snow 1988: 137-8). Later, Benford/Snow (1988b: 199) condensed their approach by distinguishing more sharply between "three core framing tasks: (1) a diagnosis of some event or aspect of social life as problematic and in need of alteration; (2) a proposed solution to the diagnosed problem that specifies what needs to be done; and (3) a call to arms or rationale for engaging in ameliorative or corrective action". Grounded on these assertions, Entman (1993: 52) gave voice to what has become probably the most frequently quoted definition of framing in the political communication context by pointing out that "[t]o frame is to select some aspects of a perceived reality and make them more salient in a communicating context, in such a way as to promote a particular problem definition, causal interpretation, moral evaluation, and/or treatment recommendation for the item described".

Admittedly, it is debatable whether the concept of framing as developed in the realm of social movement literature is equally viable for understanding other political communicators such as political parties, governments, ministerial departments, etc., since they each have different resources and methods of promoting their opinions (Pan/Kosicky 2003: 44-5) and some of them tend to produce communication for legitimizing their own actions rather than for motivating support and collective action. Nonetheless, in recent years, similar framing approaches have been applied very fruitfully to a broad selection of actors involved in political communication processes (e.g. Triandafyllidou/Fotiou 1998; Benford &Snow 2000; Semetko/Valkenburg 2000; Tedesco 2001; Daviter 2007; Helbling 2013). Furthermore, as regards political parties, the parallels to social movement communication are certainly very strong, especially in the specific arena of electoral competition. There, political parties pursue the same primary goal of mobilizing supporters, with the sole difference being that the desired collective action is voting instead of other forms of political expression. Therefore, the concept is easily transferred to the context of political parties (with small parties, especially, facing many of the same difficulties and challenges as social movements). The widespread use of framing concepts by political campaign advisers, e.g. in the United States (Lakoff 2004; Luntz 2007), shows that political parties discovered the usefulness of the concept of framing quite some time ago, and have added it as a strategic element to their communicational toolbox.

In an electoral context, the nature of frames corresponds to what Rein/Schön (1996: 92) referred to as "rhetorical frames", established in policy-relevant texts and debates, in contrast to "action frames", which express inherent patterns in the actions of policy practitioners. While the former "manifest pure frames, which are, in effect 'ideal types'", the latter "tend to be more muddied, fuzzier and mixed". Because of the electoral competition context of this study, it focuses exclusively on parties' use of rhetorical frames and disregards other elements of their rhetoric on policy implementation. The ideal types expressed in their rhetorical frames are the only feasible way of delineating parties' politicization patterns. Accordingly, a policy frame might be best understood, in the words of Verloo (2005: 20), as an "organising principle that transforms fragmentary or incidental information into a structured and meaningful policy problem, in which a solution is implicitly or explicitly enclosed". However, in order to make use of this policy framing concept, it remains to be clarified how they can a) be identified and b) be cast into a valid and comprehensive typology.

A combined approach for frame identification

As already stated, frames do not exist independently but rather are linked to specific objects, such as issues of debate. Departing from Benford/Snow (1988b) and their threefold concept, the present analysis uses *problem description* (diagnosis),[54] *treatment recommendation* (prognosis)[55] and *appeal for action* (call to arms) as three basic indicators for the construction of a policy frame. Along with these hallmarks, other properties such as a specific vocabulary being used (Hertog/McLeod 2001: 148) as well as certain "word choice, metaphors, exemplars, descriptions, arguments, and visual images" (van Gorp 2007: 64) are considered as further indicators for the presence of a policy frame. However, not all of these indicators are required at once to identify a frame. Due to their synthesizing nature, frames tend to fill information gaps. In other words, through the use of frames we are still able to understand isolated pieces of information as parts of a broader meaning, even when other elements of this meaning are not expressed at the same time (Entman 1993: 52; Donati 2001: 150). This is of crucial importance for the analysis of frames in texts, because it clarifies that once a frame is established in a cultural reservoir, the use of even a single attribute can be sufficient for the activation of the respective interpretive frame. Thus, during coding of the texts, the identification of policy frames has to be conducted using multiple indicators that cannot and will not all appear together in every single text.[56] Instead, due to the different natures of different sorts of documents, they will be articulated more or less selectively. While programmatic documents will tend to offer a more extensive description of issues (and thus contain more elements of frames), short-term communication on a day-to-day basis will consist of more selective and specific descriptions of policy issues. Consequently, the present study defines two compulsory indicators for the presence of frames – "problem definitions" and "treatment recommendations" – while other indicators are regarded as facultative, but not compelling elements, of a frame within a coding unit.

---

[54] For the purpose of this project, a diagnosis is defined as the linkage of two semantic elements: a) the description of a historical or actual social condition (such as structures, measures, etc.) and b) an appraisal of that condition as being either positive or negative. The two elements do not have to appear in equal proportions but must be explicitly stated. Thus appraisal elements can appear either a) as separate, complete sentences or b) as words or phrases within descriptive sentences.

[55] The prognostic framing of a phenomenon for the present project is defined as the monocausal (unidirectional) linkage of a) a present action with b) a future social condition. Differently put, it refers to the prediction of an expected future condition as a supposed result of some specific action (or of not taking said action) in the present. In contrast to the diagnostic elements, in a prognosis only the description of a future condition has to be made in an explicit form, while the action linked to it can be identified either explicitly (by naming it) or implicitly (as in descriptions of developments expected to result from the absence of new measures). Again, elements can appear either as complete, independent sentences or as individual words or phrases within descriptive sentences.

[56] As Entman (1993: 52) puts it: "A single sentence may perform more than one of these four framing functions [defining problems, diagnosing causes, making moral judgements and suggesting remedies; O.G.], although many sentences in a text may perform none of them. And a frame in any particular text may not necessarily include all four functions."

Another question remains, namely how to label and characterize frames correctly. According to Donati, frame analysis is a translation of the analyzed text into common-sense categories of the people's "Lebenswelten", such as "no gains without cost" (Donati 2001: 164). Similarly, Nelson/Willey (2001: 248) point out that "[m]ost issue frames can be summarized by a simple tagline, such as 'reverse discrimination' or 'right to life'". The present study worked from these premises; both a general indicating label (a basic noun) and a prototypical idiomatic expression are indicated for each frame identified in party discourse. Due to the combined approach, some of these labels and idioms, as well as the characteristics of the corresponding frame, could be derived from earlier studies in the field of migration and ethnic relations, and thus they served as a foundation for the present analysis. Furthermore, this deductive step was supplemented by the inductive development of frames in consideration of the coding material consulted for the study. By combining deductive and inductive creation and verification of relevant policy frames, not only were new frames developed (capturing discourse elements that are not covered by frames suggested in previous research), but the a priori deduced frames were condensed and expressed more clearly, as well. Thus, once literature-based frame categories had turned out to be insufficient to capture the interpretive core of the material, new frame categories were constructed using the frame elements explained above. Furthermore, existing frames were expanded upon, insofar as was necessary, by the analysis of this study's material, which in some cases has led to their reformulation in more precise terms (in order to ensure accurate discrimination in the frames developed here). This analytical process attempts parsimony, i.e. to create as few frames as possible but as many as necessary in order to satisfactorily reflect the structure of Austrian electoral discourse on migration and ethnic relations (Hertog/McLeod 2001: 150). Each frame thus consists of at least a) a diagnosis of some state or aspect of social life as being problematic and in need of alteration, and b) a proposed solution to the diagnosed problem specifying what needs to be done (Benford/Snow 1988b: 199) – but is occasionally expanded upon with further indicators as well.

The next section documents the findings of the qualitative analysis of frames on migration and ethnic relations in Austrian electoral competition from 1971 to 2013. Its goal is to define the boundaries of party discourse by explicating and exemplifying the dominant lines of interpretation promoted by Austrian parties over the course of the examination period. Once the details of the set of frames have been presented, their relation to individual parties as well as their quantitative importance in Austrian electoral competition will be addressed separately in Chapter 6.

5.2   Baselines of politicization: Framing of migration and ethnic relations

How do Austrian parties frame migration and ethnic relations in electoral competition? This is the central question of this section, and it shall be answered with the findings of a combined frame analysis. Using the approach outlined above, eleven policy frames in total were identified in the electoral discourse on migration and ethnic relations since 1971. Most of these frames can be roughly categorized into two groups: one with a more *liberal* mindset and another with a more *restrictive* tendency (Lahav 2004). According to Givens/Luedtke (2005: 10), restrictiveness as applied to migration and ethnic relations may be defined as "any limitation of immigrant rights, freedoms, benefits or privileges" together with pejorative and delegitimizing stances on cultural diversity, extended immigration movements, or the presence of foreigners in general – whereas liberal positions are defined as the opposite stances (see also Ivarsflaten 2005; Statham 2003).[57] Using the juxtaposition of restrictive vs. liberal stances, a bipolar scale was created with five policy frames of migration and ethnic relations on each side. The following descriptions depict the core meaning of each frame and combine it with exemplary references drawn from analysis of the coding material. Additionally, all frames were deductively grounded on previous sources consulted during literature review that explicitly suggested categories of the same kinds and used similar definitions to delimit their meanings.

5.2.1   *Liberal frames on migration and ethnic relations*

In the liberal part of the discourse spectrum, at least five different frames can be distinguished that express an inclusive attitude on migration and ethnic relations:

- *(Human/Basic) rights:* The most fundamental of all liberal frames references the *"indivisibility of (human) rights"* and thus connects questions regarding the treatment of minorities and migrants with a basic rights perspective (Fujiwara 2005; Helbling 2013). In view of this, it harshly criticizes the flouting of fundamental human rights in refugee policy and in the application of immigration regimes (especially with regard to family reunification), and decries the social and political exclusion of ethnic minorities or foreigners.

> The right to share a family life is a fundamental right. We claim that it should be equally valid for all immigrants. A prerequisite therefore is the right to family reunification, without quotas or restrictions. (*Greens*, Manifesto, 2006)

---

[57] It is important to note that the term "liberal" in this context is used only in its narrow political sense (i.e. adressing policies that promote the freedom of individuals without regard to their sex, class, ethnicity, etc.) and does not consider its (politico-)economic use.

As a consequence, the rights frame promotes a humanitarian perspective and calls not only for the implementation of all existing human rights, but also advocates for new rights to be established – especially within the context of ethnic and religious minorities and, to an increasing extent, also with regard to refugees (Larsen et al. 2009). Correspondingly, special emphasis is placed on the right to refuge and the right to family reunification, but questions of religious freedom are also commonly framed using a rights perspective. At times its scope may be extended further, as in appeals for more support of disadvantaged ethnic groups, who are to be enabled to assert their basic rights as humans and/or citizens (e.g. by facilitating access to multilingual documents, advisors, etc.) (Wengeler 2003). Even in the context of labor market regimes, rights are applied as a frame, such as by the LIF:

> Austrian immigration policy finally has to develop concepts that offer legal immigrants a right to labor market integration. Who rightfully resides on Austrian soil must be entitled to work and choose its workplace here without chicane. (Liberal Forum, Manifesto, 2002)

Thus, in a rights frame, rights are treated only in an inclusive manner and both the juridical framework as well as its execution across all potential subgroups (according to ethnicity, religion, or residence status) are addressed.

- *Participation:* Based on the concept of an 'emancipation' frame (outlined by Vliegenthaart 2007: 37), the present framework suggests a slight expansion of this frame toward the concept of "participation" in a broader sense (Roggeband/Verloo 2007: 277). In this perspective, discursive strategies stress the necessity of policies that ensure equality for diverse groups living in a society by promoting their self-empowerment. As a consequence, the participation frame commonly appears in the topical context of migrant integration or the integration of ethnic and religious minorities (Lavenex 2005). Its central argument revolves around the notion of *"integration through modes of participation"*, implying that participatory offers help to overcome existing exclusion of people living in a common polity, and can be expressed as by the ÖVP in 2002:

> Political authority has to ensure that people living on Austrian soil – regardless of their different ethnic or cultural background – find the opportunity to participate in social, economic and public life on an equal and fair basis. The inclusion of these different groups into the political and social constitution of the country has to be conveyed to the Austrian population in order to achieve a mutual understanding and acceptance. Participation of immigrants in the social and political structures can and should be facilitated by the institutions of the active civic society. (People's Party, Manifesto, 2002)

This perspective needs to be further specified in two regards. Firstly, the participation frame differs from a rights perspective in that it expresses the need for facilitation and support not as fundamental rights in a narrow sense, but rather only as options for individual inclusion. Thus its foundation is less compulsory than the notion of positive rights or lawfully documented entitlements (as outlined above); instead it introduces softer instruments that promote individual and group empowerment that may be provided where useful and in actual demand. Secondly, the perspective of participation does not designate its instruments as obligations (which characterizes another frame – the assimilationist – instead), but merely as facilitations for participating in a wide range of individually and socially fruitful processes. Concrete examples would be measures for more inclusive adult and school education, sponsored language programs, facilitation of citizenship acquisition, and support with administrative procedures for people of a different native language.

- *Multiculturalism:* The concept of multiculturalism serves as a common interpretive framework in discourse all over Europe, and thus has already been identified as an important frame by previous authors (e.g. Vliegenthaart 2007; Roggeband/Verloo 2007: 278; Scholten 2011; Helbling 2013). In essence, the frame expands on the principle of *"diversity as a social boon"*, primarily in a normative sense but also with respect to the historical heritage of multicultural influences in a country's identity (meaning, most importantly to the Austrian case, the ethnically diverse history of the Austro-Hungarian Empire). The frame diagnoses a lack of acceptance and appreciation for modes of living or religion other than the hegemonic ones. It criticizes modes of active and passive discrimination and – in its most explicit form – tendencies toward compelling cultural assimilation. Conversely, the multicultural frame aims to overcome patterns of uniformity by supporting measures that actively promote diversity (e.g. multilingualism initiatives, or training of educators in intercultural competence), such as in the following example:

> In the multicultural society, tolerance becomes the touchstone for democracy. However, this does not imply a simple mutual laissez-faire but active respect of language and culture of minorities. (…) Minority questions are question of coexistence und culture. No ethnic or language group, as numerically superior and powerful it might perceive itself, may claim to have created a culture that is superior to all the others. (…) The comprehension of a common responsibility is the foundation for a new culture of coexistence. It develops and enriches human and social contacts in ethnically mixed regions. It rejects nationalistic and ethnocentrist patterns of thinking and politics by following the principle of interethnic and multicultural communication. It demands a political and cultural guideline for multilingual regions that creates the foundations for multilingualism. Its goal is to overcome the minority status of the smaller language and thus create a so-

cial and public framework that is inevitable for the survival of the minority culture. (Greens, Manifesto, 1990)

With this perspective, the multiculturalism frame substantially differs from weaker conceptions that merely focus on tolerance and acceptance of diversity, which leaves the power relations between majorities and minorities unaffected (see the solidarity frame). Instead, its explicit emphasis on the value of plurality promotes policies that preserve and encourage all patterns of cultural and religious diversity.

- *Solidarity:* Unlike the multicultural perspective, this frame is based on the moral value of tolerance and revolves around the principle of *"mutual coexistence instead of intergroup competition"* (Vasta 2010). Consequently, it primarily opposes the abuse of ethnic or religious minorities as scapegoats and their being played off against each other as well as against a supposed majority culture. It overtly opposes any form of xenophobia and exploitation of disadvantaged and vulnerable groups as demonstrating a lack of solidarity (Roggeband/Verloo 2007; Larsen et al. 2009), yet it refrains from proactive calls for diversity – such as in the following statement of the SPÖ:

> [T]he SPÖ sets an example for a common, conjunctive and peaceful way of coexistence in Austria and opposes exclusion, incitement, division as well as increasing radicalization that we experienced again during this election campaign. 'It's not about ignoring or euphemizing problems and difficulties that might very well evolve with the coexistence of people. On the contrary, it's about the emphasis that we may only solve these problems by a joint effort and that we may not get divided by populist paroles of right-wing instigators. All of us, together constitute this country of Austria, which we can be proud of', explaines SP-spokeswomen Laura Rudas. (Social Democrats, Press release, 26 September 2008)

Besides these rather general appeals, the frame is also closely associated with critical narratives of victimization, which are commonly observed in the context of asylum seekers or the suppression of women from ethnic or religious minorities (van Gorp 2005; Vliegenthaart/Roggeband 2007). In light of these diagnoses, the solidarity frame calls upon political actors and society to show solidarity and compassion for the discriminated groups (ethnic minorities, religious minorities, asylum seekers, etc.) (Lakoff/Ferguson 2006). It emphasizes the importance of working with instead of against each other, and thus demands that priority should be given to social cohesion as well as forums of common discourse that promote mutual understanding. Solidarity framing differs from the previous frames in that it does not explicitly promote diversity; but rather calls for greater significance to be accorded to the principle of tolerance. It also makes no explicit references to the promotion of minority participation, and its demands are pleas for recognition and charity rather than claims of positive rights.

- *Cosmopolitanism:* Similarly to the notion of an access-frame (Roggeband/Verloo 2007), a cosmopolitan frame expresses the most flexible perspective on immigration and access to fundamental sectors like labor, welfare system, education, and the like. It characterizes transnational mobility as a traditional pattern in Europe and also points out the necessity of migration from a social, economic and even cultural angle. As a consequence, it argues for an *"accessible regime of immigration and transnational migration"* (Balabanova/Balch 2010). It diagnoses tendencies toward shutting/closing and exclusionary policies on a national level. Similar bulkheading behavior is identified on a European level, more specifically with regard to the European Union ("fortress of Europe") (Favell/Hansen 2002). As a direct response to these diagnoses, the frame promotes "the opening up of the national boundaries and the process of international integration" (Kriesi et al. 2006: 922). It calls for a migration-friendly policy on both the national and the European level that reflects the transformed conditions of mobility in the 21st century, helps to overcome the problems caused by aging population pyramids, and also offers more flexibility to the economy; it is therefore tied to calls for facilitation of access to Europe or Austria, more flexible incorporation into the labor market, etc.:

> The only alternative to the misery of the previous "Gastarbeiter"-regime is a coherent regime of Immigration and Migrant Integration. Only such a new regime corresponds to the enlightened and humanitarian tradition of Europe as well as the conditions of increasing internationalization and mobility. The populist talk of "closing the borders" for immigration is unrealistic and produces massive insecurity for foreigners, which implies disadvantageous consequences for all residents of our country. (Greens, Manifesto, 1994)

In the Austrian context specifically, the frame frequently references the historical duty to maintain a spirit of openness considering the country's role in the Nazi regime, as well as its post-war position as a bridge between East and West (resulting from the country's declaration of neutrality) and its role as a United Nations headquarters. From a common European perspective, references in this context often emphasize the continent's (historical) global ties to the Asian and African continents, as well as its image of being at the vanguard of modernity ('cradle of enlightenment') and a global promoter of liberal values.

5.2.2 Restrictive frames on migration and ethnic relations

At the opposite side of the ideological spectrum, restrictive frames express a more or less exclusive character with regard to migration and ethnic relations. Again, these perspectives can be differentiated into five frames:

- *Genuineness:* Reversing the liberal notion of 'rights', this frame creates a normative framework using the notions of 'legitimacy' and 'genuineness'. Hence the frame is built on the diagnosis of widespread *"abuse of too liberal regimes"* in the fields of immigration, asylum, social system, labor market etc. that is said to be exploited by non-nationals who are not genuinely entitled. The most obvious target groups of these frames are clandestine migrants who illegally live and work within the country's borders (Lakoff/Ferguson 2006). Less obviously, common examples for this kind of discursive framing are the cases of asylum seekers who, it is suspected, willfully delay and dissimulate in the process of screening ("bogus asylum seeker"), as well as non-nationals exploiting the welfare system or damaging the labor market through illicit work, and couples accused of being in bogus marriages – so called "import brides" (Roggeband/Vliegenthart 2013: 531). These illicit groups are consequently contrasted with legitimate counterparts, such as the genuine asylum seeker, ambitious and hardworking labor migrants, etc., and their juxtaposition constitutes the core of this perspective:

> Asylum seekers are far from equally shared across the European Union. Instead the refugee smuggling industry and illegal migration have become the routine. (…) Therefore we will campaign on the international level for an adaption of the Geneva Convention to the changing conditions of mass migration. Just by such an adaption it might be ensured, that protection and refuge is granted to those, who are in actual need of it while abuse of asylum regimes becomes permanently reduced. (Alliance for the Future of Austria, Manifesto, 2006)

In response to this juxtaposition of perceived abuse and entitled groups, the genuineness frame demands more measures that sharpen the distinction between those groups, better identification of illegitimate groups, and a more restrictive approach with regard to the latter. Common suggestions in this frame are stronger restrictions on asylum procedures, increased penalties for abuse or non-compliance, stronger limitation of welfare aid, and rigorous expulsion of abusers (Nickels 2007). Thus a genuineness frame is applied entirely from exclusionary principles, since the distinction of genuine and illicit groups is hardly ever addressed with a focus on the rights of the former instead of the identification and reduction of the latter.

- *Benefit:* The benefit frame is the most utilitarian perspective within the discourse on migration and ethnic relations: it is entirely restricted to an evaluation of costs and benefits for the host society (Kretsedemas 2012; Helbling

2013). By its precepts, immigration should be allowed for only those essential sectors in which the receiving country is short of human resources. Accordingly, the frame criticizes the ousting of the native and local population and thus demands that priority ought to be given to nationals in preference to foreigners in a broad range of regulated fields such as labor market access, educational system access, and so on. This hierarchic perspective is linked to the explicit claim that, in order to gain any legitimacy, immigration (in general) and foreign individuals (in particular) need to contribute particular requested benefits to the host country, such as filling vacant gaps in the labor market, facilitating economic improvement, increasing professional know-how, etc.

> We have and we will value the great accomplishments that immigrants and Neo-Austrians have contributed to our country. However, unrestricted immigration is no suitable model for the future of our country. Therefore we will develop a model that enables us to actively control the immigration of only those people that Austria needs for ensuring its economic growth. (...) Thus, immigration – except of the question of family reunion – has to be limited to those areas that are vital for the further development of our country (such as specific economic sectors, science and research). (People's Party, Manifesto, 2006)

Conversely, if these requirements are not met, the benefit frame strictly opposes granting access or even further residence of the immigrant population. As a consequence, it demands measures that promote beneficial immigration only with selective access to residence permits and the labor market, time limits on residence permits, and a major focus on the expected contribution of foreigners to the public interest, and thus may even lead to calls for rigorous inspection of rigid criteria for granting residence permits, or for a stricter expulsion regime (Wengeler 2003; Nickels 2007). As has been shown, the benefit frame is strictly different from previous frames in that it argues solely from utilitarianism, and its rigidity can manifest in different degrees of restrictiveness. Moreover, unlike the cosmopolitan perspective, the frame is used solely restrictively to designate existing regimes that are deemed too open (but never ones that are the opposite).

- *Assimilation:* This frame is directly opposed to the multiculturalist frame and expresses an assimilationist approach (Scholten 2011) that calls more or less concretely for the *"preservation of a guiding culture"* (see also Helbling 2013). In its most extreme form, it diagnoses a threat to Austrian identity posed by foreign ethnicities or religions – e.g., by asserting an Islamization of Austria or Europe – and consequently demands measures to counteract these influences. A more moderate version of the assimilation frame diagnoses a reluctance to assimilate on the part of foreigners and/or ethnic minorities (who are accused of offending assumed national or European basic values), and therefore primarily calls for the subordination of those groups to hegemonic values as shown here:

> The will of immigrants to integrate is an indispensable requirement for their permanent residence in Austria. It may not be confined to the will to live and work in our country. It also consists of the willingness to learn the German language and to unconditionally accept the legal order of our country. Additionally it also implies to devote oneself to the historic and cultural background of our country as well as to accept the social order that is based on freedom, tolerance and equality of chances. All of these prerequisites have been considered in the new citizenship law. (…) For the People's party the conferral of citizenship represents the conclusion of a successful process of integration in Austria that has to be marked by identification with our country on the part of the applicant (People's Party, Manifesto, 2006)

Measures to this end comprise a broad range of extremity, from bans on specific religious practices and demands for obligatory adaptation of foreigners to Austrian language and culture to mandatory courses about Austrian culture, values, and history (Hell 2005). Beyond that, the assimilation frame frequently raises a gender issue, alleging incompatibility between "Western" and "Muslim" views of women. The compulsory nature of the assimilation frame is a constitutive element, since it distinguishes this strand of discourse from more inclusive perspectives (such as the participation frame described above).

- *Security:* One of the most salient frames during the last decade links immigration and the presence of ethnic minorities to a scenario of threat and insecurity for the Austrian population. Consequently, it demands *"tightened security measures against criminal aspects of immigration and asylum"* (Lakoff/Ferguson 2006; Huysmans/Squire 2009; Helbling 2013). Its diagnoses revolve around descriptions of heightened danger of crime, physical violence and, more generally, the violation of law – such as by specific religious communities (mainly targeting Islam and its practices as well as in connection with fundamentalism), by illegal entrants (commonly in connection with petty crime or drug trafficking), and as part of so-called "crime tourism" in border regions. As a consequence, the security frame urges more restrictive measures against non-nationals who commit a criminal offence (such as facilitated expulsion, restrictions for re-entries, and a tightening of incarceration conditions) as well as stronger use of preventive measures such as intensified border control, police surveillance, and stronger sentences (Huysmans 2000; Bigo 2002; Buonfino 2004; Larsen et al. 2009). For example:

> The most disturbing chapter in the context of legal and illegal immigration is the high level of crime among foreign population, currently at about 40%. (…) The damage that is inflicted on the national econ-

> omy extends to billions of Schilling, the annual damage caused by
> shoplifting alone is estimated at 6 billions. The increase in crime rate
> caused by foreigners is a symptom of the unregulated immigration to
> Austria. Thus, guestworkers who have been residing in Austria long-
> since and who comport commendably are cast in a negative light by
> the misguided immigration policy caused by Social Democrats and
> People's Party. (Freedom Party, Press release, 6 September 1994)

The core message of the security frame thus closely resembles a traditional
"law & order" discourse, but compounds it twofold by ethnicizing security
problems and securitizing immigration and asylum at the same time. Beyond
that, a pattern that has become characteristic of the securitization frame is its
combined emphasis of both a national and a transnational (European) perspective, with the latter contributing to the significant growth of the frame's
representation in discourse to cover almost all levels and areas in recent years
(under the umbrella of the EU's "area of freedom, security and justice").

- *Relief:* The discursive core of the relief frame inherently centers on a notion
  of resources and their scarcity within a given society. Thus it is characterized
  by a diagnosis of limited capacities of admission, and of an overburdening of
  the labor market, welfare system, and housing possibilities because of immigration, which can (no longer) be afforded (Kretsedemas 2012). Analogous
  problem definitions are applied with regard to asylum, which is portrayed to
  cause stresses that overexert the country's capacities. In contrast to the previous restrictive frames, the relief perspective minimizes its use of devaluating
  or delegitimizing references, and instead argues with a *"full boat"* metaphor.
  On a national level, the relief perspective is occasionally linked to criticism
  of unequal distribution of encumbrances (such as in the case of refugee
  flows):

> An increased wage level in the pre-accession countries would be an
> indispensable must for their accession to the EU, commented FPÖ-MP
> Reinhard Bösch. Not only permanent immigrants but also daily com-
> muters in the border regions would pose a threat for the domestic la-
> bor market. (…) Due to its geopolitical location as well as its econom-
> ic structure Austria would be affected extraordinarily by an EU-
> enlargement. According to recent studies, the Central and Eastern Eu-
> ropean immigrants would move predominantly to Austria and Germa-
> ny. 'Incautious EU-enlargement would clearly exceed the absorbing
> capacities of the domestic labor market', Bösch concluded. (Freedom
> Party, Press Release, 13 November 2002)

As a consequence, among the measures suggested to ameliorate this burden
are a stop to further immigration, quicker enforcement of asylum procedures,
withdrawal of residence permits for the long-term unemployed, an independent social security system for non-nationals, and the support of the countries

of origin to avoid emigration (Wengeler 2003). Its detachment from the previous frames makes it a somewhat less accusatory perspective that usually is
not linked to collective or individual allocation of blame to immigrants or
ethnic minorities (thus it often exhibits a depersonalizing manner).

The eleventh and final frame exists outside of the dichotomy of liberal and restrictive tendencies because it is utilized in both contexts in the same way:

- *Administration:* The administration perspective is a largely depersonalized
  framing of immigration and, more specifically, the question of asylum. It diagnoses an insufficiency of regulation in the policy fields of immigration and
  asylum and thus regularly serves the purpose of reducing political responsibility, since it locates the reasons for problems – whether too much or too little migration or ethnic diversity – on a structural level. Thus its problem definitions refer to administrative difficulties, understaffed authorities, judicial
  complexity and the like. Accordingly, this diagnosis is linked to calls for additional resources and staff, for simplification of laws and procedures, for
  clearer criteria for immigration and asylum, and for the formulation of rules
  for the coexistence of social groups that are to fix the "rights and duties for
  all members of society" (Nickels 2007).

To conclude, Table 13 summarizes the set of policy frames identified by the
study's combined approach, and separates liberal from restrictive perspectives
on migration and ethnic relations. This set of frames is able to capture the discursive spectrum of Austrian electoral competition on these issues between 1971
and 2013. By this means it enables to trace parties' politicization strategies on a
longitudinal basis and to take them as a basis for a quantitative analysis based on
the notion of salience theory.

Table 13:   Policy frames on migration and ethnic relations

Liberal	Neutral	Restrictive
Rights		Genuineness
Participation		Benefit
Multiculturalism	Administration	Assimilation
Solidarity		Security
Cosmopolitanism		Relief

Note: The frames identified in this table represent nominal codes of perspectives about migration and ethnic
relations. Thus except of their allocation to the three different segments of the discursive spectrum no hierarchy
or numeric relation between these frames is implied.

5.2.3 Synopsis

This chapter aimed to introduce the concept of framing, the study's approach of
frame identification as well as the findings produced by a qualitative frame

analysis of party discourse. The set of frames presented in the previous section is able to capture the discursive spectrum of Austrian party competition on migration and ethnic relations since the 1970s. Despite their apparent abstraction, these frames offer diversity sufficient to portray the competing interpretations in electoral politicization.[58] Obviously this implies neither that the identified frames represent the only frames in all of Austrian political discourse (in other discursive contexts, such as parliamentary debates, media coverage, etc., further frames might be just as well applied as those discussed here), nor that there do not exist different frames in political discourse in other country contexts (e.g. Wengeler 2003; Lakoff/Ferguson 2006; Vliegenthaart 2007; Scholten 2011; Kretsdemas 2012).

However, as outlined previously, this set of policy frames was elaborated using a combination of inductive and deductive exploration. Hence, although it is developed mainly from Austrian party discourse, it may serve as a generalizable foundation for other national contexts as well. This gives the findings of this exploratory chapter intrinsic value, since they may contribute to future case studies, or even enhance country-comparative research of party politicization on migration and ethnic relations. Moreover, considering the condensed nature of the electoral form of politicization, the limited range of frame perspectives is quite a reasonable result. In sum, this set of eleven frames helps to track the baselines of electoral competition between Austrian parties over a time frame of four decades without digressing into specific discursive subtleties of individual elections. The distinction between different types of liberal and restrictive perspectives on migration and ethnic relations demonstrates that parties do indeed find different and changing ways of interpreting a set of issues which are an increasingly contested policy field throughout Europe today.

These findings constitute the framework for a quantitative content analysis of Austrian electoral competition, which shall be discussed in the next chapter. As part of this quantitative study, section 6.3 sheds light on the question of how these policy frames are applied by Austrian parties and whether there are discernible strategy shifts over the course of the examination period.

---

[58] For the analysis of press releases the addition of a residual code has become necessary due to the text structure of press releases. Press releases regularly contain individual coding units that are included in the text of the document, but do not express a specific position (even though they can be identified to be related to the issues of migration and ethnic relations). These text fragments obviously are part of a party's overall discourse which made it necessary to include them for the measurement of parties general issue salience. In order to be able to collect these references, a residual code labelled „indeterminate" was applied in cases where no explicit position could be identified and the respective code will be added to the descriptions in the quantitative chapter of the book.

6. The politicization of migration and ethnic relations: quantitative patterns of competition

How important are migration and ethnic relations in Austrian electoral competition? What sorts of framing tendencies prevail in the debate, and what kind of developments over time can be identified? Which parties are the main drivers of politicization, and what patterns of consistency or divergence exist between them? These are the core questions investigated in this chapter, which aims to reveal the structure of party politicization on a quantitative basis both from an aggregate (party system) perspective as well as by looking at individual parties. As the previous chapters have demonstrated, a number of factors make active and contentious party politicization of migration and ethnic relations highly expectable in the Austrian case: the historical legacy of a multicultural monarchy, recurring actual experiences with immigration and asylum in the 20th century, predominantly negative and pressing attitudes among the Austrian population, and the co-evolution of niche parties potentially attracted to these issues – to name only the most important. The spectrum of frames developed in the previous chapter already revealed the range of policy perspectives characterizing Austrian electoral debate. However, the question of whether and to what degree these patterns have emerged over time and become potential hallmarks of Austrian competition needs to be evaluated on a quantitative basis.

Accordingly, this chapter presents the findings of a content analysis conducted as outlined in Chapter 4. Its primary goal is to deliver data on the basic quantitative patterns of Austrian electoral discourse on migration and ethnic relations. Thus it will focus on descriptive analysis of the dependent variables, i.e. Austrian parties' strategies in terms of general issue emphasis, topical preferences and policy frames, whereas the conjunction with the explanatory framework will be conducted separately (see Chapter 7). Starting with the descriptive part, all sections are based on the fundamental assumption of salience theory that parties will grant the most attention to those issues that are of the greatest relevance for them. The descriptive findings are presented as follows:

First, the topic of general issue emphasis is examined by presenting an overview of the development of cross-party *issue salience* in the electoral context as well as individual parties' specific roles. The expectation here is that increased involvement of political parties in competition over migration and ethnic relations will materialize in an increase of the salience of these issues on the electoral level per se, irrespective of the topical details or the direction of politicization (6.1).

Second, party politicization is analyzed on a topical basis by dissecting the electoral debate into its overall "issue dimensions" and further into its specific prevailing *subtopics* of migration and ethnic relations. This section is grounded on the presumption that political parties will accentuate particular topical aspects according to the associated advantages and ownership patterns, thereby contributing to the formation of discursive clusters. The first conclusions will be drawn of topical proximity both between parties and between campaign channels (6.2). Third, the analysis goes beyond the topical dimension of the debate by examining parties' issue positions. Based on the assumption that parties will employ different frames to politicize migration and ethnic relations and thus grant more prominence to some positions than to others, this section highlights the dominant *policy frames* applied by Austrian parties as well as discursive coalitions among them (6.3). Finally, in the concluding remarks, these findings are condensed by fitting them into an integrated description of party politicization of migration and ethnic relations (6.4) that aims to provide a basis for the discussion of potential explanatory factors in the subsequent and penultimate chapter of this book.

6.1   The importance of emphasis: Issue salience

The issues of migration and ethnic relations have become characteristic themes in the majority of contemporary Western democracies. Yet this commonness disguises the fact that in most countries, these issues have been subjected to historical processes of public debate, which has turned once depoliticized (or at least non-public political) issues into essential elements of public and electoral debate. This process of "issue evolution" (Carmines and Stimson 1986; 1989; 1993) illustrates how "an issue moves from the limited 'policy' environment to the larger stage of partisan politics" (Carmines and Stimson 1986: 902). "Critical moments" which catalyze the development of a new conflictive issue, along with its partisan character and the ensuing mass polarization, potentiate the issue so that it leaves an "indelible imprint on the party system" (Carmines and Wagner 2006: 70). Accordingly, the core questions for the analysis of party politicization in a specific country (such as Austria) are when and under what circumstances the issue at stake starts to gain the attention of a broader spectrum of relevant parties. These must be answered before this process can be explained. Therefore, the initial step of the analysis focuses on the relevance of migration and ethnic relations on the party system level, i.e. the extent to which these issues have become subject to electoral politicization in the Austrian party system at all.

6.1.1   Issue evolution and establishment: Salience of migration and ethnic relations

In order to gain an overview of the absolute relevance of migration and ethnic relations in Austrian party competition, the average salience among relevant parties serves as a first point of reference. Accordingly, Figure 6 plots the historic development of electoral politicization of migration and ethnic relations by the average of relevant parties' individual scores in each election. These salience scores are compared between both levels of campaign communication under examination: programmatic communication (i.e. manifestos) and day-to-day campaigning (i.e. press releases).

Figure 6: **Average salience of migration and ethnic relations per election, 1971-2013 (in %)**

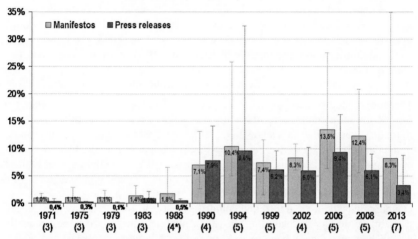

Note: The bars indicate the average salience of migration and ethnic relations among all relevant parties prior to or after a given election (number of relevant parties in brackets). The average is based on individual parties' relevant wordshare in relation to total wordshare of each party manifesto or a party's press releases per election. The dotted lines indicate the range between minimum and maximum party score per election. For the complete data table, see Appendix 1.

* According to the parliamentary group of the Greens, for the 1986 election there are no Green party press releases available in the archives.

Comparing the two campaign channels, a striking correspondence between issue salience in manifestos and press releases is evident, with emphasis in press releases being only slightly lower. The parallel development of the programmatic to the day-to-day salience of migration and ethnic relations is clearly evident. On both channels, a continuous depoliticization of the issue is obvious throughout the 1970s and early 1980s, as from 1971 to 1986 migration and ethnic relations were almost non-existent aspects in the electoral debate, averaging only 1.3% of the total programmatic and 0.4% of the total press release communication. In contrast, in 1990 the importance of migration and ethnic relations increased dramatically and subsequently remained at a high level into the present (in the post-1989 era, they reached an average of 9.6% in manifestos and 6.9% in press releases). Thus, 1990 undoubtedly saw the birth of a new campaign issue; this finding confirms Plasser/Ulram's (1990: 317) observation that the 1990 elections were the first to make "the immigration question an issue". Since then, the issue has developed into a characteristic cornerstone of electoral competition in Austria, with increasing involvement of ever more parties, as the minimum/maximum range indicators in Figure 6 demonstrate. From 1990 onwards, the intensity of politicization has remained consistently high, with peaks in 1994, 2006, and 2008. These peaks resulted from both the particular composition of the party spectrum (which will be the focus of the next section) as well as topical reasons that arose during these elections. To be more specific, the particular context created by the FPÖ's "Austria first" petition in 1993 constituted the main driver for an intensified debate in 1994, while in 2006, the topic fueling electoral politicization was the role of clandestine workers in the care sector (including a case in Chancellor Schüssel's family), which linked immigration to a traditionally important policy field in Austria: health and elderly people.

The congruency of campaign levels, however, has started to dissolve after the turn of the millennium; the difference was slight in 2002 and 2006 but all the more dramatic in the years since 2008. Although a declining trend is apparent on both channels, the sharp decline in day-to-day campaign communication diverges from the slight decrease in programmatic salience. The continued growth of this gap in 2013 shows that although migration and ethnic relations are firmly established as contested issues for the party spectrum as a whole, the heyday of campaigning about migrants and minorities may be over. This is particularly true for day-to-day campaigning, in which parties, especially the most recently established newcomers, have focused predominantly on other issues than migration and ethnic relations. Programmatically, however, all parties have put migration and ethnic relations on their agendas by now and address the issues to a respectable degree (with only one exception in 2013, which will be further investigated below).

In a nutshell, despite the recent decline in the number of press releases, the status of migration and ethnic relations as established, core issues of electoral competition is beyond doubt. The increased relevance of these issues in Austrian electoral competition since the late 1980s parallels patterns observed in other European countries. Still, the question remains: who are the main drivers of these electoral tendencies? The only way to determine whether migration and ethnic relations have been equally contentious issues for all parties or have instead been "owned" by specific actors is to examine party-specific results.

6.1.2 Engage or refrain? Individual party strategies of issue emphasis

Parties' appeals in politicizing migration and ethnic relations are expected to be far from equal. As outlined in Chapter 3, various assumptions have been made regarding the engagement of niche and mainstream parties in the Austrian context. While the former are predicted to actively engage in the politicization of migration and ethnic relations due to their quest for new issues orthogonal to the established cleavages owned by mainstream parties, the latter have been assumed to refrain from politicization for exactly the opposite reason (i.e. their lack of ownership). In order to verify this basic assumption and to identify the actors most responsible for the growth in overall issue salience over time, Figure 7 draws a time series comparison of the campaign emphasis of each party.

Figure 7:   **Salience of migration and ethnic relations per election. Individual parties, 1971-2013**

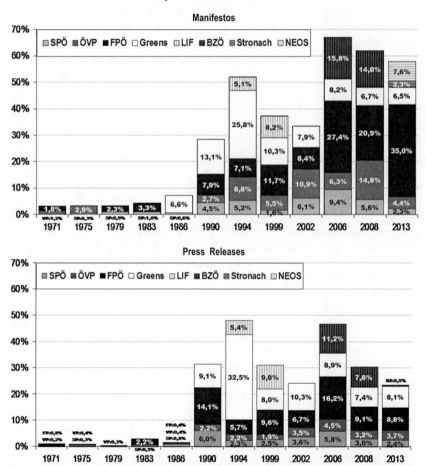

Note: No press releases are available for the Greens in 1986. Low salience-scores have been offset for legibility. Data labels: SP (SPÖ), VP (ÖVP), FP (FPÖ), BZ (BZÖ). For the complete data table, see Appendix 1.

Individual party scores reveal heterogeneous patterns of politicization that feature some prominent characteristics and illustrate the changing approaches of individual parties. To begin with the period of minor politicization during the 1970s and 1980s, individual party scores highlight that the FPÖ added migration and ethnic relations to its electoral agenda – at least marginally – as early as the pre-Haider era. Even if these shares by no means compare to those of the 1990s and onward, they nonetheless indicate that awareness of these issues already existed in earlier decades, but had not yet attracted overt politicization. This impression is reinforced by the ÖVP's occasional references and by a Green party that immediately picked up migration and ethnic relations in its first successful appearance on the federal party stage in 1986. In fact, the only party consistently depoliticizing the issue before 1986 was the SPÖ. In short, migration and ethnic relations were indeed marginal issues rather than non-issues. However, this conclusion can only be drawn for the programmatic level; in day-to-day competition, there was radio silence until the late 1980s. Despite the tentative signs of awareness in earlier decades, the heyday of active electoral politicization still only kicks off in 1990, with both surprising as well as predictable patterns:

Lack of continuous radical right domination

Most strikingly, the results clearly counter the common assumption of permanent domination of the radical right in the politicization of migration and ethnic relations, as such domination cannot be identified from the outset in either manifestos or press releases. On the contrary: The Greens clearly were the more active party in programmatic communication until 1994 (and the issues received more emphasis from the ÖVP in 2002), while on the day-to-day campaign level, Greens and FPÖ alternately dominated politicization from election to election. It is especially noteworthy that the issues gained almost no attention from the FPÖ in the immediate aftermath of the internal FPÖ upheaval in 1986. Neither in manifestos nor in press releases was there any notable reference to migration and ethnic relations on the part of the FPÖ, even though, in the very same election, the Greens actively politicized these issues for the first time. It was only in 1999 that the FPÖ became the principal actor both in programmatic and day-to-day campaign communication, yet it took a couple of years and a second internal split of the FPÖ in 2005 for this circumstance to reach its peak.

Thus, electorally, migration and ethnic relations have not been primarily dominated by radical right politicization, but rather have been (or have become) vital issues on other parties' agendas too. Accordingly, this confirms that the "single-issue party" label has hardly ever been valid for the FPÖ and does not accurately describe its utilization of the issues of migration and ethnic relations (Mudde 1999). Furthermore, it raises the question to what degree the internal split in 2005 was the cause for the drastic intensification of politicization by the re-launched FPÖ ever since. Confronted with another right-wing opponent (the BZÖ) and its similar addressing of these issues, the remaining members of the FPÖ, guided by new party leader Heinz-Christian Strache, appeared eager to prove themselves to be the "rightful owners" of the anti-immigrant party label. This pushed the FPÖ's engagement to another level of intensity: The party not only massively raised the salience of the issue in all its electoral manifestos since 2006 (with a peak in 2013), but has also remained the most active party on the day-to-day campaign level in recent elections. As a result of the conflict on the far right flank of the party spectrum, right-wing domination of the issues of migration and ethnic relations had become an obvious consequence by 2008 and was mitigated only by the BZÖ's decision to shift its party profile toward an entirely centrist and neoliberal stance, as a result of which it almost completely cut the issues of migration and ethnic relations from its 2013 campaign agenda.

The prominent but declining role of liberal and left-libertarian parties

With the role of radical right parties being less pronounced than expected, the immediate question is how the role of parties in the far-left spectrum – which, on the cultural axis in the Austrian case after 1960, is limited to left-libertarian and liberal parties – can be described. Left-libertarian parties arose in the Austrian political spectrum much later than in other European democracies, in which such parties emerged as early as the 1970s. As shown in Chapter 3.2, since 1986 the Greens have established themselves as the most prominent left-libertarian party in Austrian politics; hence it is all the more important to discuss in depth their role in politicizing migration and ethnic relations. The findings reveal the preeminence of the Greens in the first years after their entrance on the Austrian electoral stage in 1986. When both electoral dimensions are combined, the Greens emerged as the principal actor emphasizing migration and ethnic relations in the electoral context from 1986 until 1994. This pattern, however, began to erode by the end of the 1990s, with the Greens continuously cutting back their politicization. The average percentage of issue salience of both campaign channels combined has steadily decreased since then. While the retreat in 1999 and 2002 resembled the hesitant performances of other parties, since 2006 the growing emphasis placed by the radical right and, to some extent, the mainstream parties as well) put the Greens on the second circle of the hierarchy. In the 2008 elections, the party finally reached its lowest salience-values in the last two decades, indicating a profound transformation of the party's profile in this regard, which continued in 2013.

Further hindering the role of left-libertarian politicization is the fact that the decrease of Green politicization was compounded by the absence of a second left-libertarian party. During its parliamentary presence from 1994 to 1999, the LIF acted as a powerful promoter of migration and ethnic relations and thus helped to create a libertarian phalanx in opposition to the radical right. With the LIF dropping out of parliament in 1999 and the Greens lowering their issue focus, the liberal/left-libertarian presence altogether lost its electoral prerogative for the last decade. However, this may be about to change with the surprising emergence of the NEOS in the 2013 election, which added a new libertarian voice to the Austrian party system. Although the newcomers have only addressed the issues on the programmatic level so far, their presence may elicit a resurgence in the left-libertarian presence and politicization of migration and ethnic relations. This depends on whether or not the NEOS manage to establish themselves as a permanent presence in the Austrian party landscape, which remains to be seen.

Fluctuating mainstream party emphasis

The changing patterns in niche party behavior are accompanied by a concomitant shift of emphasis on the part of the mainstream parties over the course of the examination period as they participated more and more in competition on migration and ethnic relations. However, the obvious question as to which of the rival mainstream parties is the more active has a pretty clear-cut answer.

Considering the party that was expected to engage more actively, the *center-right* mainstream party (ÖVP), a close look at the two channels of campaign communication reveals an interesting discrepancy: Programmatically the party showed some engagement during the early 1970s, followed by a lack of politicization until the end of the 1980s, and a fluctuating pattern of emphasis from election to election ever since. To focus on the developments since the 1990s, in five out of seven elections the ÖVP put considerably more emphasis on migration and ethnic relations than its center-left counterpart, the SPÖ. In the years since 2002 the party has recorded its highest average emphasis, with a peak of about 15% in 2008, the strongest emphasis ever put on migration and ethnic relations by an Austrian mainstream party. This increased focus made the ÖVP the most active (2002) and the second most active (2008) party in electoral competition over migration and ethnic relations, which demonstrates the increasing relevance of these issues to the party's profile. The steady increase, however, came to an end in the 2013 election with a cutback in emphasis to only 4.4% (a salience-level the party started with in the early 1990s). This jump from its highest programmatic emphasis in 2008 to a very modest rating in 2013 is a signal of a changing approach on the part of the ÖVP's leadership – an approach that matches the party's strategy during the preceding legislation period. Interestingly, however, the ÖVP's strong emphasis in its manifestos up until 2008 was never associated with politicization on the day-to-day campaign level, as migration and ethnic relations were dramatically less prominent in the party's press releases. In fact, up until 2008, the party was the weakest actor in addressing those issues through the day-to-day campaign channel, which was in sharp contrast to its vigorous programmatic engagement. These findings reveal a twofold strategy on the part of the ÖVP, one of frequently signaling the importance of migration and ethnic relations on a programmatic basis but avoiding equivalent engagement in day-to-day competition on the issues during the hot election campaign period.

Conversely, the *center-left* mainstream party (SPÖ) is characterized by a pattern of salience that is much more consistent between programmatic and day-to-day campaign communication. Unlike the ÖVP, the SPÖ never displayed such discrepancies across campaign channels but instead almost continuously showed covariant development in its politicization (with slightly lower issue salience in press releases than in manifestos). This confirms the expectation issued in Chapter 3, that for the SPÖ the strategic value of migration and ethnic relations is lower than for its center-right rival, a conclusion that is reinforced by the party's salience scores from election to election: During the 1970s and 1980s, politicization on the part of the SPÖ was scarce or even non-existent, reflecting the party's strenuous efforts to depoliticize migration and ethnic relations on an electoral level. Only in 1990 did it start to address the issue to a somewhat greater degree, although with far less intensity than the Austrian niche parties. While programmatically the SPÖ remained among the least active parties and mostly lagged behind its center-right counterpart, it continuously exceeded the ÖVP on the day-to-day campaign basis – in large part because both mainstream parties' engagement in day-to-day competition over migration and ethnic relations was comparatively low anyway. The only exceptions featuring a stronger electoral emphasis on the part of the SPÖ were in 1990 and 2006, two elections that were shaped by particular situational stimuli (the abrupt increase of migration and ethnic relations after the fall of the Iron Curtain in 1990, and the lively debate on clandestine care workers in 2006). However, even if it has never caught up to the ÖVP, on average the SPÖ, too, has increased its competitive efforts and, in the post-millennium years, has granted higher salience to migration and ethnic relations millennium than it did in the 1990s – a pattern that holds on both campaign levels. Yet, like the ÖVP, the SPÖ drastically cut back its emphasis on migration and ethnic relations in 2013. This remarkable change, in line with that of its coalition partner, raises the question of the motives underlying the mainstream parties' recent pullback, a question which will be tackled in Chapter 7.

Table 14:   Average salience of migration and ethnic relations. Mainstream vs. niche parties, 1990-2013 (in %)

	Manifestos		Press releases	
	Mainstream parties	Niche parties	Mainstream parties	Niche parties
1990	3.6	10.5	4.1	11.6
1994	7.0	12.6	2.3	14.5
1999	3.5	10.1	2.2	8.8
2002	8.5	8.1	3.6	8.5
2006	7.8	17.1	5.2	12.1
2008	10.2	13.9	3.1	8.1
2013	3.3	10.2	3.0	3.5
Avg.	6.3	11.8	3.3	9.6
Std.-dev.	2.8	3.0	1.1	3.5
pre-millennium	4.7	11.1	2.9	11.7
post-millennium	7.5	12.3	3.7	8.0

Note: Mann-Whitney-test for difference between mainstream and niche parties: Manifestos (U=42, p<.05, r=-.48), Press releases (U=4, p<.001, r=-.81)

Still, the overall comparison between mainstream and niche parties (Table 14) permits only one conclusion: The introduction of migration and ethnic relations to electoral discourse was first and foremost a niche party achievement, and only little by little has the topic been taken up by Austrian mainstream parties. Since the outset of active politicization in 1990, niche parties significantly outdid their mainstream rivals (with FPÖ/Greens/Liberals showing higher shares than SPÖ/ÖVP) – a pattern that is even more clear-cut on the day-to-day campaign level than in programmatic communication. While on average, mainstream parties dedicated only 2.9% of their press releases to migration and ethnic relations, niche parties emphasized it more than three times as much (10.1%). Programmatically the gap is less distinct, yet the clear predominance of niche parties remains the same (mainstream parties 5.9%, niche parties 11.4%). Since the millennium, this predominance has started to wane: The SPÖ and ÖVP have started to politicize migration and ethnic relations more actively (7.5% among manifestos and 3.7% among press releases), while niche parties have only slightly increased their programmatic salience (12.3%) and have actually started to reduce their emphasis on the day-to-day campaign channel (8.1%). In summary, even though niche parties remain the dominating voices in the electoral context, the narrowing gap suggests that by now, migration and ethnic relations have turned into essential subjects for the political mainstream, too.

Divergence of issue salience between campaign channels

The overall tendencies of party politicization indicate a distinct colinearity in the relation between programmatic and day-to-day campaign communication. Individually, parties differ in the degree of consistency with which they emphasize the two campaign levels, though – as the findings demonstrate – not quite the way that was suggested by the theories discussed in Chapter 2.

Table 15: Divergence of salience between campaign channels. Party rankings and rank differences, 1990-2013

	Greens			LIF			NEOS			SPÖ			ÖVP			Stronach			BZÖ			FPÖ		
	Manifestos	Press Releases	Rank-Difference	Manifestos	Press Releases	Rank-Difference	Manifestos	Press Releases	Rank-Difference	Manifestos	Press Releases	Rank-Difference	Manifestos	Press Releases	Rank-Difference	Manifestos	Press Releases	Rank-Difference	Manifestos	Press Releases	Rank-Difference	Manifestos	Press Releases	Rank-Difference
1990	1	2	1	-	-	-	-	-	-	3	3	0	4	4	0	-	-	-	-	-	-	2	1	1
1994	1	1	0	5	3	2	-	-	-	4	4	0	2	5	3	-	-	-	-	-	-	3	2	1
1999	2	3	1	3	2	1	-	-	-	5	4	1	4	5	1	-	-	-	-	-	-	1	1	0
2002	3	1	2	-	-	-	-	-	-	4	3	1	1	4	3	-	-	-	-	-	-	2	2	0
2006	4	3	1	-	-	-	-	-	-	3	4	1	5	5	0	-	-	-	2	2	0	1	1	0
2008	4	3	1	-	-	-	-	-	-	5	5	0	2	4	2	-	-	-	3	2	1	1	1	0
2013	3	2	1	-	-	-	2	6	4	5	4	1	4	3	1	5	6	1	7	5	1	1	1	0
Avg. Rank Difference	1.0			1.5						0.6			1.4						0.7			0.3		

Note: Mann-Whitney-test for difference between mainstream and niche parties: (U=146, p>=.05, r=-.06).

As Table 15 demonstrates, there is little evidence of any discrepancy between mainstream and niche parties' divergence between campaign channels; instead, other differentiators appear to be at work. When the parties are ranked by emphasis instead of using absolute salience scores,[59] the ones most consistent across campaign channels over time are evidently those which politicize the most or the least actively. Hence, even though the FPÖ is not the programmatically most active party in the beginning, it establishes itself as the main actor on both campaign levels after the millennium and attaines the lowest average divergence of ranks between programmatic and day-to-day campaigning (0.3). Similarly, the second populist radical right party, the BZÖ, is also among the most consistent parties (0.7), since it mostly ranks second during the Haider era and ranks last on both levels after its shift to a centrist profile. In the center-left area of the party spectrum, the SPÖ is quite consistent too, since it ranks among the least active parties throughout in competition over migration and ethnic relations, with an average rank-difference of 0.6. The most inconsistent parties are the ÖVP (1.4) and the LIF (1.5). While the latter is generally more active on the day-to-day level than in its manifestos, the ÖVP, on the other hand, is much more active on the programmatic level, which is separated from its day-to-day campaign activities by a wide gap. The Greens' divergence patterns are in the center, between those of the remaining parties, with an average rank-difference of 1.0 – a value that is quite continuous over time. Hence, in evaluating parties' consistency between campaign levels, neither the party type (mainstream/niche) nor the ideological party family can account for the variance identified.

Methodical digression: Comparison with CMP data

Reflecting on the study's findings, it is important to revisit the methodical question addressed in Chapter 4, regarding the comparison of the salience-scores with those of the "Comparative Manifesto Project" (CMP), as some discrepancies come to light.[60] Overall, the CMP's counting procedure produces lower sa-

---

[59] Due to the divergence of average salience between programmatic and day-to-day campaign channels, the comparison of absolute (metric) salience measures can produce quite misleading results, which is why an ordinal solution of parties' rank order – from most active to least active party – was used instead. This way, potentially large – and misleading – metric differences are circumvented in cases where a party still scores the same rank on both campaign levels in relation to the remaining opponents.

[60] Using only the three available CMP-codes that specifically refer to the issues of migration and ethnic relations ("national way of life", "multiculturalism" and "underprivileged minority groups") and excluding broader codes that might also include aspects (such as "law and order"), the following salience-scores can be derived for elections since 1990: *1990:* SPÖ (1.1), ÖVP (2.0), FPÖ (2.8), Greens (8.4); *1994:* SPÖ (4.6), ÖVP (5.7), FPÖ (2.8), Greens (11.6), LIF (4.7); *1999:* SPÖ (2.4), ÖVP (1.8), FPÖ (9.9), Greens (4.5); *2002:* SPÖ (6.4), ÖVP (5.4), FPÖ (3.3), Greens (6.3); *2006:* SPÖ (5.0), ÖVP (8.1), FPÖ (10.2), Greens (4.9), BZÖ (8.4); *2008:* SPÖ (3.8), ÖVP (7.7), FPÖ (8.9), Greens (5.2), BZÖ (5.5).

lience-scores and leads to a slightly different order of parties' ranks during the 1990s, whereas after the millennium they are more in line with the findings of this study. More importantly, though, in some elections, certain parties' scores appear to be misleading: Especially the FPÖ's scores in 1990, 1994 and 2002 seem too low (and indicate that the party was among the least active actors), while in 1999 they appear to be somewhat high when compared to the scores of the remaining parties and this study's findings.

There are two reasons for this discrepancy: Firstly, owing to the different evaluation method of the CMP (which does not count words, but rather quasi-sentences), the CMP does not take into account the length of each such quasi-sentence. The approach adopted here tries to avoid this uncertainty by relating the number of words to the total wordshare of a manifesto, and thus is arguably a more nuanced measure that also allows for better comparison of different campaign channels (featuring different styles of communication). Secondly, a more specific problem is that the CMP uses few and somewhat broad codes to refer to the issues of migration and ethnic relations. Codes such as "national way of life" or "multiculturalism" leave out certain aspects of migration and ethnic relations (such as asylum, immigration-regimes, etc.), while others of the CMP's codes such as "underprivileged minority groups" or "law and order", mingle them with aspects that go far beyond. Thus, while one could in some way overlook the first problem of different counting procedures, the second problem poses a more serious obstacle for migration researchers using the CMP's data (for these difficulties see also Benoit/Laver 2007, Alonso/Claro da Fonseca 2011, Ruedin/Morales 2012, Ruedin 2013, Zulianello 2013). Thus the coding tool suggested by this study is expressly designed to capture the nuances within the electoral discourse on migration and ethnic relations.

6.1.3 Synopsis

In Chapter 2, the concept of salience was discussed as a central strategy of political parties in their electoral campaigns. Due to a growing number of parties and the increasing importance of issue-based electoral competition in Western democracies, the selective emphasis of particular issues has become a common pattern of politicization (Budge/Farlie 1983; Budge 1987; Carmines/Stimson 1993; Petrocik 1996). Applying the concept of salience theory to Austrian electoral competition on migration and ethnic relations reveals the first tendencies of Austrian party competition: From a party system perspective, salience of migration and ethnic relations was limited during the 1970s and 1980s, increased slightly in 1986, and has subsequently taken on a significant role in Austrian electoral competition – its importance increasing during the 1990s and peaking in 2006 and 2008 before dropping slightly in 2013. This shows that migration and ethnic relations have become established as issues of electoral competition in Austria. Furthermore, the recent drop in 2013 indicates that these issues are not continually growing in importance, and shows instead the normalization of a policy debate that has become a natural part of the Austrian political agenda and for which by now, autonomous government institutions (such as the State Secretariat for Integration) have been established.

These overall patterns, however, are highly dependent on the individual approaches of different parties. As expected, niche parties dominated the scene throughout the whole examination period, while mainstream parties increased their emphasis much more slowly from election to election. However, some surprising findings come to light, such as that until the mid-1990s, the Greens were the most active party in emphasizing migration and ethnic relations programmatically, while on the day-to-day campaigning channel they alternated with the FPÖ. However, since the internal split in the FPÖ, the radical right has established unequivocal dominance in electoral politics. As for the mainstream parties, conflicting results emerge between the campaign channels, with the ÖVP exceeding the SPÖ in terms of programmatic salience, while the SPÖ is more active than the ÖVP on the day-to-day campaign level. In day-to-day campaign communication, both mainstream parties remained far behind the engagement of niche parties, while in their manifestos, both parties (and in particular the ÖVP) occasionally approached niche party salience, especially in the post-millennial period. Thus, while mainstream party involvement in programmatic competition can be said to be increasing, it remains comparatively limited in press releases. This indicates that although mainstream parties are increasingly identifying migration and ethnic relations as relevant issues for party competition, they are not keen to engage in daily struggle with their niche party opponents.

6.2   The topical structure of competition: Issue dimensions and subtopics

So far, the analysis has been limited to the general importance of migration and ethnic relations to the electoral appeals of Austrian political parties. However, these findings leave us rather puzzled about the specific contents and ideological directions of electoral discourse. Although the previous section demonstrated that all parties included migration and ethnic relations in their electoral platforms sooner or later, this by no means implies that they actually address the same aspects in their politicization efforts. In fact, the core argument of salience theory can also be applied to another level, the subtopical, since it may even prove beneficial for a party to avoid addressing the same aspects that its opponents do in favor of singling out those subtopics of migration and ethnic relations which offer the most authentic starting points for politicization – ideally those linked to the party's characteristic clientele. This raises questions on two levels of abstraction: what strategies do individual parties pursue in subtopical terms, and how do these influence the greater patterns of electoral discourse on migration and ethnic relations?

In order to delve into these questions and to get a better picture of how electoral preferences are distributed, the next section unravels the topical structure of the discourse. In the first step, the section focuses once more on the party level and investigates the degree of coherence of the electoral debate on migration and ethnic relations, i.e. to what extent the topical patterns of competition differ between campaign channels and elections (6.2.1). Secondly, it concentrates on individual parties, asking which subtopics are preferred by individual political parties and how they deviate between campaign channels (6.2.2).

6.2.1 What's the story about? Core themes of electoral debate

As discussed in Chapter 4, there are various approaches to breaking down political discourse into its thematic components. Pursuant to the outlined research goals, the topical structure of electoral politicization is analyzed in two steps. First, the section focuses on broader "issue dimensions" (distinguishing between "asylum", "immigration", "integration" and "diversity"), as these core dimensions structure not only the public debate but also the operational logic of political authorities. Second, the topical structure of party politicization also needs to be dissected on a more nuanced, policy level of abstraction, accounting for the cross-sectional character of migration and ethnic relations, which are vitally linked to other policy fields such as *labor, crime & security, education, social & family issues* and so on (as suggested in Chapter 4, Table 12). Starting with the party system level, Table 16 shows the average salience of issue dimensions and subtopics over time. Comparing both of the campaign channels under consideration reveals rather striking differences in the dispersion of issue dimensions and subtopics, in the nature of the aspects that predominate in the debate, and finally in the concreteness with which these aspects are politicized. Each of these differences shall be discussed independently.

Balance vs. narrowness of politicization

As Table 16 clearly shows, campaign levels differ in terms of their topical density. While programmatic communication addresses subtopics and issue dimensions in a more balanced way, day-to-day campaigning is much more concentrated on particular aspects of the debate. For the most part, there is a single issue dimension in day-to-day campaign communication that exceeds the remaining dimensions by far – a pattern that is particularly striking until 2006, after which the picture has become more even. Conversely, the issue dimensions in party manifestos are more balanced, with no election showing such prevalence of any issue dimension as some do in press releases.

This pattern of a more balanced discourse on the programmatic level in contrast to a narrower selection of issue dimensions in day-to-day campaign communication continues in the circulation of concrete subtopics. Again, the findings reveal a far narrower picture in press releases in contrast to the more balanced distribution of subtopics in programmatic discourse. In six out of seven elections, at most two subtopics dominated the day-to-day level of electoral competition, whereas the number of actively emphasized subtopics is much higher on the programmatic level, as are their average salience scores. Drawing on standard deviation as an indicator for the topical density further substantiates the conclusion that discourse is narrower on the day-to-day campaign level, since the scores exceed those of programmatic communication in every election except those of 1990 and 2008.

This remarkable divergence is the first piece of evidence for the important role that the campaign channel plays in structuring party politicization, and also forces us to discuss the question of subtopics separately for each campaign channel. Finally, the table also shows that the variety of subtopics being addressed on both campaign channels increases the longer migration and ethnic relations remain established issues of electoral competition; discourse has become more differentiated, especially in the post-millennial period, and more obviously in manifestos than in press releases.

Table 16: **Average shares subtopics & issue dimensions (unweighted), 1990-2013 (in %)**

	1990		1994		1999		2002		2006		2008		2013		Avg.	
	MF	PR	MF	PR	MF	PR	MF	PR	MF	PR	MF	PR	MF	PR	MF	PR
Asylum general	**13**	4	**14**	3	**17**	7	8	**16**	6	3	2	**11**	7	**18**	**10**	9
Asylum Procedures	5	10	**11**	3	**14**	**11**	4	**42**	9	6	7	7	7	**28**	8	**15**
Citizenship & Voting	1	0	3	0	4	1	4	3	4	3	2	6	5	3	3	2
Crime & Border Control	5	**26**	5	**14**	**15**	**28**	8	1	**11**	6	**16**	**20**	5	5	9	**14**
Education	8	**17**	4	2	4	0	**11**	1	9	8	8	6	**14**	**11**	8	6
Gender Relations	0	0	0	0	0	1	0	1	1	2	3	5	2	0	1	1
Foreign Politics	0	3	0	0	0	0	0	0	1	2	3	0	0	0	0	1
Housing & Settlement	1	0	0	0	0	0	1	0	1	0	0	1	0	0	0	0
Immigration general	8	**21**	9	**12**	**16**	**11**	8	4	**10**	**10**	**10**	5	**10**	9	**10**	**10**
Integration general	4	0	5	0	3	2	7	2	**14**	2	7	5	9	0	7	2
Internat. Migration	4	0	4	0	0	0	1	0	6	1	0	1	0	0	2	0
Labor	**30**	3	8	**14**	**11**	2	**18**	**16**	**15**	**35**	**11**	3	**11**	2	**15**	**11**
Religion	0	0	0	0	**11**	1	0	0	1	7	**13**	4	1	1	4	2
Science	3	0	1	**14**	1	1	4	0	1	2	4	**11**	3	0	2	4
Social & Family	1	0	2	**19**	2	2	3	0	5	1	3	2	5	3	3	4
Societal Model	**17**	9	**19**	5	3	1	**15**	4	7	6	9	6	**17**	4	**12**	5
Xenophobia	1	6	**14**	**13**	0	**33**	7	9	0	7	3	8	5	**15**	4	**13**
Sum	*100*	*100*	*100*	*100*	*100*	*100*	*100*	*100*	*100*	*100*	*100*	*100*	*100*	*100*	*100*	*100*
Std.-dev.	*7.5*	*7.8*	*5.6*	*6.5*	*6.2*	*9.6*	*5.2*	*10.3*	*4.8*	*7.9*	*4.6*	*4.7*	*4.9*	*7.8*	*-*	*-*
Asylum	19	18	25	6	31	22	13	60	17	12	13	30	15	29	19	28
Immigration	43	51	25	67	42	44	32	21	41	54	40	31	29	24	35	41
Integration	21	10	17	8	13	5	33	7	35	15	22	21	36	23	24	12
Diversity	17	22	33	19	14	30	23	13	7	21	25	18	21	24	22	20
Sum	100	100	100	100	100	100	100	100	100	100	100	100	100	100	100	100
N (words)	5174	19881	6142	14108	4650	19163	6066	18181	4699	32966	3536	22088	5962	12500		
(parliamentary parties)	(4)	(4)	(5)	(5)	(5)	(5)	(4)	(4)	(5)	(5)	(5)	(5)	(7)	(7)		

Note: Results show averages of individual party salience of each subtopic in each party's relevant wordshare in an election. MF (manifestos), PR (press releases). The most salient subtopics are highlighted in bold letters.

Predominant subtopics of electoral competition

In order to deal with the different ways in which topics are politicized between the two campaign channels, first a closer look is given to the programmatic level. Among manifestos, salience turns out to be quite balanced between subtopics in most elections, as emphasis is placed on a greater number of subtopics, and no single subtopic is considerably more important than any other (1990 being the only exception to this rule). This indicates that the absence of centripetal influences makes manifesto communication more heterogeneous, though even programmatically some subtopics do exceed others in importance:

One characteristic pattern of programmatic communication is a large number of abstract references to *societal models* without direct links to concrete policy suggestions. These general calls for societal configurations and majority/minority relations (such as appeals for multiculturalism and demands for diversity or minority rights from one side and pleas for cultural hegemony and assimilation from the other) are archetypal patterns in programmatic debate (12%). *General references to immigration* (10%) and *asylum* (10%) also rank among the most salient subtopics in party manifestos, as do general references to *integration* (7%) – findings which further substantiate the notion that discourse in manifestos is more generalist. Thus programmatic communication often includes elements that do not point to any specific policy measure but rather comprise general remarks on the issue dimensions of immigration, asylum, migrant integration or ethnic diversity. These remarks essentially contribute to the development of ideological frames of interpretation, which explains their appeal for programmatic communication.

Aside from these common generalizations in programmatic communication, some repeatedly salient subtopics are linked to specific policy areas. Among these policy-specific links, one field in particular shows higher salience than any other, which is the question of immigrant *labor* (15%). Labor aspects of migration and ethnic relations ranked among the most important subtopics in six out of seven elections and have the highest average salience score of all programmatic subtopics. The labor debate centers on the question of labor market access for non-nationals, the definition of labor immigration quotas and the fight against clandestine employment. Another example for a policy aspect that has repeatedly been raised in programmatic competition is the discussion of *asylum procedures* (8%), which have been relevant throughout the last two decades. Together with general references to asylum, they constitute an important share of the electoral debate surrounding forced migration and refugees, especially during the 1990s. Other issue links only seem to have developed over time, especially the policy area of *education* (8%), which is emphasized as an aspect of integrating ethnic minorities. It was already a permanent but low-salience aspect of programmatic communication throughout the 1990s, but it increased in importance around the turn of the millennium. Its most prominent suggestions have included schooling policies (such as facilitation measures for immigrant pupils), organization of multicultural classes (as opposed to calls for segregated education), early interventions to influence the learning capacities of children with immigrant backgrounds, and others. Increasingly, it has also addressed adult education by stressing the need for language programs, cultural and administrative courses, and other similar means of enabling adult citizens of migrant backgrounds to participate more actively in society. Another growing policy subtopic of programmatic debate has been the role of *crime & border control* (9%). With the sole exception of the election in 2002, the salience of crime and border control in connection with migration and ethnic relations has continuously increased since 1999 and remained a thriving subtopic of programmatic communication ever since. This is evidence for an increasing police and security perspective in the debate (Gächter 2008: 16), which is informed by the global post-9/11 discourse on securitization. However, the recent drop of salience in the 2013 election may signal an end to this development. Finally, there are some subtopics on the programmatic level that seemed to come and go, such as *religion* (which was highly important in 1999 and 2008) and condemnation of *xenophobia* (which ranked as the most salient subtopic in 1994). Furthermore, a vast number of subtopics, although existent, remained only minor parts of the programmatic debate, such as *social & family* policies and references to *international migration and mobility*, as well as *housing/settlement, gender relations, science* and *foreign relations*.

In comparison to these programmatic patterns, the distribution of subtopics on the day-to-day channel of *parties' press releases* is much narrower. In every election other than 1994, there was a maximum of two subtopics (and usually only one) that dominated day-to-day competition at the expense of all the remaining subtopics. Interestingly, though, those dominating subtopics vary from election to election:

In 1990, *general references to immigration* (21%) as well as the question of *crime & border control* (26%) dominated an electoral debate shaped by the circumstances of the recently collapsed Iron Curtain and increasing migratory influx to Austria. Securing the country's eastern borders, introducing visa requirements for Polish and Romanian immigrants, and combatting illegal immigration and illicit work became the most controversial subjects during the hot election campaign. In 1994, *social & family issues* (19%) were the most salient element of the debate, but the most prominent subtopics were quite evenly balanced. In 1999, once again immigrant *crime & border control* (28%) and – even more importantly – the subtopic of *xenophobia* (33%) clearly outdid the other subtopics due to an increase in debate between SPÖ, ÖVP and FPÖ over the state of Austrian border control and illegal immigration to Austria as well as a collective outcry from all parties against a number of xenophobic statements made by FPÖ members during the election campaign. The hot election campaign period in 2002 was dominated by refugee policy – more concretely, by *asylum procedures* (42%) – throughout the whole examination period. This was primarily the result of a heated debate over a shift of responsibilities in Austrian refugee assistance (the installment of the private company "European Homecare" and weakening of the role played by Austrian NGOs), which was initiated after the ÖVP took over the Ministry for the Interior. Similarly, in 2006, once again there was one dominant subtopic that attracted the attention of all competing parties during the hot period of the election campaign, namely the question of illegal immigrant *labor* (35%) – in a debate that ensued from the uncovering of a clandestine care worker in the family of then-chancellor Wolfgang Schüssel. The election campaign of 2008 was the first to show a more balanced politicization of different subtopics among press releases. While *crime & border control* were slightly more important than other subtopics, they did not dominate the debate as heavily as has been the case in previous elections. However, the 2013 election reproduced a familiar pattern, with references to *asylum procedures* (28%) being by far the most salient aspect of the debate owing to the coincidence of a pressing European debate on Syrian refugees escaping the civil war on the one hand with a group of asylum seekers squatting the famous Votive Church in Vienna in order to protest against their impending expulsions, on the other. In summary, the pattern of subtopcis addressed has fluctuated across elections, although some subtopics (*crime & border control, asylum procedures, xenophobia* and *labor*) have emerged more regularly than others. Thus, compared to programmatic communication, the narrower picture of topical emphasis in day-to-day campaign communication has been striking. This picture has been accompanied by another contrast between programmatic and day-to-day campaign communication, i.e. in the share of generalist vs. policy-specific subtopics.

Generalist vs. policy-specific discourse

The role of generalist issue categories emerges as a distinct feature that distinguishes programmatic from day-to-day campaign communication (Table 17).

Table 17:   **Mean shares of generalist & policy-specific subtopics, 1990-2013 (in %)**

	Generalist		Policy-specific	
	MF	PR	MF	PR
1990	44.8	35.7	55.2	64.3
1994	49.4	13.5	50.6	86.5
1999	28.2	17.2	71.8	82.8
2002	39.5	24.4	60.5	75.6
2006	34.3	21.2	65.7	78.8
2008	25.1	30.1	74.9	69.9
2013	40.3	43.6	59.7	56.4
Avg.	*37.4*	*26.5*	*62.6*	*73.5*
Std.-dev.	*8.1*	*9.8*	*8.1*	*9.8*

Note: Generalist subtopics refer to the four codes *asylum general, immigration general, integration general,* and *societal model*. Policy-specific subtopics refer to the remaining codes.

Mann-Whitney-test for difference between manifestos and press releases: Generalist subtopcis (U=320, p<=.001, r=-.40), Policy-specific subtopics (U=386, p<.05, r=-.30).

Compared to programmatic communication, the salience of *generalist refer-ences to asylum, immigration, integration* or *societal models* turns out to be sig-nificantly lower in press releases. On the whole, generalist subtopics were more salient in every election except for 2008 (on average, they reached 37.4% in manifestos, compared to only 26.5% in press releases) – a result that is not sur-prising in the least, owing to the nature and purpose of election manifestos. With regard to programmatic communication, these generalist references constitute a vital means to generate coherent narrations for an issue. As a consequence, gen-eral references to asylum, societal models, integration and immigration ranked among the most salient subtopics. Manifestos contribute much more strongly to the emergence of overarching storylines, which constitute an interpretational framework for the specific aspects of the daily debate. Day-to-day campaign communication such as press releases affords neither the time nor the space nec-essary for the development of such storylines and consequently relies less heavi-ly on generalization. The higher prevalence of concrete subtopics instead (espe-cially *crime & border control* and *xenophobia,* but also *education, science* and *social & family issues)* shows the difference in the way day-to-day campaign communication is used by political parties. Unlike programmatic appeals, it puts ideology and policy goals into concrete terms by articulating more specific sug-gestions of political action. Furthermore, it operates much more strongly on the basis of statistics, exemplification with individual cases, references to actual leg-islative conditions, and direct responses to other statements made in the debate. Due to this forum-like character of press releases, a more repetitive but also more practical debate arises, with generalist appeals often being restricted to brief statements. Hence, the subtopics found in programmatic campaign com-munication match those found in the day-to-day channel of press releases only imperfectly.

In sum, there is distinct evidence for the need to distinguish between campaign communication channels in any analysis of electoral competition. Different ob-jectives between communication channels lead to dramatically different forms of party discourse and thus have to be weighed against each other carefully. On the day-to-day level, parties are much more limited in their topic selection, yet they also engage in more policy-specific politicization than they do in program-matic communication. These patterns, and especially their links to the book's explanatory framework, will be discussed more extensively in Chapter 7. Fur-thermore, they will continue to oblige us to discuss the campaign channels sepa-rately. This will be especially important when moving on to the individual party level, investigating whether certain parties are more responsible than others for this incongruence in politicization, and whether some parties participate more in the discourse on specific subtopics. These are the central questions of the next section.

6.2.2 Pushing their agendas: Individual party emphasis of issue dimensions and subtopics

How do political parties differ in the way they approach migration and ethnic relations in election campaigns? This fundamental question is of vital importance if we are to avoid the misinterpretations that arise when relying solely on cross-party tendencies. Thus this section will investigate whether there is any variance in the politicization patterns of individual Austrian parties. Is parties' politicization characterized by a focus on specific issue dimensions and subtopics or by a heterogeneous pattern? Are there clear party-to-subtopic links, i.e. do certain parties politicize some issue dimensions and subtopics more than others? Can we find clusters of parties that resemble each other?

Parties' emphasis of issue dimensions

In order to shed light on these questions, Table 18 starts with a comparison of individual parties' emphasis on four overarching issue dimensions. Examining these general issue dimensions of *asylum, immigration, integration* and *diversity* already brings the first variance patterns to light.

As the average salience scores of issue dimensions show very clearly, questions of immigration account for the largest share of electoral politicization by Austrian parties, a finding which is valid for both campaign channels in question. The focus on the immigration dimension was most pronounced during the 1990s, whereas it lost some of its importance after the millennium (with the exception of 2006). This occurred as part of a diversification over time of the electoral debate as the center of the debate shifted and other aspects grew to be considered equally important (such as the role of migrant integration, which gradually became a more important issue dimension after the millennium). The role of refugee and asylum questions, however, as well as the debate about diversity politics, remained relatively stable over time, though at a lower level than questions of immigration control.

Focusing more closely on individual parties, the findings document that mainstream parties and populist radical right parties resemble each other quite distinctly in that they are the most active drivers of debate on the immigration-dimension. In contrast, both left-libertarian parties deviate from that pattern, either by being generally balanced across all issue dimensions (the Greens) or by focusing more actively on diversity aspects instead (the LIF). Aside from their shared focus on immigration aspects, however, mainstream parties also resemble each other in their emphasis of other dimensions. The ÖVP has complemented its immigration focus with sporadic emphasis on the asylum dimension (especially in 1990, 1999 & 2002) and, rarely, on diversity (1994), while the integration dimension has been gaining in importance since 2006. Similarly, the SPÖ has intermingled its focus on immigration with an erratic emphasis on asylum (most pronouncedly in 1999 & 2002) and increasingly, especially since 2002, on the integration dimension, whereas diversity was of great importance only in

2013. The Greens differ the most radically from the remaining party spectrum in that they have repeatedly put the asylum dimension at the top of their agenda and have also addressed diversity aspects recurrently throughout the whole examination period. With the repeated emphasis on the integration dimension in their programmatic statements, along with their lower emphasis on immigration than the other parties, the Greens' topical patterns of politicization are the most deviant in the party spectrum. Similarly, the LIF – in its few appearances – also deviated from the mainstream and populist radical right parties quite considerably, putting the most emphasis on diversity and asylum.

Table 18: Shares of issue dimensions per election. Individual parties, 1990-2013 (in %)

		SPÖ		ÖVP		FPÖ		Greens		LIF		BZÖ		Stronach		NEOS	
		MF	PA	MF	PA	MF	PA	MF	PA	MF	PA	MF	PA	MF	PA	MF	PA
1990	Asylum	15	20	24	33	24	10	14	8								
	Immigration	**56**	**55**	**53**	**53**	**58**	**58**	5	36								
	Integration	24	16	9	3	18	22	31	0								
	Diversity	4	10	14	11	0	10	**51**	**57**								
1994	Asylum	18	9	11	0	0	14	**55**	9	**43**	0						
	Immigration	**47**	**72**	34	**61**	20	**66**	16	**68**	8	**66**						
	Integration	26	7	17	2	11	10	20	23	12	0						
	Diversity	9	12	**38**	37	**69**	9	10	1	38	34						
1999	Asylum	**48**	11	15	28	16	11	**46**	28	31	31						
	Immigration	52	**66**	**73**	38	**72**	**80**	13	20	0	15						
	Integration	0	2	11	8	12	4	22	6	18	4						
	Diversity	0	22	2	26	0	4	18	**46**	**51**	**51**						
2002	Asylum	10	**62**	28	**73**	15	40	0	**63**								
	Immigration	22	18	**40**	14	**58**	**50**	7	0								
	Integration	**53**	8	14	9	17	10	**47**	2								
	Diversity	15	13	19	4	10	1	46	35								
2006	Asylum	19	4	12	7	22	6	22	32			10	9				
	Immigration	52	**64**	32	**59**	36	40	35	35			**50**	**71**				
	Integration	29	12	**56**	20	38	24	30	5			23	12				
	Diversity	0	21	0	15	4	30	13	29			17	9				
2008	Asylum	8	11	11	27	7	**47**	25	35			14	31				
	Immigration	28	37	**47**	**45**	**41**	21	**45**	15			**41**	**37**				
	Integration	**46**	**39**	16	27	18	11	13	14			16	16				
	Diversity	19	13	26	1	**34**	22	17	**36**			29	17				
2013	Asylum	14	33	8	12	22	29	32	**57**			-	-	6	-	9	-
	Immigration	30	0	29	30	17	**43**	**34**	20			-	-	**52**	-	10	-
	Integration	25	9	**51**	**34**	**38**	15	28	18			-	-	14	-	**58**	-
	Diversity	**31**	**59**	12	23	23	13	6	5			-	-	29	-	23	-
Avg.	Asylum	19	21	15	26	15	22	28	**33**	**37**	15	12	20				
	Immigration	**41**	**44**	**44**	**43**	**43**	**51**	22	28	4	41	**45**	**54**				
	Integration	29	13	25	15	22	14	27	10	15	2	20	14				
	Diversity	11	21	16	17	20	13	23	30	**44**	**42**	23	13				

Note: Results show individual party salience of each dimension in relation to a party's relevant wordshare. The most salient issue dimension for each party is highlighted in bold letters.

Most important subtopics

The trends in the development of issue dimensions, however, need to be evaluated in more detail by considering the politicization patterns of specific subtopics. Table 19 reveals the dominant subtopics in debate by showing the average share of each subtopic in relation to each party's relevant wordshare.

Mainstream parties: Considering the *SPÖ's* working class origins, it is hardly surprising that, on average, the focus in SPÖ manifestos as well as in its press releases (18% and 16%) is on *labor* aspects of migration and ethnic relations. This is the only subtopic that is of major importance to both campaign levels, whereas other subtopics receive distinctly different degrees of attention. For example, references to *immigration in general* are much more common in the SPÖ's manifestos (13%) than in its press releases (8%). Likewise, references to *integration in general* are more prevalent in the party's programmatic communication, averaging 11% in SPÖ manifestos and growing in relevance from 2002 on, but averaging only 1% in the SPÖ's day-to-day campaigning. In contrast, questions of *crime & border control* are of clear importance in day-to-day communication (16%) but only occasionally feature in the party's programmatic messages (6%); similarly with the subtopic of *xenophobia* which, on average, is actually the most salient subtopic in SPÖ press releases (19%) while being mostly disregarded in the SPÖ's manifestos (2%). A similar pattern of inconsistency holds for issues of asylum, with references to *asylum in general* being more frequent in manifestos than in press releases (14% vs. 9%), whereas on the day-to-day basis, references to *asylum procedures* are more common (10% vs. 4%). Interestingly, though, the SPÖ began to de-emphasize asylum on both campaign channels after the turn of the millennium; both subtopics drop in importance after 1999 (manifestos) and 2002 (press releases), a pattern that was interrupted only by the party being forced to address asylum more directly in 2013 due to the ongoing Syrian refugee crisis. Thus, besides a permanent focus on labor, the remaining subtopics vary in importance between campaign channels and elections. As a consequence, the range of subtopics is much more balanced in the SPÖ's case than in any other party's.

Table 19: Shares of subtopics per election. Individual parties, 1990-2013 (in %)

Manifestos

	1990				1994					1999					2002				2006					2008					2013							Avg.					
	SPÖ	ÖVP	FPÖ	Greens	SPÖ	ÖVP	FPÖ	Greens	LIF	SPÖ	ÖVP	FPÖ	Greens	LIF	SPÖ	ÖVP	FPÖ	Greens	SPÖ	ÖVP	FPÖ	Greens	BZÖ	SPÖ	ÖVP	FPÖ	Greens	BZÖ	SPÖ	ÖVP	FPÖ	Greens	BZÖ	Stronach	NEOS	SPÖ	ÖVP	FPÖ	Greens	LIF	BZÖ
Asylum general	15	24	9	3	15	5	5	3	12	48	11	15	9	–	8	11	14	–	6	7	16	–	2	4	2	6	–	2	5	1	18	8	–	6	6	14	4	9	11	8	6
Asylum Procedures	–	–	15	6	–	6	–	–	31	–	4	15	9	–	11	16	–	–	11	5	5	20	4	4	3	11	25	3	9	6	10	–	3	–	3	3	6	19	7	31	4
Citizenship & Voting	–	13	–	2	–	–	–	14	–	–	8	4	7	–	9	–	–	6	3	4	8	20	–	–	–	–	8	–	5	5	10	6	–	7	3	2	3	4	7	–	–
Crime & Border Control	6	–	–	–	20	–	–	–	–	–	50	23	–	18	–	7	24	6	9	17	8	7	14	6	26	11	13	25	–	16	10	–	25	–	–	6	20	11	3	–	20
Education	16	14	–	–	9	8	5	–	–	–	–	–	–	–	5	2	7	7	7	13	13	9	4	14	9	5	5	12	34	17	9	3	12	–	–	12	6	7	7	–	8
Foreign Politics	–	–	–	–	–	–	–	–	–	–	–	–	–	–	–	–	–	–	–	–	–	1	–	–	–	–	–	–	–	7	–	–	–	–	–	–	2	1	1	–	–
Gender Relations	–	–	–	2	–	–	–	1	–	–	–	–	–	–	2	1	8	–	3	3	–	–	3	–	4	2	8	–	–	9	1	5	8	–	–	–	1	1	1	–	5
Housing & Settlement	–	–	–	–	–	–	–	–	–	–	–	–	–	–	–	–	18	8	–	13	4	15	10	2	2	8	32	9	9	6	21	2	9	–	–	13	6	10	13	–	9
Immigration general	9	20	–	4	14	10	9	7	8	6	4	8	8	14	10	8	18	–	3	24	1	7	18	21	7	4	–	4	10	22	1	12	4	–	10	11	11	6	6	11	–
Integration general	4	9	–	4	11	2	4	2	12	4	2	–	14	–	4	10	8	–	7	7	19	13	9	–	–	–	–	–	–	22	–	–	17	–	22	3	2	3	2	3	4
International Migration	12	–	5	–	8	4	7	7	–	6	6	43	4	–	33	12	17	12	34	4	4	3	17	17	6	19	–	11	14	4	11	6	29	22	8	18	12	22	8	–	14
Labor	22	40	33	24	14	14	15	4	–	2	2	–	–	51	–	–	–	29	–	1	7	1	–	–	18	18	–	29	7	1	1	5	–	4	–	4	3	4	1	26	14
Religion	11	–	–	–	6	–	–	1	–	–	4	2	–	–	5	9	3	5	3	1	–	5	1	14	5	–	–	–	7	9	–	5	–	–	–	6	2	1	1	1	–
Science	–	–	–	–	–	–	–	–	–	–	–	–	–	–	12	–	–	–	3	14	1	–	–	–	–	–	–	–	–	24	2	2	–	–	–	4	2	–	1	–	–
Social & Family	4	14	7	2	7	7	–	1	–	4	2	6	2	–	12	11	10	30	3	14	4	30	1	14	5	11	–	–	7	12	24	2	–	–	–	6	2	8	2	–	2
Societal Model	4	34	33	49	37	4	5	5	20	2	4	–	17	–	9	11	11	16	–	4	13	–	17	19	8	16	1	–	11	12	21	6	–	2	–	7	7	11	12	17	10
Xenophobia	–	–	37	4	18	37	5	–	18	1	2	–	1	–	6	8	–	16	–	7	–	16	–	8	19	8	–	15	11	2	–	14	–	14	14	2	2	2	5	6	9
Sum	100	100	100	100	100	100	100	100	100	100	100	100	100	100	100	100	100	100	100	100	100	100	100	100	100	100	100	100	100	100	100	100	100	100	100	100	100	100	100	100	100

$x^2=3158$; df=36; Cramér's V=.507*** (1990)

$x^2=5828$; df=48; Cramér's V=.447*** (1994)

$x^2=8013$; df=48; Cramér's V=.640*** (1999)

$x^2=4419$; df=45; Cramér's V=.505*** (2002)

$x^2=3381$; df=60; Cramér's V=.374*** (2006)

$x^2=3613$; df=56; Cramér's V=.470*** (2008)

$x^2=1416$; df=75; Cramér's V=.420*** (2013)

Press Releases

	1990 SPÖ	ÖVP	FPÖ	Greens	1994 SPÖ	ÖVP	FPÖ	Greens	LIF	1999 SPÖ	ÖVP	FPÖ	Greens	LIF	2002 SPÖ	ÖVP	FPÖ	Greens	2006 SPÖ	ÖVP	FPÖ	Greens	BZÖ	2008 SPÖ	ÖVP	FPÖ	Greens	BZÖ	2013 SPÖ	ÖVP	FPÖ	Greens	BZÖ¹	Stronach	NEOS	Avg SPÖ	ÖVP	FPÖ	Greens	LIF	BZÖ
Asylum general	4	11	1	-	-	-	7	9	-	6	28	1	-	-	16	29	18	-	1	4	2	4	3	-	6	33	9	9	33	5	21	34	-	-	-	8	12	12	8	-	6
Asylum Procedures	13	15	9	2	-	-	7	-	-	5	-	11	18	20	41	42	21	61	3	3	1	20	2	-	13	7	2	2	-	8	8	23	-	-	-	10	12	9	20	-	7
Citizenship & Voting	-	2	-	-	9	-	1	-	-	-	5	-	-	5	2	1	10	-	-	6	-	5	2	3	5	2	19	2	-	-	11	6	-	-	-	1	3	4	2	10	8
Crime & Border Control	21	34	21	28	12	23	22	8	13	48	21	65	-	2	-	3	-	-	4	1	15	-	11	24	18	23	7	13	19	19	6	-	-	-	-	16	17	22	4	9	23
Education	16	-	23	27	-	2	8	-	-	-	-	-	-	-	2	2	-	-	9	12	11	-	7	13	10	2	2	36	9	34	1	13	-	-	-	7	9	6	6	1	4
Foreign Politics	-	-	-	3	-	-	-	-	-	5	-	1	-	-	4	-	-	-	1	1	-	7	-	18	3	-	1	1	-	-	-	-	-	-	-	3	1	-	1	1	0
Gender Relations	7	4	-	-	-	-	-	-	-	-	-	-	-	-	-	-	-	-	1	2	2	2	-	-	-	-	-	-	-	-	-	-	-	-	-	1	1	-	-	-	0
Housing & Settlement	1	-	-	-	-	-	-	-	-	-	-	-	-	-	-	-	-	-	-	-	-	-	-	1	1	1	4	11	-	-	-	-	-	-	-	-	-	-	1	-	0
Immigration general	17	20	35	11	19	11	25	-	3	5	12	13	18	10	2	3	13	-	2	11	6	3	26	7	7	1	1	1	11	11	25	9	-	-	-	7	11	17	6	7	18
Integration general	1	1	-	-	1	-	1	-	-	1	4	-	2	2	3	2	-	2	1	6	1	6	-	1	14	1	6	1	-	1	6	1	-	-	-	1	3	1	1	1	2
International Migration	1	-	1	-	-	-	-	-	-	1	-	-	-	-	-	-	-	-	4	1	-	1	-	-	1	-	-	-	-	-	-	-	-	-	-	2	-	-	1	1	0
Labor	11	-	2	-	31	8	14	-	15	4	-	2	2	-	16	10	37	2	47	38	25	30	38	17	18	15	12	4	-	-	8	-	-	-	-	16	9	13	5	7	19
Religion	-	-	-	-	-	1	-	-	-	1	5	3	-	-	1	-	-	-	1	3	-	2	8	1	1	-	1	7	-	-	-	5	-	-	-	-	6	-	1	3	6
Science	-	-	-	-	7	1	5	10	35	-	-	-	4	-	-	1	-	-	5	5	6	-	-	5	1	3	2	-	-	-	-	-	-	-	-	4	6	1	3	17	3
Social & Family	-	-	-	-	10	8	-	80	-	2	-	3	-	-	2	1	-	15	3	8	6	14	-	5	7	7	3	5	4	15	4	11	-	-	-	2	1	2	14	1	3
Societal Model	2	7	8	18	4	15	7	1	-	1	1	1	2	2	1	1	-	20	5	6	-	1	-	9	-	1	11	-	-	6	6	-	-	-	-	2	6	5	1	8	6
Xenophobia	6	4	-	12	8	22	1	1	34	21	26	1	57	60	13	4	1	1	17	4	14	-	14	9	1	30	2	1	59	2	2	5	-	-	-	19	10	1	20	47	1
Sum	100	100	100	100	100	100	100	100	100	100	100	100	100	100	100	100	100	100	100	100	100	100	100	100	100	100	100	100	100	100	100	100	-	-	-	100	100	100	100	100	100

1990	1994	1999	2002	2006	2008	2013
$x^2=9947$; df=30; Cramér's V=.337***	$x^2=39591$; df=56; Cramér's V=.543***	$x^2=23623$; df=60; Cramér's V=.481***	$x^2=16637$; df=45; Cramér's V=.470***	$x^2=26849$; df=60; Cramér's V=.413***	$x^2=24963$; df=60; Cramér's V=.472***	$x^2=13082$; df=48; Cramér's V=.489***

Note: For each election and party, the absolute number of relevant press release addressing migration and ethnic relations has been considered (see Appendix 1). Association between variables for each election was calculated using each party's word count weighted by the average wordshare of all competing parties, *** $p \leq 0.01$, two-tailed test.

[1] In 2013 the BZÖ issued only one relevant press release (on asylum procedures), which was too little material to be included into our topical analysis (since it would have represented a severe distortion of the party's average preferences).

As for the *ÖVP, crime & border control* turns out to be by far the most important subtopic. On average, it is the most-addressed issue both in manifestos (19%) as well as in press releases (17%); hence, the ÖVP not only surpasses the SPÖ in the focus of its emphasis but even approaches the scores of the radical right populists. Another important subtopic on both campaign channels is the aspect of immigrant *labor*, although its relevance is slightly lower than in the case of the SPÖ, FPÖ or BZÖ (averaging 12% in programmatic material and 9% in day-to-day campaigning). Thirdly, *asylum in general* also ranks among the subtopics of greatest importance to the ÖVP in both campaign channels, although its salience is more consistent in manifestos (9%), whereas in press releases (12%) its emphasis varies from election to election. Yet, like the SPÖ, the ÖVP emphasizes some subtopics more strongly on one campaign channel than on the other, such as *societal models* (11%) and *integration* (11%) in the party's programmatic communication, and *asylum procedures* (12%), general *immigration* (11%), and *xenophobia* (10%) in its press releases. Thus the ÖVP's topical emphasis largely resembles that of its mainstream counterpart (especially in its treatment of the subtopics of labor, crime & border control and asylum), although the ÖVP focuses on slightly fewer subtopics and consequently exhibits a narrower topical selection than the SPÖ.

Radical right parties: A number of similar patterns show between the populist radical right parties, the *FPÖ* and the *BZÖ*, and the mainstream parties. Most importantly, both radical right parties put very high emphasis on the subtopics of *labor* and *crime & border control*. The FPÖ is the actor that most stridently emphasizes labor in its campaigns, averaging 22% in its manifestos and 13% in its press releases, while crime & border control scores an average salience of 11% and 22%. By contrast, the BZÖ, in its two relevant appearances, stressed crime & border control more heavily than any other party in the spectrum, with the topic reaching 20% on average in its manifestos and 23% in its press releases, while labor accounts for 14% and 19%. Another commonality between the two populist radical right parties is their emphasis of *immigration in general*, both in programmatic and day-to-day campaign communication (FPÖ: 10% and 17%; BZÖ: 9% and 18%), which even exceeds the scores of the mainstream parties. However, there are also differences between FPÖ and BZÖ, e.g. when it comes to the relevance of asylum issues. While for the FPÖ, references to *asylum in general* account for an average of about 10% of both campaign channels (although it fluctuates from election to election), neither asylum in general nor asylum procedures are of notable importance for the BZÖ. On the other hand, the aspect of *religion* is more heavily emphasized by the BZÖ (at least in its manifestos, with an average of 14%) than it is by the FPÖ. Even more divergent is their degree of focus on *integration in general*, which is of low relevance for the FPÖ, but of considerable programmatic relevance for the BZÖ (on average,

11%).[61] Nevertheless, despite these isolated differences, the populist radical right parties seem to focus mostly on similar subtopics.

Liberal and left-libertarian parties: Compared to the remaining party spectrum, the strategies of both Greens and LIF diverge remarkably. To start with the Greens, their most prominent subtopic is *asylum procedures*, which reaches an average of 19% in their manifestos and 20% in their press releases. Thus the Greens, along with the LIF, are the actor granting the most importance to procedural aspects of asylum politics beginning in the 1990s and continuing through to recent elections. Moreover, the Greens are also the most active party by far when it comes to discussing *societal models* in general terms, with an average of 17% in programmatic communication and 8% in press releases. Together with the LIF, they also repeatedly draw attention to *xenophobia* (with an average of 6% in Green manifestos and 20% in press releases). The only emphasis that the Greens have in common with the parties already discussed is that of *immigration in general* (at least in programmatic communication; 13%). However, what distinguishes the Greens most clearly from other competitors is the party's remarkable emphasis on *social & family* issues in day-to-day campaign communication (14%), which makes the Greens the only party to repeatedly politicize this subtopic to a noteworthy degree. The *LIF*'s patterns largely resemble those of the Greens, although its results are based on only two relevant electoral performances. The party's strong focus on *asylum procedures* (30% in manifestos and 10% in press releases), the relevance it grants to *xenophobia* (9% in manifestos and 47% in its press releases), and its programmatic concern with *societal models* (10%) closely link the LIF to the Greens. What distinguishes the two parties is the LIF's focus on *science* aspects of migration (17% among press releases) and its programmatic emphasis on *religion* (26%).

As for the newcomers in 2013, their topical preferences can only be identified on the programmatic level, though there are some similarities between them: *Team Stronach* puts the most emphasis on general references to immigration (28%) and general conceptions of a *societal model* (29%), whereas its only policy-specific subtopics are those of immigrant *labor* (22%) and the rejection of *xenophobia* (14%). On the other hand, the *NEOS*' most-highlighted subtopic by far is *education* (26%), but like the Team Stronach, they also place emphasis on general references to the *societal model* (20%) and *xenophobia* (14%). The NEOS, however, are unique in their general emphasis of *integration* (10%).

---

[61] This result can be traced back to the BZÖ's interest in continuing its ownership of those integration policies which had been introduced by the ÖVP-FPÖ coalition at the insistence of the FPÖ, nearly all of whose ministers subsequently moved to the BZÖ (including front runner Peter Westenthaler, minister of Defense Herbert Scheibner, minister of Social Affairs Ursula Haubner, and of course Jörg Haider, her brother and the new party's central figure).

To complete the picture, there are a number of subtopical aspects that are of minor importance to all parties. Of these minor subtopics, the aspect of *education* retains the most importance. *Science* aspects of migration and ethnic relations are accorded greater importance by the SPÖ, ÖVP and LIF, while in the manifestos of the Greens and the BZÖ's press releases *citizenship & voting* occupies a place of some importance. *Religion* is most important to the LIF and BZÖ in their programmatic appeals, but is of less relevance for the remaining parties. Finally, apart from isolated exceptions in single elections, the aspects of *gender relations, foreign politics,* and *housing/settlement* remain of little relevance to any party throughout the whole examination period.

Summarizing the findings on similarities in emphasis of subtopics between parties, it can be observed that right-wing populist parties (FPÖ/BZÖ) and left-libertarian or liberal niche parties (Greens/LIF) differ not only ideologically but also in their topical preferences. While the emphasis of right-wing parties is placed on the aspects of labor and crime & border control, left-wing parties instead stress subtopics such as asylum procedures, societal models, and xenophobia. This distinguishing pattern apparently holds only to a degree; overall, however, the findings show a medium to strong correlation between parties and subtopics throughout the whole examination period – basically due to these characteristic issue alignments of the parties at the fringes, but corroborated by the behavior of the Austrian mainstream parties. The profile of subtopics addressed by both Austrian mainstream parties much more strongly resembles the selection of the populist radical right parties (especially with regard to labor or crime & border control) than that of left-wing parties. This is especially true in programmatic campaign communication, while on the day-to-day campaign channel, the picture shifts at the end of the 1990s, with themainstream parties becoming more equidistant to the fringes.

A systematic way of visualizing these similarities and differences within the party spectrum is to plot city block distances between pairs of parties on a heat map to indicate the degree of divergence between them (Table 20).

Table 20:   Divergence of subtopics between individual parties, 1990-2013

Year	Party	SPÖ	ÖVP	FPÖ	Green	LIF	BZÖ	Stronach	NEOS	SPÖ	ÖVP	FPÖ	Green	LIF	BZÖ	Stronach	NEOS	Heat Map / Bisected city block distance
		Manifestos								Press Releases								
1990	SPÖ		48	41	64	-	-	-	-		32	32	39	-	-	-	-	0
1990	ÖVP	48		58	55	-	-	-	-	32		42	46	-	-	-	-	1-19
1990	FPÖ	41	58		61	-	-	-	-	32	42		35	-	-	-	-	20-29
1990	Greens	64	55	61		-	-	-	-	39	46	35		-	-	-	-	30-39
1994	SPÖ		47	71	53	58	-	-	-		43	36	83	55	-	-	-	40-40
1994	ÖVP	47		35	62	56	-	-	-	43		44	81	42	-	-	-	50-59
1994	FPÖ	71	35		78	55	-	-	-	36	44		87	63	-	-	-	60-69
1994	Greens	53	62	78		52	-	-	-	83	81	87		89	-	-	-	70-79
1994	LIF	58	56	55	52		-	-	-	55	42	63	89		-	-	-	80-89
1999	SPÖ		77	77	82	100	-	-	-		45	35	63	61	-	-	-	90-99
1999	ÖVP	77		46	66	94	-	-	-	45		65	61	57	-	-	-	100
1999	FPÖ	77	46		72	99	-	-	-	35	65		70	72	-	-	-	
1999	Greens	82	66	72		69	-	-	-	63	61	70		14	-	-	-	
1999	LIF	100	94	99	69		-	-	-	61	57	72	14		-	-	-	
2002	SPÖ		48	50	62	-	-	-	-		23	42	39	-	-	-	-	
2002	ÖVP	48		40	60	-	-	-	-	23		46	50	-	-	-	-	
2002	FPÖ	50	40		64	-	-	-	-	42	46		76	-	-	-	-	
2002	Greens	62	60	64		-	-	-	-	39	50	76		-	-	-	-	
2006	SPÖ		42	44	55	-	39	-	-		30	51	45	-	42	-	-	
2006	ÖVP	42		53	43	-	34	-	-	30		42	42	-	31	-	-	
2006	FPÖ	44	53		55	-	54	-	-	51	42		61	-	38	-	-	
2006	Greens	55	43	55		-	42	-	-	45	42	61		-	59	-	-	
2006	BZÖ	39	34	54	42	-		-	-	42	31	38	59	-		-	-	
2008	SPÖ		57	50	82	-	62	-	-		42	63	60	-	56	-	-	
2008	ÖVP	57		36	77	-	34	-	-	42		60	49	-	53	-	-	
2008	FPÖ	50	36		75	-	44	-	-	63	60		73	-	43	-	-	
2008	Greens	82	77	75		-	71	-	-	60	49	73		-	66	-	-	
2008	BZÖ	62	34	44	71	-		-	-	56	53	43	66	-		-	-	
2013	SPÖ		43	68	45	-	-	61	36		78	69	54	-	-	-	-	
2013	ÖVP	43		64	53	-	-	83	42	78		67	67	-	-	-	-	
2013	FPÖ	68	64		67	-	-	59	55	69	67		43	-	-	-	-	
2013	Greens	45	53	67		-	-	57	55	54	67	43		-	-	-	-	
2013	BZÖ	-	-	-	-	-		-	-	-	-	-	-	-		-	-	
2013	Stronach	61	83	59	57	-	-		56	-	-	-	-	-	-		-	
2013	NEOS	36	42	55	55	-	-	56		-	-	-	-	-	-	-		

Note: Calculations show bisected city block distance of subtopics between parties (with 0=absolute congruence and 100=absolute divergence).

As the distance matrix shows, the Greens and the LIF are the parties that deviate the most from the remaining party spectrum (although not for the same reasons, as they also differ from one another). The parties resembling each other most closely are the mainstream parties (with only few exceptions, such as programmatically in 1999 and in the day-to-day campaign during the 2013 election). As regards the Austrian niche parties, the FPÖ exhibits much more similar topical preferences to those of the mainstream parties than the left-libertarian parties do, as does the BZÖ, though it seems to have begun to diverge in 2008. As a result, the electoral discourse is focused on a set of issues dominated by populist radical right parties rather than those favored by left-libertarian and liberal parties, although the most recent election in 2013 indicates that this circumstance may be about to change.

Intra-party campaign divergence

Finally, proceeding from the inter-party to the intra-party dimension of campaign diversion, it remains to be determined whether Austrian parties are consistent campaigners, or in other words, to what extent parties are able and willing to politicize the same subtopics in day-to-day campaign communication as they originally outlined in their programmatic statements. Do some parties show a greater degree of coherence between manifestos and press releases than others? And in particular, do mainstream parties differ from niche parties in that regard? In order to shed light on these questions, Table 21 shows the city block distance of subtopics between manifestos and press releases for every party in every election (with 100 expressing absolute difference and 0 expressing total congruence).

**Table 21: Divergence of subtopics between campaign levels.
Individual parties, 1990-2013**

Party families:	liberal/left-libertarian		Social democratic	Conservative	Radical right	
Party:	Greens	LIF	SPÖ	ÖVP	BZÖ	FPÖ
1990	74		49	67		53
1994	88	79	50	47		62
1999	66	79	90	47		63
2002	68		59	50		56
2006	55		43	58	50	38
2008	57		57	52	60	50
2013	58		87	47	-	45
Avg.	*67*	*79*	*62*	*52*	*55*	*52*
Std.-dev.	*10.9*	*0.1*	*17.2*	*7.1*	*5.1*	*8.4*

Note: Team Stronach, NEOS and BZÖ in 2013 are not considered, since they did not address migration and ethnic relations on both campaign levels. Scores based on bisected city block distance between 0 (no divergence) and 100 (absolute divergence).

Mann-Whitney-tests for difference between mainstream and niche parties (U=92, p>.05, r=-.23) and between parties left and right of the center (U=61, p<.05, r=-.45).

As Table 21 shows, the degree of campaign divergence varies from election to election for all parties, with the SPÖ (Std.-dev. 17.2) and the Greens (Std.-dev. 10.9) being the most fluctuating parties, followed by the FPÖ (Std.-dev. 8.4) and the ÖVP (Std.-dev. 7.1). The study's original hypothesis on parties' average divergence of subtopics is not confirmed: Mainstream parties and niche parties do not differ in divergence consistently. On the contrary, campaign divergence seems instead to vary along a left-right axis, since parties left of the center show a significantly higher average divergence than parties right of the center do. While the SPÖ (62) oscillates between massively divergent (1999, 2013) and less divergent (1990, 2006) elections, the Greens (67) seem to display a linear development from highly divergent politicization (up until 2002) to a more consistent pattern after 2006 (although they still remain above the average scores of parties right of the center). These left parties are accompanied by the LIF, which – although only relevant in two elections – scores the highest average divergence in subtopics of all parties (79).

On the opposite side of the spectrum, all rightist parties are characterized by average divergence scores distinctly below those of leftist parties, with the ÖVP and FPÖ being the most consistent (52) and the BZÖ close behind them (55). In a nutshell, rightist parties – with their strong focus on labor, crime & border control, and general asylum issues – appear to have less difficulty sticking to their subtopics on both channels, whereas leftist parties (which address a broader variety of subtopics) are either not as eager or simply not able to promote one cohesive storyline across campaign levels.

6.2.3 Synopsis

What lessons can be drawn from the analysis of the differing topical emphasis placed by Austrian parties? First of all, it can be concluded that the very nature of different campaign channels strongly influences the way parties politicize certain subtopics more than others. While programmatic communication in election manifestos offers parties more freedom to highlight a variety of different aspects of questions of migration and ethnic relations, conditions on the day-to-day level of election campaigning are distinctly different. On the day-to-day level, various centripetal influences such as public agendas, media agendas, and external events severely limit parties' options in selecting subtopics, forcing them to jump on the subtopics of current relevance. The result is a much narrower, centripetal pattern of topical emphasis, with fewer subtopics being more salient than in programmatic communication. This finding is an important contribution to the general understanding of electoral politicization and its diverse contexts, showing how parties use different communicative strategies to further their agendas. Some parties appear to be more successful than others in setting consistent topical priorities. As the analysis of parties' campaign divergence has demonstrated, rightist parties (ÖVP, FPÖ, BZÖ) have less difficulty in sticking to a coherent set of subtopics and emphasizing them by and large to the same degree on both levels of campaigning, whereas leftist parties (SPÖ, Greens, LIF) are significantly more divergent in that regard – which goes some way toward explaining the higher overall divergence during the 1990s (with two left-libertarian parties) than in the post-millennial elections (with two populist radical right parties).

When taking a closer look at the subtopics that are emphasized the most, the demarcation line leans toward the left even more. This means that a striking similarity between populist radical right parties (FPÖ, BZÖ), conservatives (ÖVP), and social democrats (SPÖ) stands in stark contrast to a wildly different choice of subtopics on the part of the left-libertarian and liberal parties (Greens, LIF). While the former stress subtopics such as *labor* and *crime & border control* in their campaigns, the latter put more emphasis on *asylum procedures, societal models* and *xenophobia*. These findings indicate that populist radical right parties may be more successful in influencing the topical selection of mainstream parties than left-wing parties.

However, what remains unclear is whether mainstream parties' preoccupation with the radical right's concerns results in a convergence of party positions or whether these subtopics simply serve as battlegrounds between mainstream parties and populist radical right parties. This is the core question of the next section, which aims to unravel Austrian parties' positions on the issues of migration and ethnic relations. Do parties change their positions over time, or do they staunchly stick to the same stances? And are there discursive coalitions of any kind that share the same type of policy frames?

6.3 Contested positions: Policy frames in electoral competition

As discussed in Chapter 2, altering the salience of an issue or specific subtopic is only one of several techniques that parties may apply as part of their electoral issue management. Of even greater importance are the actual policies that parties promote, which serve as another essential instrument in their strategic repertoires. In order to shed light on these strategies, this section focuses on the policy frames forwarded by political parties.

As explained in Chapter 4, electoral discourse has been encoded using a framework of eleven different policy frames, each of them expressing a particular perspective on migration and ethnic relations that together reflect the variety of policy positions in Austrian electoral discourse at a medium level of abstraction. Ten of these frames have been arranged on a bipolar graph of liberal versus restrictive positions. This approach permits a two-step analysis of parties' issue positions: Firstly, it allows the evaluation of the general trends in electoral discourse over time in order to get an overview of whether and how the debate might have changed over the course of the examination period (6.3.1). Secondly, digging deeper, it enables comparison of the frames that a party has been applying in its electoral politicization in order to evaluate how closely those particular choices resemble those of other parties (6.3.2).

6.3.1   Liberal or restrictive? The overall direction of electoral politicization

Tendency of the party system

This section begins to approach the policy tendencies in Austrian electoral competition by identifying patterns on the party system level. The core question here is whether and how strongly Austrian electoral discourse as a whole leans in either a liberal or restrictive direction. To answer this question, the average of parties' individual shares of policy frames is evaluated, following the assumption that parties will occupy more than one frame at a time during an election campaign. To once again demonstrate the logic of the study's framing approach, Table 22 lists all of the frames, and gives the relation of each to either a restrictive or liberal perspective, including its average share on both campaign levels in every election since 1990.

Table 22:   Mean shares of policy frames, 1990-2013 (in %)

		1990		1994		1999		2002		2006		2008		2013		Avg.	
		MF	PR	MF	PR	MF	PR	MF	PR	MF	PR	MF	PR	MF	PR	MF	PR
liberal	Multiculturalism	6	2	2	0	6	1	4	2	3	0	6	0	9	1	5	1
	Cosmopolitanism	4	0	4	11	2	3	5	1	2	3	1	2	9	4	4	3
	Participation	**14**	7	**10**	1	**11**	1	**24**	4	**13**	4	**10**	6	**12**	8	**13**	4
	Rights	**15**	9	**22**	**17**	**26**	**12**	**16**	**17**	**13**	**15**	**10**	8	6	**15**	**15**	**13**
	Solidarity	**11**	**21**	**18**	**18**	8	**37**	9	**22**	6	**11**	8	**17**	**12**	**33**	10	**23**
restrictive	Benefit	**10**	5	6	**10**	4	2	3	3	**11**	**21**	**10**	6	**17**	3	9	7
	Genuineness	7	7	9	**11**	3	**10**	7	**22**	8	**12**	3	**11**	4	**12**	6	**12**
	Assimilation	3	2	**10**	5	2	1	4	2	**15**	**10**	**18**	**12**	**14**	6	9	6
	Relief	**19**	**29**	**11**	7	**23**	4	**13**	**16**	**13**	**11**	9	**10**	4	7	**13**	**12**
	Security	5	**10**	5	**13**	**15**	**24**	9	0	9	8	**20**	**19**	6	7	10	**12**
	Administration	6	3	2	3	1	2	5	7	8	1	6	2	7	0	5	3
	indeterminate		4		4		4		3		3		6		3		4
	Sum	100	100	100	100	100	100	100	100	100	100	100	100	100	100	100	100

Note: Results show the average share devoted by parties to each frame in relation to the total wordshare of politicization of migration and ethnic relations for each election. MF (Manifesto), PR (Press releases). The most salient frames are highlighted in bold letters.

When the average salience of each frame across all parties and elections is calculated, the relation of restrictive to liberal frames in both campaign channels appears to be rather balanced. However, few elections are actually alike, and there are distinct differences between the two campaign channels in their most salient frames. Of the restrictive frames, *relief* and *security* score the highest average scores in both campaign channels, although the high salience of the former is much more continuous than that of the latter, especially on the programmatic level. *Security* and *benefit* frames are raised rather sporadically and never dominate the debate for long. Calls for stronger *assimilation* of immigrants and ethnic minorities grow over time and thus are of much greater importance after the millennium, in particular on the programmatic level, while the *genuineness* frame, on the other hand, is of much greater relevance in the day-to-day electoral debate. In the liberal spectrum of the discourse, patterns are slightly more distinct: Here, *participation* and *rights* outdo the remaining frames in importance quite clearly. Both of them are highly salient on the programmatic level nearly throughout, whereas in press releases, the call for *solidarity* is the most emphasized frame (together with a *rights* perspective that is equally important on both levels of campaigning). The two remaining frames lag well behind those three dominant frames, although both an explicitly *multiculturalist* frame as well as *cosmopolitan* demands for an open migration regime are intermittently emphasized.

However, the change in the direction of electoral discourse is better captured by focusing on liberal frames, which clearly shows the shift in the overall direction of Austrian party competition over the examination period. Figure 8 presents the average of Austrian parties' position scores for each election by calculating the mean of the liberal-restrictive scores of all relevant parties in that election. Liberal-restrictive scores are assigned according to the net total of liberal minus restrictive frameshares on a scale between +100 (absolutely liberal) and -100 (absolutely restrictive). This gives us a rough overview of electoral politicization and its development since the upswing in the 1990s.

Figure 8: **Liberal-restrictive-tendency of electoral politicization. Party system level, 1990-2013**

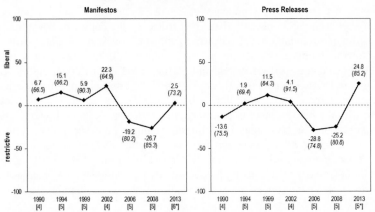

Note: Mean values denote average position of all relevant parties on a bipolar scale with +100 (absolutely liberal) and -100 (absolutely restrictive) stances. Polarization values (in parentheses) denote standard deviation of means. Values in squared brackets denote the number of effective parties considered in the respective election.

* Due to the total depoliticization of migration and ethnic relations in the BZÖ's manifestos and in the BZÖ's, Team Stronach's and the NEOS' press releases, in 2013 the number of parties considered is limited to 6 for manifestos and only 5 for press releases.

From this general bipolar perspective, the findings indicate a transformation of electoral discourse in the post-millennial period compared to the 1990s. The discourse undergoes a shift that appears to be in line with the changes in the spectrum of relevant parties: With the exception of one data point (press releases in 1990), up until 2002 there is a slight predominance of liberal framing, thanks to the presence of two left-wing niche parties that counterbalance the neutral and restrictive stances of the rest of the party spectrum. Although this tendency is not very pronounced, it holds until 2002, with the four remaining parties holding rather balanced positions on migration and ethnic relations. With the transformation of the party spectrum in the new millennium, the politicization of these issues experiences yet another shift. The exit of the liberal LIF, along with the presence of another populist radical right party starting in 2005, has resulted in prevailingly restrictive framing. This disparity is even more pronounced than the liberal advantage before 2002, especially in programmatic communication. When the different campaign channels are compared, the patterns resemble one another by and large, with day-to-day campaign communication being of slightly more restrictive nature than programmatic campaigning. In 2013, however, it is clear that the patterns of the first post-millennial decade have come to an end. While programmatically the overall direction of competition has returned to a fairly balanced mean position, on the day-to-day campaign level, the debate has become more liberal than ever before.

Focusing on the polarization of policy framing, approximated by parties' standard deviation from the mean tendency of debate, up until 2013 there is an evident link between the number of effective parties and the degree of deviation, at least on the programmatic level: Thus in manifestos polarization is at its lowest in elections with only four relevant parties contending (1990, 2002) and is higher in elections contested by five relevant parties (1994, 1999, 2006, 2008). Accordingly, polarization increases from 1990 to 1999, drops sharply in 2002, and then increases again until 2008; the findings in 2013 then reverse the previous pattern, with the highest number of competing parties producing a lower degree of deviation. On the day-to-day level of campaigning, however, polarization is more diffuse, marked by fluctuation from one election to the next without any clear-cut pattern emerging over time. Hence, while programmatically an increase in the number of competing parties usually goes along with an increase in polarization, this pattern does not seem to hold for the day-to-day level of campaigning.

Directions of individual parties

These changes in direction and level of polarization raise the question of who drives these changes. Given that there is quite a considerable range of essential tendencies represented, how do individual parties contribute to the system-level developments? Figure 9 shows the parties' positions along a liberal-restrictive axis, and tracks them over time.

Figure 9:   **Party positions on a bipolar axis (liberal/restrictive).**
                       Time-series, 1990-2013

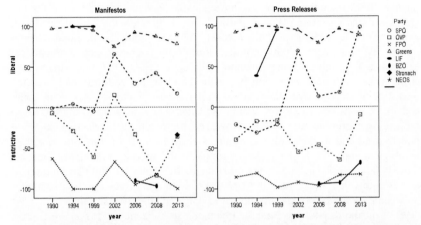

Note: For each party/election, the average of liberal (+) and restrictive (-) frames is calculated. Shares are based on each party's relevant wordshare per data point (see Appendix 1) with +100 (absolutely liberal) and -100 (absolutely restrictive) stances. Central dotted line denotes equilibrium value between liberal and restrictive frames.

Kruskal-Wallis-test for differences between ideological families: Manifestos, H(3)=24.16, p<.01; Press Releases, H(3)=24.12, p<.01. Post hoc tests (Mann-Whitney) confirm statistically significant differences between all families.

The findings confirm some of the predictions made in the conceptual sections: Most notably, Austrian *niche parties* move along the fringes of the liberal-restrictive spectrum, but remain remarkably stable throughout the whole examination period. Both in programmatic as well as in day-to-day campaigning, liberal/left-libertarian parties (Greens/LIF) maintain a predominantly liberal stance on migration and ethnic relations, while radical right parties (FPÖ/BZÖ) are continuously located at the restrictive end of the spectrum (only in one case – the LIF's day-to-day campaign in 1994 – does the campaign strategy approach a more balanced share of positions). This unambiguous behavior of the Austrian niche parties is hardly surprising, since they are largely constrained to particular positions regarding migration and ethnic relations that remain stable over the whole course of the examination period. Furthermore, the new niche parties that emerged in the 2013 election have adopted positions that are similar to those of their predecessors and related party families, at least programmatically. Hence, while the NEOS – cooperating with the former LIF – take the most liberal position of all of the 2013 manifestos (and thus align with the remaining niche parties), Team Stronach is the only minor party that adopts a balanced approach, though it leans slightly toward restrictive positions (much like the ÖVP). On the day-to-day campaign level, however, both parties refrain from addressing the issue at all, which is why no actual position could be determined (the same is true for the BZÖ).

In contrast, the contribution of the *mainstream parties* remains diffuse and shows a more flexible relation of liberal and restrictive frames. As a consequence, the mainstream parties are more clearly located at the center of the liberal/restrictive-spectrum. Hence, parties' distribution on the liberal-restrictive axis largely meets the expectations based on party family backgrounds. Nonetheless, even mainstream party politicization displays tendencies that are subject to change: On both campaign channels, the center-right ÖVP tends toward restrictiveness, the only exception being the 2002 snap election (which was the most liberal election overall). It is most restrictive in its press releases in 2006, and in its manifestos in 2008, which indicates that it adapted to the increased radical right presence after 2005. However, the recent 2013 election seems to have put an end to the ÖVP's continuous shift to the right; on both campaign levels – though it is still mostly restrictive – the party's framing has become more balanced once again. On the other hand, the center-left SPÖ's framing pattern is ambivalent throughout the 1990s. While in manifestos the SPÖ vacillates between neutral (1990), slightly liberal (1994) and slightly restrictive tendencies (1999), on the day-to-day campaign channel, its tendency is toward restrictive frames throughout. With the turn of the millennium, however, the SPÖ distinctly shifted its framing toward a pronouncedly more liberal stance on both campaign levels, aligning itself more closely with the left-wing parties. In 2013 the party's strategy deviated stronger than ever before between campaign levels: While programmatically the party sougth to return to a more balanced share of liberal and restrictive frames, the day-to-day campaign was based entirely on liberal frames (dominated by appeals for solidarity against radical right parties' xenophobia).

To recapitulate: This plot of party tendencies along a bipolar axis gives a first glimpse of how mainstream parties' policies on migration and ethnic relations can develop over time under niche party pressure. While the center-right ÖVP gives increasing preference to restrictive frames over the course of the examination period (with a recent cutback in 2013), the center-left SPÖ proves indecisive throughout the 1990s, but clearly puts more weight on liberal frames after the turn of the millennium. These first indications, however, need to be verified with deeper analysis, which is why the next section focuses on the specific frames forwarded by individual parties. This will help to determine whether niche and mainstream parties merely seem similar when evaluated in terms of their liberalness or restrictiveness, or whether they actually position themselves along the same lines of interpretation.

6.3.2 Promoting policies: Party preferences and inter-party frame-proximity

The abstraction of party positions to a bipolar axis is a gross simplification and disregards the actual diversity of frames available on any particular issue. For this reason, it is necessary to take a closer look at the frames applied by Austrian parties in order to confirm the general results discussed in the previous section. The central questions with regard to party positions are: Which specific positions do parties hold on issues surrounding migration and ethnic relations? Are there clear-cut links between specific parties and frames, and do they change over time? And finally, are there discursive coalitions of parties using the same frames in politicization?

Individual party framing of migration and ethnic relations

Although Austria was known to have one of the most stable party systems in Western Europe, since the mid-1980s, the composition of the party spectrum has undergone a number of changes as newcomers arrived (and in some cases, departed again). In the process of these changes, individual parties' stances on migration and ethnic relations may have changed; the goal of this section is to identify these changes. To begin with, Table 23 tracks individual parties' preferred frames from election to election in an attempt to capture the development of parties' policy framing.

As regards Austrian niche parties, the findings on their issue positions confirm the unambiguous patterns that were expected in Chapter 3.

Radical right parties: As stated previously, radical right parties show similar patterns of restrictiveness. The FPÖ devotes 92% of its programmatic politicization and 93% of its day-to-day politicization to restrictive frames, whereas the BZÖ manages to top these figures with 96% restrictive frames in its manifestos and 94% in its press releases. With regard to their preferred frames, however, the populist radical right parties differ from each other slightly. For the FPÖ, the most prominent frame overall is *relief* (averaging 30% in manifestos and 25% in press releases), which characterizes immigration as a burden on the host society. It continuously ranks among the party's most salient frames and constitutes a cornerstone of its approach up until the present. The second major frame advanced by the FPÖ is its constant suspicion of a lack of *genuineness*, particularly in the context of asylum but also in allowing immigrants access to the welfare state. It is a particularly persistent frame among the FPÖ's press releases (on average, 26%), whereas programmatically it waxes and wanes, but maintains an average score of 16%. For the BZÖ, the call for the *assimilation* of immigrants into a perceived *Leitkultur* ("guiding culture") of the host society (covering its language, cultural and ethical norms, and social mores) is the most salient frame overall – though more actively in manifestos (34%) than in press releases (13%). It is followed in importance by a strong emphasis on *security* concerns tied to migration and ethnic relations, which the BZÖ addresses approximately equally on both campaign levels (MF: 24%, PR: 22%). Needless to say, both parties also use the other restrictive frames (such as the benefit perspective, which gains in importance after the millennium) even more prominently than most of the other parties. However, relief, genuineness, and security stand out as the most enduring of the restrictive set of frames.

Table 23: Shares of policy frames per election. Individual parties, 1990-2013 (in %)

Manifestos

		1990				1994					1999					2002				2006					2008					2013							Avg.					
		SPÖ	ÖVP	FPÖ	Greens	SPÖ	ÖVP	FPÖ	Greens	LIF	SPÖ	ÖVP	FPÖ	Greens	LIF	SPÖ	ÖVP	FPÖ	Greens	SPÖ	ÖVP	FPÖ	Greens	BZÖ	SPÖ	ÖVP	FPÖ	Greens	BZÖ	SPÖ	ÖVP	FPÖ	Greens	Stronach	NEOS	BZÖ	SPÖ	ÖVP	FPÖ	Gm	LIF	BZÖ
Liberal	Multiculturalism	-	-	10	14	-	-	-	14	-	-	-	-	4	31	-	1	-	16	-	-	-	14	1	16	2	-	10	-	8	-	-	4	7	37	1	3	2	1	8	16	1
	Cosmopolitanism	11	-	7	23	6	-	-	25	12	-	4	-	4	38	5	14	3	47	3	-	-	7	7	3	-	-	13	-	5	13	2	25	-	11	-	5	4	-	8	25	-
	Participation	25	9	-	23	11	4	-	37	49	-	2	-	78	-	35	12	17	8	19	22	2	27	-	34	-	8	37	-	17	4	-	21	-	29	-	20	8	-	24	40	-
	Rights	5	24	4	29	19	3	-	23	39	-	-	-	14	31	22	17	8	17	26	6	2	20	-	11	3	-	28	-	14	1	-	17	27	3	-	15	6	3	35	20	1
	Solidarity	1	14	2	25	12	17	-	-	-	-	-	-	-	-	21	4	2	8	7	-	-	20	-	11	-	-	28	-	10	2	-	-	-	14	-	13	6	18	18	20	14
Restrictive	Benefit	4	22	15	1	6	18	18	-	-	-	-	-	-	-	4	3	3	3	6	9	25	-	15	14	9	13	-	13	9	35	4	-	42	-	-	6	9	18	1	-	8
	Genuineness	16	5	7	-	5	21	20	-	-	-	-	-	-	-	-	5	25	-	4	5	21	-	9	9	2	5	-	8	9	2	18	-	6	-	-	4	6	16	-	-	8
	Assimilation	4	-	8	-	-	16	33	-	-	-	-	-	-	-	-	3	14	-	3	17	20	-	34	3	18	34	-	34	21	23	26	-	11	2	-	4	12	19	-	-	34
	Relief	19	8	48	-	13	13	29	-	-	-	-	52	-	-	13	15	22	-	8	11	25	-	22	6	11	24	-	10	7	11	23	-	8	-	-	16	10	30	2	-	16
	Security	-	19	-	-	20	7	1	-	-	19	-	-	-	-	5	19	13	-	5	18	6	-	14	6	47	14	-	33	23	9	-	-	-	-	-	2	4	25	2	-	24
	Administration	16	-	6	-	9	2	-	-	-	6	-	-	-	-	-	21	1	-	18	12	1	8	2	8	8	1	13	-	9	22	-	10	-	-	-	9	10	1	4	-	1
	Sum	100	100	100	100	100	100	100	100	100	100	100	100	100	100	100	100	100	100	100	100	100	100	100	100	100	100	100	100	100	100	100	100	100	100	100	100	100	100	100	100	100
		χ²=4046; df=30; Cramér's V=.574***				χ²=6501; df=40; Cramér's V=.528***					χ²=8468; df=40; Cramér's V=.658***					χ²=4811; df=30; Cramér's V=.527***				χ²=5240; df=40; Cramér's V=.466***					χ²=4095; df=40; Cramér's V=.500***					χ²=3613; df=40; Cramér's V=.489***												

Manifestos

Frame		1990				1994					1999					2002				2006					2008					2013							Avg.					
		SPÖ	ÖVP	FPÖ	Greens	SPÖ	ÖVP	FPÖ	Greens	LIF	SPÖ	ÖVP	FPÖ	Greens	LIF	SPÖ	ÖVP	FPÖ	Greens	SPÖ	ÖVP	FPÖ	Greens	BZÖ	SPÖ	ÖVP	FPÖ	Greens	BZÖ	SPÖ	ÖVP	FPÖ	Greens	BZÖ	Stronach	NEOS	SPÖ	ÖVP	FPÖ	Gm	LIF	BZÖ
Liberal	Multiculturalism	-	-	10	14	-	-	11	-	-	-	-	-	-	31	-	1	1	16	-	-	-	14	1	16	2	-	10	-	8	-	-	4	-	7	37	3	2	1	8	16	1
	Cosmopolitanism	11	-	-	7	6	-	-	14	-	-	4	-	4	-	5	14	3	-	3	-	-	7	-	3	-	-	-	-	5	13	-	25	-	-	11	5	4	4	8	-	-
	Participation	25	9	-	23	11	4	-	25	12	-	2	-	14	38	35	12	3	47	19	22	-	23	-	34	3	-	13	-	17	4	-	21	-	-	29	20	8	-	24	25	-
	Rights	5	24	4	29	19	3	-	37	49	17	4	-	78	31	22	17	8	17	26	6	2	27	1	2	3	8	37	-	14	1	-	17	-	-	3	15	8	3	35	40	-
	Solidarity	1	14	2	25	12	17	-	23	39	30	6	-	2	-	21	4	2	8	7	-	-	20	-	11	-	-	28	-	10	2	-	17	-	27	14	13	6	1	18	20	1
Restrictive	Benefit	4	22	15	1	6	6	18	-	-	-	2	15	2	-	-	3	25	-	6	9	25	-	15	2	9	13	-	13	-	-	35	4	13	42	-	6	9	18	1	-	14
	Genuineness	16	5	7	-	5	21	6	-	-	-	1	13	-	-	-	5	25	-	4	5	21	-	9	2	2	5	-	8	9	2	18	-	8	-	6	4	6	16	-	-	8
	Assimilation	4	-	8	-	13	16	33	-	-	-	8	52	-	-	13	3	14	-	3	17	20	-	34	3	18	34	-	34	-	23	26	2	34	11	11	4	12	19	-	-	34
	Relief	19	8	48	-	20	13	29	-	-	52	12	52	-	-	-	15	22	-	8	11	25	-	22	11	11	24	-	10	7	-	11	-	10	8	-	16	10	30	-	-	16
	Security	-	19	-	-	-	-	1	-	-	52	53	19	-	-	5	19	13	-	18	6	-	-	14	47	14	-	-	33	-	23	-	-	33	-	-	2	2	10	-	-	2
	Administration	16	-	6	-	9	2	1	-	-	20	7	-	-	-	-	21	1	-	-	18	8	1	12	8	8	1	13	-	9	22	1	10	-	2	2	9	10	4	1	-	1
	Sum	100	100	100	100	100	100	100	100	100	100	100	100	100	100	100	100	100	100	100	100	100	100	100	100	100	100	100	100	100	100	100	100	100	100	100	100	100	100	100	100	100

Statistics by election:

1990	1994	1999	2002	2006	2008	2013
$x^2 = 4046$; df=30; Cramér's $V = .574$***	$x^2 = 6501$; df=40; Cramér's $V = .528$***	$x^2 = 8468$; df=40; Cramér's $V = .658$***	$x^2 = 4811$; df=30; Cramér's $V = .527$***	$x^2 = 5240$; df=40; Cramér's $V = .466$***	$x^2 = 4095$; df=40; Cramér's $V = .500$***	$x^2 = 3613$; df=40; Cramér's $V = .489$***

Note: For each election and party, the absolute number of relevant wordshare addressing migration and ethnic relations is indicated in the legends. Association between variables for each election was calculated using each party's word count weighted by the average wordshare of all competing parties, *** $p \leq 0.01$, two-tailed test.

1 In 2013 the BZÖ issued only one relevant press release (on asylum procedures), which was too little material to be included into the topical analysis (since it would have represented a severe distortion of the party's average preferences).

Liberal & left-libertarian parties: Unsurprisingly, the liberal & left-libertarian parties' framing is diametrically opposed to that of the right. The Greens' share of liberal frames averages 94% in their manifestos and 96% in relevant press releases, whereas the LIF addresses liberal frames in every one of its manifestos and in 78% of its press releases. As regards the most prevalent frames of these parties, they share a similar pattern in the sense that their appeals for, *rights* and *solidarity* are by far their most frequently addressed frames. Since their earliest beginnings, the Greens have appealed more strongly than any other party to a *rights* frame, which is linked to the treatment of immigrants and ethnic minorities of various origins, but in particular that of refugees seeking asylum in Austria. Thus it is the party's most salient frame overall (MF: 35%, PR: 36%), whereas the LIF highlights a rights perspective primarily in its programmatic appeals (40%), and less intensively on the day-to-day campaign level (15%). Aside from the prominent rights frame, both parties also repeatedly advance *solidarity*-framed appeals for recognition and against growing xenophobia, scapegoating, and other mistreatment of minorities, though much more on the day-to-day campaign level (Greens: 44%; LIF: 41%) than in programmatic communication (Greens: 18%, LIF: 20%). Other liberal frames carry only occasional relevance in either one of the campaign channels: Most prominent are programmatic entreaties for expansion of migrants' options for *participation* (Greens: 24%, LIF: 25%), while active appraisals of *multiculturalism* gain importance only in the LIF's manifestos (16%), as do calls for a *cosmopolitan* system of migration control in the LIF's press releases (20%). Obviously, both left-libertarian parties almost entirely avoid restrictive frames.

Mainstream parties: Regarding the Austrian *mainstream parties*, the analysis of issue positions reveals a different picture from that of the niche parties, but also shows that the mainstream parties differ from each other as well, featuring quite distinct patterns of frames addressed. The one thing that the mainstream parties have in common is that both of them emphasize frames in a more balanced way than the niche parties do. Thus, not only does no single frame stand out as much as in niche parties' politicization, but the mainstream parties also address a greater number of different frames on both sides of the liberal-restrictive spectrum. The only frames that both mainstream parties avoid are a *multiculturalist* perspective as well as *cosmopolitan* appeals to make migration regimes more flexible – this is a strong indicator of the limits of discourse. However, this commonality is overshadowed by a substantial number of differences: Closer examination of the *SPÖ*'s most important frames shows that they vary, both between elections and across campaign channels, making the SPÖ the most ambivalent actor in terms of policy framing, as well. In its programmatic communication, the party puts the most emphasis on *participation* (20%), *rights* (15%) and *solidarity* (13%) on the liberal side and on *relief* (16%) on the restrictive side of the spectrum (although the latter declines in importance after the millennium). Liberal frames retain or even increase in their importance in the SPÖ's manifestos after the millennium, and restrictive frames decrease in importance after 1999 (with the *benefit* frame being the sole sample of high – yet fluctuating – relevance thereafter). On the day-to-day campaign level, the SPÖ's framing pattern turns out to be more ambiguous, however: Here, *solidarity* is the only frame that retains its importance throughout the whole examination period (which is in line with the party's ideological foundations), whereas other frames erupt only in particular elections and vanish in others – like *participation* or *rights* in the liberal discourse spectrum, as well as *relief, security, benefit* and *genuineness* in the restrictive spectrum. This high degree of fluctuation prevents any clear-cut, continuous interpretation of the SPÖ's framing on the day-to-day campaign level, although on the whole, a slight predominance of liberal frames can be observed. Noteworthy, though, is the SPÖ's obvious avoidance of cultural frames such as *multiculturalism* or *assimilation*, which marks a conspicuous difference from its mainstream counterpart.

There is less ambiguity as far as the *ÖVP* is concerned, with its tendency toward certain restrictive frames being more distinct than any predilection of its mainstream counterpart. Restrictive frames clearly prevail over liberal frames in both campaign channels (even more strongly among manifestos than press releases). Programmatically the party's dominant concerns are *security* (25%), calls for *assimilation* (15%), and demands for *relief* from burdensome immigration regimes (10%), while no liberal frame scores a double-digit share. Even more distinctly, on the day-to-day campaign level, all of the restrictive frames gain double-digit scores, as opposed to only one in the liberal spectrum (*solidarity*). Thus, while the ÖVP repeatedly stresses solidarity – in line with its ideological core of Catholic Christian charity – as a core principle in dealing with minorities and immigrants, overall its framing tends to be predominantly restrictive. Nevertheless, as described above, there is a temporal component to these findings in that the ÖVP's policy framing is less restrictive during the 1990s than in post-millennium elections. The most persistent of the restrictive frames are *relief* and *security*, while the other restrictive frames fluctuate in importance from election to election. Liberal frames appear mostly during the 1990s and – after years of increasing restrictiveness – emerge once again more visibly in 2013. This supports the conjecture that the ÖVP leadership intends to return to a more balanced position on migration and ethnic relations, both in the party's government policy as well as its electoral behavior.

Finally, both of the mainstream parties accord higher salience to *administration* framing than the rest of the party spectrum due to their stronger proclivity for making neutral statements. This is a direct consequence of being the main actors in Austrian politics on migration and ethnic relations and thus having a greater need to avoid direct conflict with their previous policies and activities.

Framing coalitions among Austrian parties

To summarize these findings on parties' issue positions, the result is an even clearer pattern than that which emerged when looking at subtopics earlier on. The dividing line in the Austrian party system's issue positions on migration and ethnic relations cuts between the Austrian mainstream parties and separates a predominantly liberal spectrum (SPÖ, Greens, and LIF) from a predominantly restrictive spectrum (ÖVP, FPÖ, and BZÖ).

While the framing patterns of the niche parties remain more or less stable over time, mainstream party patterns turn out to be in a state of flux. The formerly ambiguous positioning of the SPÖ shifts toward more liberal frames after the millennium, while the already restrictive tendency of the ÖVP intensifies in the decade after 2002 before finally returning to a more balanced pattern in 2013. These findings transfer to correlation coefficients that are even higher for frames than for subtopics throughout the examination period. Thus the Greens, LIF, and SPÖ mostly overlap in their use of a *rights* frame and share the rest of the liberal frames. On the other side of the framing spectrum, a strong superposition of ÖVP, FPÖ, and BZÖ in their use of the *relief* and *security* frames can be observed, though they show a considerably lower degree of commonality with regard to other restrictive frames.

Once again, a more effective method of visualizing these inter-party frame coalitions is calculating distances between the competing parties' positions. Table 24 uses bisected city block distance to display the difference in framing between each pair of parties – with values ranging between 0 (= no differences, i.e. absolutely congruent framing) and 100 (= absolute difference, i.e. no framing congruencies whatsoever).

Table 24: Divergence of frames between individual parties, 1990-2013

		Manifestos								Press Releases							
		SPÖ	ÖVP	FPÖ	Green	LIF	BZÖ	Stronach	NEOS	SPÖ	ÖVP	FPÖ	Green	LIF	BZÖ	Stronach	NEOS
1990	SPÖ		69	57	63	-	-	-	-		29	34	64	-	-	-	-
	ÖVP	69		66	52	-	-	-	-	29		40	78	-	-	-	-
	FPÖ	57	66		83	-	-	-	-	34	40		90	-	-	-	-
	Greens	63	52	83		-	-	-	-	64	78	90		-	-	-	-
1994	SPÖ		49	76	52	58	-	-	-		41	36	74	47	-	-	-
	ÖVP	49		44	76	76	-	-	-	41		43	72	44	-	-	-
	FPÖ	76	44		100	100	-	-	-	36	43		92	75	-	-	-
	Greens	52	76	100		28	-	-	-	74	72	92		66	-	-	-
	LIF	58	76	100	28		-	-	-	47	44	75	66		-	-	-
1999	SPÖ		78	48	81	83	-	-	-		43	42	62	60	-	-	-
	ÖVP	78		65	85	93	-	-	-	43		59	66	61	-	-	-
	FPÖ	48	65		98	100	-	-	-	42	59		100	100	-	-	-
	Greens	81	85	98		56	-	-	-	62	66	100		19	-	-	-
	LIF	83	93	100	56		-	-	-	60	61	100	19		-	-	-
2002	SPÖ		46	68	40	-	-	-	-		66	85	32	-	-	-	-
	ÖVP	46		51	61	-	-	-	-	66		27	88	-	-	-	-
	FPÖ	68	51		74	-	-	-	-	85	27		97	-	-	-	-
	Greens	40	61	74		-	-	-	-	32	88	97		-	-	-	-
2006	SPÖ		37	70	37	-	69	-	-		48	57	44	-	57	-	-
	ÖVP	37		49	65	-	40	-	-	48		54	69	-	39	-	-
	FPÖ	70	49		97	-	26	-	-	57	54		89	-	35	-	-
	Greens	37	65	97		-	94	-	-	44	69	89		-	87	-	-
	BZÖ	69	40	26	94	-		-	-	57	39	35	87	-		-	-
2008	SPÖ		68	73	56	-	75	-	-		48	55	53	-	60	-	-
	ÖVP	68		42	88	-	27	-	-	48		49	88	-	33	-	-
	FPÖ	73	42		91	-	24	-	-	55	49		91	-	32	-	-
	Greens	56	88	91		-	98	-	-	53	88	91		-	98	-	-
	BZÖ	75	27	24	98	-		-	-	60	33	32	98	-		-	-
2013	SPÖ		49	63	35	-	-	56	53		65	92	29	-	-	-	-
	ÖVP	49		57	63	-	-	75	75	65		65	53	-	-	-	-
	FPÖ	63	57		94	-	-	40	96	92	65		87	-	-	-	-
	Greens	35	63	94		-	-	73	43	29	53	87		-	-	-	-
	Stronach	56	75	40	73	-	-		76	-	-	-	-	-	-	-	-
	NEOS	53	75	96	43	-	-	76		-	-	-	-	-	-	-	-

Heat Map — Bisected city block distance:
0 · 1-19 · 20-29 · 30-39 · 40-49 · 50-59 · 60-69 · 70-79 · 80-89 · 90-99 · 100

Note: Calculations show bisected city block distance of frames between parties in column and row (with 0=absolute congruence and 100=absolute divergence).

The comparison of parties' framing proximity substantiates the general tendencies shown on the bipolar liberal-restrictive scale, although there is distinct variance between the two campaign channels. Parties at the fringes of the spectrum demonstrate highly consistent frame choices in their manifestos, with the Greens and LIF overlapping in their preference for *rights*, *solidarity*, and *participation* frames, and the FPÖ and BZÖ sticking to the restrictive set of frames.

For the mainstream parties, the distance patterns in their programmatic framing once again show the changing character of their politicization during the 1990s, especially when one considers their proximity to the radical right FPÖ: The SPÖ and FPÖ converge in 1990 and 1999 due to their common utilization of a *relief* frame, which contrasts with closer framing between the ÖVP and FPÖ in 1994 (when they share a larger set of restrictive frames, including *relief, assimilation, genuineness*, and *benefit*). Since the watershed in 1999, however, the distance between the SPÖ and FPÖ has continually increased, with the SPÖ giving more weight to frames like *regulation, rights*, and *participation*, while the center-right ÖVP has moved its position toward the framing of the radical right parties, emphasizing *security, assimilation, relief*, and *benefit* more prominently. However, as already found in the case of overall salience and topical focus, the election of 2013 has put an end to some of the framing strategies pursued by parties during the last decade. Although the SPÖ is still slightly farther away from the FPÖ's framing than its center-right counterpart, the gap has narrowed once again. Yet these changes do not appear as distinctly on the day-to-day level of campaigning. Here, both mainstream parties show rather consistent framing compared to the FPÖ throughout the 1990s. The center-left SPÖ shows even more proximity to the FPÖ than the center-right ÖVP – a contrast to the findings on programmatic communication. These patterns are reversed after the 1999 elections as the SPÖ's framing shifts away from that of the radical right parties much more than does the ÖVP's (which conforms more closely to the manifesto data).

Still, the differences in press releases are far less distinct than those in manifestos, which can be ascribed to the specificity of elections. Press releases, being instruments used for short-term communication and rapid-response strategies, are much more sensitive to short-notice developments during a hot election period. In the more recent elections, especially, divergence patterns can be traced to such short-term developments: While the campaign of 2006 was heavily influenced by the exposing of an illegal home care worker in the employ of the family of then-chancellor Wolfgang Schüssel, the 2008 campaign was shaped by the ongoing economic crisis and debates on economic policy. In light of these situational influences, analysis of day-to-day communication via press releases also lends support to the theory that mainstream parties adopt opposing courses on migration and ethnic relations in response to pressure from the radical right, with the center-left distancing itself and the center-right maintaining if not reinforcing the framing of the radical right.

Intra-party consistency between campaign channels

Regarding the positional aspects of party politicization, we are also confronted with questions of intra-party consistency between different campaign channels. In order to shed light on these, once again bisected city block distance measurement is applied in order to evaluate each party's consistency between its programmatic and day-to-day issue positions.

Table 25: Divergence of frames between campaign levels. Individual parties, 1990-2013 (in %)

	Liberal/Left-libertarian		Social democratic	Conservative	Radical right	
	Greens	LIF	SPÖ	ÖVP	BZÖ	FPÖ
1990	30		49	42		24
1994	30	69	36	42		32
1999	71	63	59	56		51
2002	61		40	45		40
2006	40		46	43	34	27
2008	36		44	35	17	48
2013	39		68	49		25
Avg.	44	66.0	49	44	26	35
Std.-dev.	15.8	2.7	10.5	6.1	8.1	9.9

Note: Team Stronach and NEOS in 2013 are not considered, since they did not address migration and ethnic relations on both campaign levels. Scores based on bisected city block distance between 0 (no divergence) and 100 (absolute divergence).

Mann-Whitney-test for difference between mainstream and niche parties: U=82.5, p>.05, r=-.29. Kruskal-Wallis-test for differences between ideological families: H(3)=7.13, p>.05.

Comparing party families in Table 25, the differences discovered only roughly resemble the findings regarding parties' topical preferences. In the average divergence of issue positions between campaign channels, similar patterns among Greens (44), social democrats (49), and conservatives (44) become apparent, while divergence is slightly lower for the radical right parties (FPÖ: 35, BZÖ 26) – which means that in the Austrian case their use of frames is more consistent between programmatic and day-to-day campaigning, though not in a statistically significant sense. Again, there is no evidence whatsoever for a differentiation between mainstream and niche parties, while ideology at least partially seems to explain the differences found. As was already the case for subtopics, the findings show a greater divergence of frames on the part of the liberal/left-libertarian parties than the radical right parties, which more consistently stick to similar positions in both manifestos and press releases. This finding corroborates the conclusion drawn in the previous chapter that, for radical right parties and their agendas, it is easier to stick to a cohesive set of frames throughout a campaign, whereas other parties try to address a greater variety of different perspectives. Ultimately, the finding may also be a result of the different types of party organization: The very centralized nature of populist radical right parties, in contrast to the decentralized organization of the Greens and other left-libertarian parties, may very well be a cause of these differences in frame homogeneity – a thesis that could be the subject of future examination.

6.3.3 Synopsis

Where do Austrian parties stand on migration and ethnic relations? Do they alter their positions over time? And do they form discursive coalitions by approximating the framing strategies of other parties? These questions have been at the center of this section, and the findings are quite substantial: For the niche parties, policy frames follow a static pattern in accordance with their grossly liberal or restrictive tendencies. Austrian niche parties almost universally stick to either restrictive framing (FPÖ, BZÖ) or liberal framing (Greens, LIF) and thereby constitute the cornerstones of the discursive spectrum. Within the range of their overall or orientations, however, niche parties certainly do vary in their choices of policy frames, with frames fluctuating in importance from election to election.

Mainstream parties, on the other hand, behave much more ambiguously, with a more balanced ratio of liberal to restrictive frames and a greater number of frames applied. This is in line with the greater number of subtopics addressed by mainstream parties, but even more so with their inconsistent behavior over time. In what might be the biggest difference between mainstream and niche parties, both SPÖ and ÖVP adjust their framing from election to election, which has two analytical consequences: Firstly, it materializes in remarkable shifts along the liberal-restrictive axis (the SPÖ moving from balanced to liberal, the ÖVP shifting from slightly restrictive to more restrictive and back), and secondly, it leads to varying proximity to the radical right parties (with the SPÖ moving away from and the ÖVP mostly approximating FPÖ/BZÖ framing after the millennium).

Thus what has become apparent already with regard to subtopics is even more substantial with regard to issue positions. While the 1990s were characterized by rather restrictive stances on the parts of the FPÖ, ÖVP, and SPÖ in opposition to uniformly liberal stances taken by the Greens and LIF, the dividing line has been redrawn after the millennium. In the elections of 2002, 2006 and 2008 we see an even more cohesive circle of restrictive actors (consisting of the FPÖ, BZÖ and ÖVP) set against a less cohesive pair of liberal actors (made up of the Greens and SPÖ). The recent election in 2013, however, seems to have brought a slight shift in orientation: While the FPÖ marches on with an ever more restrictive approach, the ÖVP appears to have returned to a more balanced approach (a tendency that already foreshadowed during the preceding legislation period and cristallyzed in the establishment of a State Secretariat for Integration). In the liberal spectrum, the SPÖ is going different ways across campaign channels, i.e. moving back to the center programmatically (approaching its coalition partner, the ÖVP) while becoming more liberal than ever in its day-to-day campaign. The Greens remain one of the most liberal parties on both campaign levels, though they are joined by the newcomers in 2013, the liberal NEOS. The other newcomer, Team Stronach, resembles the ÖVP in its slightly more restrictive stance, while the BZÖ's reorientation of its party profile (including an unexpected depoliticization of migration and ethnic relations) has led to its dropping out of the Austrian parliament.

6.4 Conclusion: Migration and ethnic relations as a structuring conflict

The descriptive sections of this book highlighted different aspects of parties' strategies of electoral politicization of migration and ethnic relations. Based on the theoretical premises, three main strategic options were isolated in an electoral context characterized by selective competition over policy issues: *Issue salience*, i.e. increasing and decreasing salience of an issue in general (6.1), *topical emphasis*, i.e. highlighting some aspects of an issue at the cost of others (6.2), and *policy framing*, i.e. adopting specific frames of interpretation (6.3). On all three dimensions of competition the quantitative analysis of Austrian electoral competition from 1971 to 2013 revealed considerable differences, both between elections as well as between parties.

Section 6.1 demonstrated that the development of electoral competition on migration and ethnic relations is a product of the late 1980s: Unexpectedly, it was the Greens who, in 1986, were the first party to add these questions to their programmatic agenda more visibly. They were joined by the populist radical right FPÖ and the Austrian mainstream parties (SPÖ, ÖVP) in 1990. From 1990 onwards the issues have remained vital aspects of electoral competition on both programmatic and day-to-day campaign levels. Until the mid-1990s the Greens led in politicization on the programmatic level, while in press releases they alternated with the FPÖ in being the most active party. However, since 2002 and the split of the FPÖ and BZÖ, radical right parties have become by far the most active parties, while the Greens have cut back their politicization on both campaign channels. As for the mainstream parties, the data indicates greater involvement in programmatic competition on the part of the ÖVP than the SPÖ, with salience occasionally even exceeding that of niche parties. On the day-to-day campaign level, however, both mainstream parties shy away from stronger participation in the competition over migration and ethnic relations and thus show low salience, with the SPÖ being slightly more active than the ÖVP.

As a consequence of these results, it can be concluded that migration and ethnic relations arrived at the center of the political discourse during the 1990s. For niche parties the issue is an excellent vehicle to attack the established mainstream parties and their traditional campaign issues, and so migration and ethnic relations have become increasingly difficult for mainstream parties to avoid. Still, the SPÖ and ÖVP apply different strategies in dealing with this new area of conflict: The SPÖ tries to limit references to these issues as much as possible, though even during the 1990s, it was already forced occasionally to confront the issues, resulting in low salience levels with sporadic increases. Conversely, the ÖVP more actively competes on the issues, at least programmatically. These mainstream party patterns changed slightly after the turn of the millennium and the formation of a right-bloc government. Both mainstream parties increased their emphasis, at least programmatically; on the day-to-day level, however, these programmatic decisions did not materialize in an equal increase in mainstream party emphasis (unless the situational conditions during an election forced them to do so, as in the 2006 debate on clandestine care workers).

These changes in emphasis become even more comprehensible when linked to the subtopics that are politicized by Austrian parties (6.2). The comparison of parties' emphasis of subtopics reveals an interesting center of the electoral debate: A striking similarity between populist radical right parties (FPÖ, BZÖ), conservatives (ÖVP), and social democrats (SPÖ) contrasts with the left-libertarian and liberal parties (Greens, LIF). While the former put the greatest emphasis on subtopics such as labor and crime & border control, the latter address asylum procedures, societal models, and xenophobia instead. In a nutshell, these findings suggest that populist radical right parties are more successful than left-wing parties in influencing mainstream parties' choice of subtopics. Thus the general increase of emphasis put on migration and ethnic relations by various parties may not be equivalent to a unified debate. Instead, the decision to emphasize them more heavily is linked to a party's choice of subtopics and its potential opponents. As the distribution of Austrian parties' topical preferences shows, the conservative ÖVP competes mostly on subtopics that are similar to the choices of populist radical right parties, while the social democrats seem to be somewhat torn, for they emphasize diverse subtopics very selectively and thus choose ÖVP/FPÖ/BZÖ-claimed subtopics as well as some of the Greens' and LIF's favored subtopics.

Though there is a clear tendency of mainstream parties toward the subtopics emphasized by the radical right, parties do not only alter their emphasis of issues and specific subtopics but also engage in competition over how to interpret these issues and subtopics. By sticking to certain policy frames, parties try to impose their problem definitions and policy recommendations on other parties and the electoral discourse as a whole. Considering these framing strategies of Austrian parties causes the contours of the party spectrum to become even more clear-cut. As section 6.3 showed, the dividing line between restrictive and liberal frames cuts across the ideological spectrum, but takes some time to do so. While niche parties stick to their uniformly restrictive (FPÖ/BZÖ) or liberal (Greens/LIF) frames and only vary the intensity of their competition (with the Greens reducing and the FPÖ intensifying emphasis after the millennium), the mainstream parties shift even their policy stances (with the ÖVP intensifying its previously only slightly restrictive stance while the SPÖ shifts its balanced approach of the 1990s toward a predominantly liberal framing after the millennium). Thus policy framing appears to have even more influence on the changing circumstances of party competition than the previously discussed dimensions of politicization (i.e. issue salience & topical preferences). For this reason the final chapter will attempt to put the pieces of the puzzle together in order to get conclusive answers to the analytical research questions (see Chapter 7).

Migration and ethnic relations as a structuring political conflict

Still, combining the findings, a first conclusion on the relevance of migration and ethnic relations for Austrian party competition can be drawn. In the conceptual chapters, the study initially expected the issues to play an increasingly important role in structuring political conflict within the Austrian party spectrum, which can be assessed by considering the relevance of four criteria: a) considerable salience of these issues in electoral competition, b) permanence of their emphasis, c) the number and proportion of parties competing on these issues, and d) the irreconcilability of the issue positions between relevant parties. Evaluating for all four criteria, the discussion of the preceding sections demonstrated that the indicators confirm the overall notion that migration and ethnic relations have become part of a dominant political conflict structure:

Firstly, the issues have grown steadily and considerably in importance since the late 1980s in contrast to the preceding period of minimal politicization during the 1970s and early 1980s. Secondly, the increases since the 1990s were not isolated events; instead the issues have retained their importance and even witnessed another boost in salience with the establishment of a second populist radical right party in 2005. Thirdly, every relevant party engaged in politicization of these issues sooner or later during the examination period; in other words, migration and ethnic relations have become unavoidable elements of electoral competition. And fourthly, the positional patterns of competition have clearly taken on a conflictive shape perfectly in line with the conclusions of Kriesi et al. (2006), with liberal/left-libertarian parties occupying the liberal end of the positional spectrum, radical right populist parties holding the restrictive end of the spectrum, and mainstream parties fluctuating in between but increasingly following centrifugal tendencies.

Although the patterns diverge in some respects between programmatic and day-to-day campaign communication, they definitely speak the same language with regard to these four indicators: The issues of migration and ethnic relations feature all the characteristics necessary to deem them a major line of conflict that has structured Austrian party competition at the beginning of the 21st century. Following Kriesi et al. (2006), the findings would thus support the argument that migration and ethnic relations have become an integrative part of a broader "cultural dimension" of political conflict that "has become the primary basis on which new parties or transformed established parties seek to mobilize their electorate" (Kriesi et al. 2006: 950). Therefore, not only do the issues separate ideological opponents, but they also articulate the tension between established major parties and emerging or transforming niche parties.

7.   Closing the circle: Drivers of electoral politicization

The previous chapter described the quantitative dispersion in the politicization patterns of Austrian parties in their general issue emphasis, subtopical emphasis and policy framing. On each of these three dimensions, considerable evidence has been gathered demonstrating the conflicting patterns of Austrian electoral competition. It has been shown that the emergence of the issues of migration and ethnic relations in Austria was closely tied to new niche parties, that mainstream parties caught up only later, and that the approaches of the latter diverged, especially after the turn of the millennium.

In order to close the circle of this analysis of the dynamics of electoral politicization, these findings finally need to be connected to the explanatory framework developed in the conceptual chapters. Which driving motives have guided parties' politicization strategies, how are they related to one another, and what further aspects suggest themselves as explanatory factors? This chapter attempts to answer these questions and evaluates the study's hypotheses. Furthermore, it underlines the instructiveness of the Austrian case for the study of party politicization of migration and ethnic relations and draws conclusions that will help to advance the current state of scholarly debate.

7.1   Societal inputs to electoral politicization

Among the most commonly cited reasons for the intensity and direction of political debate are socio-structural patterns of migration and ethnic relations, which constitute opportunities for parties in electoral competition. Section 3.1 enumerated indicators for the patterns of migration and ethnic relations in Austria, such as the net immigration total, the number of foreign residents, and the number of applications for asylum. Since a connection between these indicators and general issue salience is difficult to discern, instead it was assumed that the link between certain issue dimensions and the corresponding empirical indicators, at least, should be apparent. Thus this section associates the salience of two specific issue dimensions, immigration and asylum, with the empirical indicators related to them (see Figure 10).

Figure 10:   **Correlation of socio-structural inputs**
with salience of issue dimensions, 1971-2013

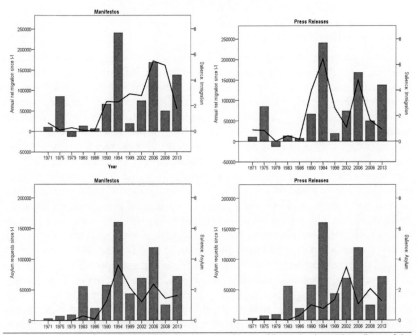

Note: In each diagram, bars denote the given socio-structural input, while graphs denote the salience of the given issue dimension. Scores for 12 elections (1971 to 2013), based on Pearson's product-moment correlation:

	Manifestos	Press releases
- Net migration since t-1 with salience immigration	r=.432	r=.781***
- Asylum requests since t-1 with salience asylum	r=.877***	r=.270

*** p ≤ 0.01, two-tailed test

For asylum requests two estimated values (1994: 160,000, 1999: 43,600) were logged, in order to account for de facto refugees, who escaped to Austria during the 1990s and were not included in official statistics on asylum applications. Following the numbers of Fassmann/Fenzl (2003), it was calculated that Austria received 13,000 Croatians in 1991 and about 85,000 Bosnians since 1992 who sought refuge from the civil wars in their home countries, in addition to about 5,000 refugees from Kosovo who were treated as de facto refugees during the Kosovo War in early 1999.

Net migration

The issue dimension most constitutive of the policy field of migration and ethnic relations is undoubtedly that of *immigration*, which is comprised of references to the permanent or periodical crossing of borders and the political aim of regulating access to certain territories. As previously stated (*H3a*), if socio-structural inputs have a general influence on politicization, then the salience of the issue dimension of immigration should be associated with the socio-structural indicator of net total migration (see Figure 10). Three peak periods of immigration, namely those starting at the end of the 1960s (1969 to 1974), at the end of the 1980s (1989 to 1993), and at the turn of the millennium (2000 to 2005), led to the expectation that the immigration dimension would show the highest salience in elections within these periods.

However, when the salience scores of the immigration dimension are compared between both election campaign channels, several conflicting patterns come to light. During the first peak in immigration starting in the late 1960s there appears to be little corresponding politicization. There are only minor references in both campaign channels in 1971, a pattern that fades even further over the course of the rest of the decade and the 1980s. Despite repeated fluctuations in the net migration, politicization of immigration aspects remains absent. Thus there is hardly any correspondence between empirical indicators and politicization for the first two decades of the examination period. The situation changes dramatically at the end of the 1980s, with immigration figures reaching their highest levels between 1989 and 1993. Unsurprisingly, these changes bring the first substantial increases in electoral references to immigration by Austrian parties on both campaign channels. Thus the election of 1990 marks a watershed in terms of electoral politicization of immigration, as this issue dimension has remained of major importance ever since. Indeed, immigration has become a fixture of both programmatic and, to a somewhat lesser extent, day-to-day electoral discourse, even though the empirical indicators of net migration have fallen since 1993. This demonstrates that the development of the issue dimension has become independent of the actual circumstances surrounding immigration. However, of the two campaign channels, day-to-day campaigning is more closely associated with net migration figures than programmatic communication is. While the new relevance of immigration in manifestos remains stable from 1990 to 2002 until it peaks in 2006 and thus shows no correlation with changes in net migration, the covariance of press releases with net migration is high (except in 2002 and 2013): Salience of immigration increases in 1990 and 1994, decreases in 2002, rises again in 2006, and falls again in 2008. Thus the correlation of day-to-day campaigning (at .781) to actual net migration is much stronger than that of programmatic communication (at .432).

These findings indicate comprehensive changes in the role of immigration in Austrian electoral competition. Once a political issue has become established on the electoral scene, it stays as long as it remains useful to any of the political competitors. This holds especially true in parties' programmatic communication, which is under much tighter control of the parties. Therefore it comes as no surprise that issue salience remains at the same level until 2002, even though actual immigration begins to decrease in the mid-1990s before increasing again from 2002 to 2006 and in 2013. However, it remains to be verified whether this discrepancy between campaign channels holds true for other issue dimensions as well.

Asylum

Including a second issue dimension reveals the difficulties of relating empirical indicators to politicization on an aggregate level. As outlined in chapter 2, Austria's geopolitical situation between East and West made it a first-line destination for refugees during the Cold War period. For more than four decades, Austria was a shelter for refugees from Eastern and Southeastern Europe. As a consequence, Austrian policies on the admission and transfer of refugees became keystones of the country's self-perception and international image after 1955. Thus, while public sentiment in Austria has been ambivalent for a long time about the notion of being an "immigration country", it had less trouble promoting itself as a "refugee country", implying that the country would remain a transit point for refugees moving on to other destinations. Connecting this somewhat positive conception of asylum with unabating numbers of asylum applications, this study suggested a link between the number of asylum requests and the intensity of politicization (*H3b*). Consequently, the asylum dimension was expected to be even more strongly politicized during the 1970s and 1980s than that of immigration; however, this expectation is not borne out.

The impression of being a refugee shelter that was evoked in Austria by the refugee inflows of 1956 and 1968 did not materialize in programmatic appeals regarding asylum in any way in the 1970s, and did so only slightly in press releases. The question of asylum started to gain more relevance among manifestos only in 1983 and among press releases in 1986. In fact, however, substantial politicization of asylum, as of immigration, did not occur until 1990. Since then, while the relevance of asylum has fluctuated from election to election, it has remained considerable. The pattern of emphasis on asylum in the two campaign channels is the inverse to that of the immigration dimension; programmatic salience follows the number of asylum applications much more closely (r=.877) than the salience of day-to-day campaign communication does (r=.270).

As described above, prior to the early 1980s, there is almost no politicization at all on either campaign channel regardless of the levels of socio-structural indicators. The increases in programmatic politicization since 1983, however, coincide with rising numbers of asylum applications. Their rise in the early 1980s generates the first electoral emphasis in 1983, and the next increase in asylum applications after the late 1980s also leads to greater politicization in 1990 in both programmatic and day-to-day campaigning. In light of the great number of "de facto" refugees in the early 1990s, which was excluded from the official statistics on asylum applications, the high programmatic salience in 1994 perfectly follows the predictions based on socio-structural inputs, whereas the salience in press releases drops in 1994 and rises only slightly in 1999, contradicting expectations. After the turn of the millennium, the discrepancy between the campaign channels is accentuated even more clearly. While programmatic salience continues to accord with the number of asylum applications, decreasing in 2002 and 2008 and increasing in 2006, the pattern of day-to-day campaign communication does not correspond at all, seeming even to be inverted. Thus the results for the asylum dimension are diametrically opposed to those for the immigration dimension, raising the question of the actual general importance of socio-structural inputs for politicization.

The contradictory findings in regard to issue dimensions make it impossible to link empirical socio-structural indicators with political parties' campaign strategies. As neither of the two campaign channels shows strong correlation with either one of the issue dimensions, the original hypothesis cannot be verified. Instead, these contradictory results should be used with caution and taken merely as circumstantial evidence for the presumed correlation between socio-structural inputs and their subsequent politicization. The range of this examination is necessarily limited by the indicators available for consideration as well as by the small sample pool of only twelve elections in a single country.

In light of these restrictions, the role of socio-structural inputs should be described in broader terms than hypothesized: Under certain conditions, the growth of socio-structural indicators such as immigration or refugee inflow can stimulate parties to jump on the bandwagon of politicization. However, this simple statement of socio-structural relevance is hardly sufficient to explain why and how political parties have emphasized the question of immigration differently over the past decades, because changes in socio-structural conditions do not consistently or directly correspond to changes in politicization. All in all, there is some evidence that changing societal inputs constitute a framework of opportunity for parties to politicize these issues in electoral debate in that they create urgency and give grounds for parties' activities. However, not only do these stimuli appear to be mediated by a number of other factors, but an issue dimension can also gain a certain independence once it has become established on the political scene. It is then detached from the real-world conditions that gave rise to it, and parties may either politicize it in anticipation of future developments or emphasize it by addressing previous events.

Public opinion

Analysis of the second suggested potential societal factor, i.e. public opinion and voter preferences, reaches a similar verdict. As stated above, due to the lack of available data and useful indicators, the study was limited to making a rather general prediction based on a couple of obvious trends in public opinion. The overall increase in Austrian antipathy toward immigration since the early 1990s, which was interrupted only by a slight decline at the end of 1990s, indicated that parties would be inclined to adopt restrictive positions. While the options for Austrian niche parties arising from changing voter attitudes are rather limited because their voters staunchly support either liberal or restrictive stances, shifts in public opinion were theorized to be of greater importance for the mainstream parties. Indeed, the mainstream parties' restrictive stances during the early 1990s suited the majority opinion amid the Austrian population. The sudden increase in immigration in combination with predominantly adverse public opinion left the mainstream parties little room to maneuver. Moreover, with the strengthening of restrictive attitudes after the millennium, the ÖVP's increasing involvement and emphasis on restrictive stances continued to bear out the conjecture. The SPÖ, however, shifted toward more liberal stances after the turn of the millennium despite the renewed antipathy and restrictiveness toward immigrants on the part of the Austrian public, which runs counter to expectations from a public opinion perspective. Clearly, considerations other than the majority opinion on migration guided the SPÖ's decision to shift its stance. In conclusion, while some of the party behavior observed is in line with public opinion, especially when majority opinion favors a party's ideological position (contrary to the findings of Adams et al. 2004), there are a number of results that demand other explanations, which will be sought by focusing on internal factors of party competition.

7.2 Internal party competition factors

In fact, the core argument of this study underlines the importance of internal party competition factors for the explanation of politicization of migration and ethnic relations. Only by accounting for the opportunities and constraints that come from within the party system can individual party behavior be explained satisfactorily. The next section shall discuss these aspects.

7.2.1 Cleavage structures and party ideologies

Political cleavages and party ideology are integral to structuring party behavior, and their importance as drivers of party politicization has been verified repeatedly. In accordance with this strand of literature, this study assumed that the more strongly an issue is linked to a cleavage owned by a party, the more strongly the issue will be politicized by that party (*H5*). Based on the historical development of the traditional cleavages in the Austrian party system, it determined that the issues of migration and ethnic relations fit into the ideological frameworks of emerging or revived niche parties, which are based on cultural and post-materialistic cleavages, rather than into the frameworks of traditional mainstream parties, which are grounded on traditional cleavages. These ideological factors were expected to influence both the general issue salience and the policy frames emphasized in a party's appeals. In operational terms, radical right parties (FPÖ and BZÖ), Greens and Liberals were expected to be the primary actors (*H5a*), and mainstream parties (SPÖ and ÖVP) to be the least active (*H5b*) in their general emphasis on migration and ethnic relations issues. These expectations were supplemented with predictions of parties' policy positions. In general tendency on a scale from liberal to restrictive, radical right parties (FPÖ and BZÖ) were expected to hold the most restrictive positions (*H6a*) and left-libertarian and liberal parties (Greens and LIF) to hold the most liberal positions

(*H6b*) on migration and ethnic relations issues. Finally, mainstream parties were expected to take more centrist positions, with center-left parties (SPÖ) tending toward liberal positions (*H6c*) and center-right parties (ÖVP) tending toward restrictive positions (*H6d*). The empirical findings produced in this study deliver strong evidence for the importance of party ideology in structuring parties' politicization of migration and ethnic relations, although they cannot explain individual party behavior entirely.

Issue salience

The expectations regarding the salience granted by parties to migration issues were largely confirmed. There is a significant difference between the average issue salience of the traditional mainstream parties (SPÖ and ÖVP) and that of new and revived niche parties (the FPÖ, BZÖ, Greens and LIF) (see Table 14). While in day-to-day campaign communication this difference holds throughout the entire examination period, with the issue salience of every niche party exceeding that of both mainstream parties in every single election, it is not as clear-cut with regard to programmatic politicization. In five out of seven elections, at least one mainstream party shows similar or even greater emphasis than at least one of the niche parties.

Nevertheless, overall the expected predominance of niche parties is broadly confirmed. When it comes to the behavior of individual parties, however, the assumptions based on the ideological perspective do not apply universally (see Figure 7). Firstly, radical right parties are far from being the most active throughout the whole examination period, with a distinct predominance of Green programmatic politicization until 1994 and of the ÖVP's programmatic politicization in 2002, while the Greens and FPÖ alternated in having the highest salience on the day-to-day level. Secondly, the issue emphasis of the Greens noticeably decreases after the turn of the millennium, leading to the salience of the mainstream parties equalling or even surpassing it, at least programmatically. Thirdly, the emphasis of mainstream parties in their programmatic appeals has occasionally increased since the turn of the millennium, nearing or even exceeding that of their niche party opponents.

Thus the influence of ideology and issue ownership on the intensity of a party's electoral politicization is not as direct as expected. Though the concept of selective emphasis as discussed in chapter 2 offers some explanation, it does not yet account for the evident variance in individual parties' electoral campaign strategies, which cannot be explained satisfyingly by cleavage theory or party ideology, since both suggest that patterns should be relatively stable. A change of mainstream parties' strategies and their rising appeals dedicated to attacking niche parties' ownership point to the importance of inter-party competition rather than to the static picture of purely cleavage-based politics. This finding leads to the conjecture discussed in section 7.3.

Issue positions

For explaining the issue positions adopted by parties, cleavage structure and party ideology serve as much more reliable predictors than they do for issue salience. The findings demonstrate that Austrian niche parties maintain stable positions throughout the examination period in perfect accordance with their ideological backgrounds. While the radical right parties are consistently the most restrictive actors, the Greens and LIF are by far the most liberal actors on issues of migration and ethnic relations.

As expected, while the mainstream parties occasionally deviate slightly, they generally stick to centrist stances, balancing restrictive and liberal positions in their campaigns. Except in one election, the center-right ÖVP is always rather restrictive on both campaign channels, a pattern which even intensifies after the watershed of 1999. The most distinct deviations appear in 2006 in its press releases and in 2008 in its manifestos, marking its adaptation to the greater radical right presence after 2005, a process that has come to an end with the 2013 election. On the opposite side of the aisle, the center-left SPÖ's positions are ambivalent throughout the 1990s, fluctuating irregularly in manifestos and being slightly restrictive overall in press releases. With the turn of the millennium, however, it clearly shifts its stances toward liberal framing in both campaign channels (see Figure 9).

These findings show that, overall, ideology is a valuable predictor of the positional strategies of Austrian parties with regard to migration and ethnic relations. This holds especially true for niche parties and to some extent for mainstream parties. However, ideology by itself cannot entirely explain the behavior of the latter over the course of the examination period. Therefore other factors must be sought to account for the variance in the mainstream parties' strategic politicization of migration and ethnic relations.

7.2.2 Party strength, coalition options and cabinet composition

How can the changes in the behavior of political parties be explained? Sections 3.2.2 and 3.2.3 introduced factors internal to the party system and intrinsic to party competition as elements crucial to explaining parties' strategic behavior, distinguishing between two distinct motives that drive parties' strategies: the pursuit of votes vs. securing government participation by prioritizing coalition considerations. Although in practice parties act out of both of these considerations simultaneously, analyzing each of them separately leads to slightly different conjectures regarding parties' actual campaign strategies.

Parties as vote-seekers

Firstly, it was argued that parties adapt their politicization based on previous electoral experiences. The first conjecture was thus that from a purely vote-seeking perspective, Austrian niche parties should continuously increase their politicization as long as this promises to increase their vote shares on election day (*H7*). With both of the main Austrian niche parties growing more or less continuously since 1986 (except for the setback of the FPÖ in the 2002 snap elections and slight losses for the Greens in 2008), they were expected to stick to migration and ethnic relations as core elements of their electoral campaigns and even to increase their emphasis over the course of the examination period. Conversely, mainstream parties were expected to adopt "dismissive" strategies (i.e. depoliticization of the issues forwarded by niche parties) in the first period of niche party success, since the incentive to change their campaign strategies (i.e. loss of votes to the niche parties) was not yet sufficient. Only once these dismissive strategies had failed were mainstream parties expected to engage more strongly with niche party issues (i.e. increase their issue salience and establish their positional stance). With the radical right FPÖ being the niche party exerting the most pressure on both mainstream parties, its ideological neighbor, the ÖVP, was expected to react sooner than the center-left mainstream party, the SPÖ, though both were expected to choose a strategy of "accommodative politicization" toward the radical right (i.e. by increasing salience and approximating the FPÖ's restrictive stance).

An initial indication of the accuracy of these conjectures lies in the salience scores of the niche parties over the course of the examination period. Table 26 compares the vote share of each niche party in every election since 1986 with its issue emphasis on both campaign channels. The evidence shows that niche parties do not invariably adjust their issue salience according to their gains and losses in the previous election. For instance, the Green party increases its issue salience from 1986 through 1994 irrespective of whether this led to success in the previous election (as in 1990) or not (as in 1994). Indeed, in 1999 the party even begins to cut back its issue salience in both campaign channels, despite its success with raising its issue salience in 1994. From 2002 on, the Greens vacillate between slight increases and slight decreases, although they gain more votes in every election except 2008. The decline in the party's emphasis in its manifestos since the 1980s and early 1990s, together with its fairly static emphasis in its press releases, confirms the insufficiency of vote-seeking considerations for explaining its politicization strategy. The case of the FPÖ similarly undermines the conjecture. The party maintains (in its manifestos) and even decreases (in its press releases) its issue salience between 1990 and 1994 despite the fact that its emphasis before helped to increase the party's vote share in the election of 1990. In 2002, again, the party cuts back its issue salience despite achieving a historic victory in 1999 on a strongly anti-immigrant platform. Only in 1999, when it increased its issue salience further following its success with high issue salience in 1994, and from 2006 onwards, after lowering of its issue salience was followed by a collapse of its ratings in 2002, can the party's behavior plausibly be related to its previous electoral experience.

Table 26: **Vote shares and issue salience of niche parties per election, 1986-2013 (in %)**

		1986	1990	1994	1999	2002	2006	2008	2013
Greens	Salience (MF)	6.6	13.1	25.8	10.3	7.9	8.2	6.7	6.5
	Salience (PR)	-	9.1	32.5	8.0	10.3	8.9	7.4	8.1
	Vote share	**4.8**	**4.8**	**7.3**	**7.4**	**9.5**	**11.1**	**10.4**	**12.4**
LIF	Salience (MF)	-	-	5.1	8.2	-	-	-	-
	Salience (PR)	-	-	5.4	9.0	-	-	-	-
	Vote share	-	-	**6.0**	**3.7**	-	-	-	-
BZÖ	Salience (MF)	-	-	-	-	-	15.8	14.0	0.0
	Salience (PR)	-	-	-	-	-	11.2	7.8	0.5
	Vote share	-	-	-	-	-	**4.1**	**10.7**	**3.5**
FPÖ	Salience (MF)	0.0	7.9	7.1	11.7	8.4	27.4	20.9	35.0
	Salience (PR)	0.4	14.1	5.7	9.6	6.7	16.2	9.1	8.8
	Vote share	**9.7**	**16.6**	**22.5**	**26.9**	**10.0**	**11.0**	**17.5**	**20.5**

Note: Salience indicates proportion of relevant words in relation to total number of words in a party's manifesto or all of its press releases for the corresponding election (see Figure 7). (MF = manifesto, PR = press releases).

For mainstream party behavior, purely vote-seeking motivations again prove insufficient to explain the empirical findings (Table 27). While both mainstream parties largely depoliticize the issues during the 1970s and 1980s, both increase their emphasis in 1990 and somewhat alter it in 1994, only to cut back their issue salience in 1999 when pressure from the radical right peaks. Thus there is no evidence for a purely dismissive strategy; instead both parties seem to respond to socio-structural inputs and the increasing politicization of the niche parties. Furthermore, the expected increasing involvement of the center-right ÖVP materializes only in programmatic politicization, in which the ÖVP's salience is generally higher than that of the SPÖ. In their day-to-day campaign communication, however, both parties show equally low issue salience until the late 1990s.[62] These findings illustrate the inconsistent behavior of the mainstream parties during the early period of the party system's transformation, since both of them seem to be in search of an adequate response to the changing competitive environment.

The election of 1999, however, marks a turning point. The mainstream parties reduce their issue salience (the SPÖ more than the ÖVP), only to revise their strategies after the turn of the millennium to emphasize the issues of migration and ethnic relations more noticeably from then on (slightly so in their press releases and more strongly in their manifestos). This seems to accord more closely with vote-seeking expectations. However, it must be qualified by consideration of the direction of mainstream parties' policy positions. While the expectation of increasingly accommodative politicization from the center-right ÖVP is borne out, the center-left SPÖ's behavior is inverted: It shifts toward a strategy of adversarial politicization against radical right positions by putting noticeably more

---

[62] The single exception to this is the SPÖ in 1990.

emphasis on liberal frames (most prominently in its manifestos, but also on the day-to-day campaign channel).

Table 27:   Vote shares, issue salience, and framing tendencies
             of mainstream parties per election, 1986-2013 (in %)

		1986	1990	1994	1999	2002	2006	2008	2013
SPÖ	Salience (MF)	0.9	4.5	5.2	1.5	5.9	9.6	5.6	2.3
	Framing (MF)	*20*	*-1*	*4*	*-5*	*66*	*30*	*42*	*17*
	Salience (PR)	0.8	6.0	2.3	2.5	3.6	5.8	3.0	2.4
	Framing (PR)	*87*	*-21*	*-31*	*-21*	*69*	*13*	*18*	*98*
	Vote share	**43.1**	**42.8**	**34.9**	**33.2**	**36.5**	**35.3**	**29.3**	**26.8**
ÖVP	Salience (MF)	0.0	4.4	8.8	6.8	11.4	6.6	14.8	4.4
	Framing (MF)	-	*-7*	*-29*	*-61*	*15*	*-33*	*-84*	*-36*
	Salience (PR)	0.4	2.2	2.2	1.9	3.5	4.5	3.2	3.7
	Framing (PR)	*100*	*-40*	*-17*	*-17*	*-55*	*-46*	*-65*	*-5*
	Vote share	**41.3**	**32.1**	**27.7**	**26.9**	**42.3**	**34.3**	**26.0**	**24.0**

Note: Salience indicates proportion of relevant words in relation to total number of words in a party's manifesto or all of its press releases for the corresponding election (see Figure 7). Framing indicates the average position of frames in the relevant wordshare on a bipolar scale between +100 (absolutely liberal) and -100 (absolutely restrictive) (see Figure 9). (MF = manifesto), PR = press releases).

In a nutshell, predictions based solely on vote-seeking considerations seem to be of limited utility for explaining Austrian parties' strategies of electoral politicization. Though party strategies seem to follow this rationale in certain periods, most notably that of party system transformation between 1986 and 1994, it cannot account completely for the behavior of any of the four parties relevant throughout the period since 1986. In order to answer the questions that cannot be resolved by the previous conjecture, further explanations must be sought.

The importance of coalition scenarios

Potential coalition options are another of the factors influencing parties' campaign strategies in multi-party contexts, since parties may subordinate policy interests to the goal of inclusion in a governing coalition. This study assumed that mainstream parties will alter their strategies on the issues of migration and ethnic relations only if niche parties manage to successfully politicize those issues. While from a vote-seeking perspective success is defined as an increase in the number and proportion of the votes won by a party, from an office-seeking perspective in multi-party competition the definition focuses instead on a party's coalition potential and its corresponding influence over other parties' coalition considerations. In developing the hypotheses stated in section 3.2.3, it was pointed out that coalition options were quite limited in the period from the mid-1980s to the mid-1990s, as both mainstream parties refused government cooperation with the radical right, while no other minimal winning coalitions were possible. With the center-right ÖVP coming under pressure from the radical right earlier and remaining stuck in its role as a junior partner in the grand coalition, its reorientation toward an accommodative stance vis-à-vis the radical right became an acceptable strategy even from a rational coalition-building perspective. Furthermore, increasing radical right success meant the majority for a potential right-bloc coalition increased as well, constituting a growing threat from the center-left SPÖ's point of view. With the formation of a right-bloc government and the advent of actual bipolarism in Austrian party competition (right government vs. left opposition) the events diverged from expectations assuming purely vote-seeking behavior. In light of increasing bipolarism (with no mediating center party) and its role as the opposition, the center-left SPÖ was expected to adopt a centrifugal strategy of adversarial politicization against the restrictive stances adopted by the right-bloc majority. Conversely the center-right ÖVP was expected to adopt more restrictive stances to meet the demands of its coalition partner, the FPÖ, in one of the FPÖ's core issues (*H8a*). As far as the niche parties are concerned, coalition considerations were expected to primarily influence their emphasis, while their positions were expected to remain constant. If participation in a government coalition is prioritized more highly than maximizing votes, then a less aggressive approach would presumably be the rational strategy in order to become or remain a viable coalition partner. Thus niche parties were expected to depoliticize migration and ethnic relations issues if they were considered to be conflictive issues vis-à-vis a potential coalition partner (*H8b*). This pattern, however, is expected to appear only after a period of increasing success in garnering votes but no success in taking offices. As a result, neither the FPÖ nor the Greens should engage in this behavior earlier than the late 1990s.

Applying these expected coalition considerations finally clarifies the findings that were not adequately explained previously. First of all, the decision of the Greens to cut back their emphasis on migration and ethnic relations after 1999 can be attributed to the party's aim to become a more viable coalition partner for both of the mainstream parties. In fact, in 2002 the first coalition talks with the center-right ÖVP demonstrated the importance of coalition considerations to the Greens. Moreover, the FPÖ's short-lived reduction of issue emphasis in 2002 might be interpreted as a similar attempt to remain a potential coalition partner for its senior partner, the ÖVP.[63] The only circumstance that contradicts this niche party pattern is the BZÖ's decision in 2006 to emphasize restrictive policies as heavily as the FPÖ, despite being a government party. Here, obviously, vote-seeking considerations and the need to sharpen the party's profile prevailed over the need to appear as a viable coalition option.

The role of coalition considerations for mainstream parties is equally unmistakable. The center-left SPÖ's decision to adopt an adversarial politicization strategy in opposition to the radical right can only be understood as rational in light of the nearly bipolar shape of Austrian party competition immediately after the turn

---

[63] After the resignation of the FPÖ's cabinet members, the remaining FPÖ team, under the lead of Herbert Haupt, overtly strove to keep close ties to its coalition partner in order to maintain its strategically valuable place in government (Müller & Fallend 2004: 829).

of the millennium. Until the mid-1990s, pressure from the radical right was considered more of an irritation than a menace, with the FPÖ drawing away votes but remaining a pariah for both mainstream parties. However, the developments of 1999 dramatically changed the conditions for mainstream party politicization of migration and ethnic relations. The formation of an ÖVP/FPÖ government after the election of 1999 turned the numerical pressure of the FPÖ into actual executive power, and thus both mainstream parties became more aware of the "usefulness" of the radical right. After 1999, electoral competition generally became more polarized between the left and right antagonists, which prompted centrifugal behavior from both mainstream parties with regard to migration and ethnic relations issues (among others). Thus expectations are met in regard to both aspects of party behavior, namely salience and policy positions. The increasing issue emphasis of the mainstream parties is a rational reaction to the changing conditions, as are the adaptations of their issue positions. While ÖVP politicization became increasingly restrictive and overlapped ever more with the frames of the radical right parties, the SPÖ's stance shifted toward slightly more liberal frames, putting greater distance between its own and radical-right parties' issue positions on migration and ethnic relations. With the right-bloc government colonizing the restrictive side of the positional spectrum, on which there were three parties clustered from 2005 on, there was simply little to gain for the SPÖ in an accommodative strategy. However, this shift in behavior, despite being quite plausibly explained by the bipolar shape of competition, is additionally linked to another factor that must be highlighted in this conclusion, i.e. ministerial responsibility.

Ministerial responsibility

With the new configuration of inter-party competition after 1999, another major influence on parties' strategic considerations becomes apparent. It is an aspect that has remained somewhat neglected in previous literature: the responsibility for issue-specific governmental departments. The present study confirms that in party-driven democracies, executive responsibility plays a decisive role in parties' electoral strategies. Historically, government responsibility for migration and ethnic relations issues was situated chiefly in two government departments, namely the Ministry of Social Affairs in the earlier period of the 2nd republic and, since the mid-1980s, the Ministry of the Interior (Bauböck/Perchinig 2006: 732). Responsibility for the portfolio lays an "intrinsic duty" upon government parties to forward these issues. For the greater part of the examination period, both government departments were held by social democrats: throughout the 1970s, obviously, under the single-party government of the SPÖ, and thereafter under first an SPÖ/FPÖ coalition and then a grand coalition of SPÖ and ÖVP. Thus, from the perspective of ministerial responsibility the SPÖ had a great incentive to include migration and ethnic relations in its electoral agenda even though the party lacked ideological issue ownership. In fact, these considerations help to explain the isolated increase in issue emphasis in the SPÖ's press releases in 1990 in contrast to its rather dismissive strategy in the other elections between 1986 and 1999. Moreover, these constraints may also account for the more restrictive tendency of SPÖ politicization during the 1990s in comparison to the post-millennial period.

After 1999, with the formation of a right-bloc government and the handing over of the Ministry of the Interior by the SPÖ to the ÖVP, the mainstream parties were given another incentive to revise their strategies on migration and ethnic relations. While the SPÖ was relieved of the necessity for the rather restrictive approach accompanying responsibility for the work of the Ministry of the Interior, the ÖVP now felt exactly that pressure. This change in office responsibility was clearly reflected in shifts in the patterns of mainstream party politicization. While during the 1990s the SPÖ had emphasized migration and ethnic relations selectively and only as long as there was a strong necessity for the government to do so (such as in 1990), its positions had remained ambivalent and somewhat more restrictive than was to be expected based on its ideological background. Relieved of this constraint after 1999, the SPÖ began to address the issues of migration and ethnic relations noticeably more actively in their electoral politicization. As a consequence, the SPÖ increased its overall issue salience on both campaign channels and, more importantly, steadily shifted its positions toward a more liberal framing. Conversely, after 1999 the ÖVP, being in charge of the Ministry of the Interior, highlighted migration and ethnic relations as one of its central campaigning fields. Not only did it retain an ideological incentive stemming from its conservative core values, but now it had acquired an executive responsibility that urged the ÖVP to emphasize the issues more prominently and to shift its positions toward a more restrictive stance. These patterns continued and even intensified after the return of the grand coalition in 2006 since office responsibility remained in the hands of the ÖVP, which in 2008 appointed hardliner ministers (Maria Fekter, Johanna Mikl-Leitner) who were even more restrictive than their predecessors (Liese Prokop, Günther Platter, Ernst Strasser) had been.

Thus, though predictions based on rational models of inter-party competition provide good explanations, they must be complemented by consideration of executive opportunities and constraints arising from ministerial responsibility in order to show the complete picture. This finding contributes to the contemporary literature on party politicization of more than just migration and ethnic relations. It demonstrates the need for stronger integration of party and governmental activities in analyses of party politicization to understand the electoral considerations of government parties in an electoral context.

7.3   The role of the campaign channel: Programmatic vs. day-to-day campaign communication

The final research goal of this study was to discuss party politicization on different campaign channels in order to capture the complexity of electoral campaigning. The distinction between programmatic and day-to-day dimensions of election campaigning raised two basic questions: firstly, how these campaign levels differ in the communicative contexts they offer for political party politicization in general, and secondly, which parties are more successful than others in translating their programmatic appeals into day-to-day communication, and how they manage to build more coherent agendas.

General differences between campaign channels

The empirical findings of this study have demonstrated considerable divergence between programmatic and day-to-day campaign communication on the party system level. Admittedly, as regards overall salience, the differences are slight, with rather similar patterns coming to light (see Table 15). Despite slightly lower salience among press releases and two outliers resulting from exceptional elections (1990 and 2006), the salience patterns of programmatic and day-to-day campaign communication resemble each other on the whole. With regard to the contents of politicization, i.e. the choice of subtopics as well as the nature of frames, however, the descriptive findings show some important differences. The distribution of the general *issue dimensions* (asylum, immigration, integration and diversity) in the party system as a whole is much more balanced in manifestos than it is in press releases. A similar relation becomes apparent in the selection of *subtopics*. Here, too, a much more narrow distribution on the day-to-day campaign basis contrasts with a more balanced distribution of subtopics in programmatic discourse (see Table 21). This evidence offers initial support for the assumption that the nature of the campaign channel determines the way that parties are able to politicize campaign issues. Moreover, programmatic communication is characterized by a greater proportion of generalist subtopics than the day-to-day campaign.

These general references constitute an important element of programmatic communication that is used to generate coherent narratives on issues. Manifestos thus contribute much more to the development of overarching storylines into which particular aspects of the daily debate can be inserted later. Obviously, constructing such storylines is an involved process that takes time and space. In press releases, however, precisely the lack of time and space makes it more difficult to generate coherent storylines with generalist remarks. Thus day-to-day campaign communication is focused instead on putting ideology and policy goals in concrete terms by articulating specific suggestions for political action. Day-to-day campaigning operates much more through the use of statistics, specific example cases, references to actual legislative conditions, and direct responses to other statements from within the debate. Due to this forum-like character of press releases, the debate that develops is more repetitive but also more practical, whereas general appeals are often limited to brief statements.

The patterns of parties' issue positions present a mixed picture. Firstly, the differences in framing are not as distinct as those in subtopics; the campaign channels show similar patterns of heterogeneity in the post-millennial period following a much narrower selection of frames in the pre-millennial period (see Table 25). This development indicates a greater diversification of framing strategies the longer the issues of migration and ethnic relations remain established on the scene of Austrian party competition, and it can be observed in both programmatic and day-to-day campaign communication. Analysis of the direction of policy framing also shows a mixed picture. While in some elections (e.g. 1990, 1994, and 2002) the mean tendency on the liberal-restrictive axis differs considerably between programmatic and day-to-day campaigning communication, in other elections (e.g. 1999, 2006, and 2008) the channels match each other closely. These findings can be traced back to specific circumstances in the corresponding elections, with that of 1999 being shaped by a united front of parties against the FPÖ's xenophobic campaign and those of 2006 and 2008 being heavily influenced by the presence of two radical right parties together with an increasingly restrictive ÖVP. In tendency, however, the day-to-day dimension of campaign communication is slightly more restrictive than parties' programmatic appeals (see Figure 9).

Overall, these isolated indications are evidence for the importance of distinguishing between dissimilar campaign channels in analyzing electoral competition. Different dimensions of election campaigning and their corresponding communication channels result in distinctly different forms of party discourse, and thus these differences need to be accounted for carefully. Not only are parties much more limited in their issue selections in day-to-day communication due to the influence of short-term agenda considerations, they are also more likely to engage in more policy-specific politicization than they do in programmatic communication. Accordingly, the study of election campaigning has to be much more explicit about the way these different campaign levels are conceptually and methodically integrated, in order to be able to draw a more representative picture of election campaign's diverse nature.

Campaign channels and individual party behavior

The second core prediction of the study was that parties would differ in the success with which they translate their programmatic appeals into consistent short-term communication on the day-to-day channel of election campaigns. Based on the discussion in section 2.3, the conjecture was made that niche parties would show more consistent politicization with regard to both subtopics and positions, while mainstream parties were expected to display more inconsistent choices of issues and positions across campaign channels (*H1 & H2*). However, as the evidence provided in sections 6.2 and 6.3 demonstrated, these predictions could not be confirmed.

The distinction between mainstream and niche parties does not account for individual parties' selections of subtopics differing between campaign channels, with mainstream parties and radical right parties showing equivalent patterns of campaign divergence (see Table 21). Only the liberal/left-libertarian parties deviate from the remaining party spectrum in that they show significantly greater divergence of subtopics between campaign channels, which may be traced back mostly to their pluralistic party organization rather than to their niche party status per se.

These results regarding subtopics are echoed in regard to framing. Although parties' framing is slightly more consistent across campaign channels than their choice of subtopics (see Table 25), there is considerable divergence nonetheless. Once more, this inconsistency cannot be explained by the difference between mainstream and niche parties. With liberal/left-libertarian, social democrat, and conservative parties being equally erratic and only populist radical right parties being more consistent in their frame selection, it seems to be ideological and organizational factors more than anything else that account for these differences. The Austrian radical right parties not only are characterized by a centralized, leadership-dominated organization, the nature of their populist appeals in the context of migration and ethnic relations also facilitates the promotion of a coherent set of frames across campaign channels – even though they might vary over time.

Above all, there is no significant difference in the consistency of the salience of mainstream and niche parties. Instead the gap appears to lie between the left and the right, with parties right of center fluctuating more strongly between programmatic and day-to-day campaign communication than parties left of center (see Table 15). Therefore the distinction between mainstream and niche parties not only fails to explain the differences in parties' ability to stick to the same issue dimensions, the same subtopics or the same frames in the debate. It also offers no explanation for the variations in issue emphasis (salience) that parties show between different campaign channels. Thus, although considerable differences between programmatic and day-to-day politicization were found, these differences are linked instead to ideological or organizational characteristics, it appears. However, the conclusions drawn by this study are evidently limited and a number of other factors might come to mind that influence parties' ability to stick to coherent campaign communication but that have not been taken into consideration here. In the following conclusive chapter this and other pending questions for future research shall be summarized.

8. Conclusion: Campaigning in radical right heartland

Migration and ethnic diversity are anything but new in European countries. They are essential characteristics of a geopolitical area that has witnessed countless border transformation processes, refugee flows and cross-national movements, resulting in ethnically diverse societies and nations. However, the recent revival of discourse on cultural and ethnic issues differs from its historic predecessors, such as the nationalist discourse of the 19th century resulting from the collapse of the old imperial order and the emergence of new state entities. In contemporary European democracies, it has been the patterns of migration (whether voluntary or involuntary) and the resulting challenge of integrating ethnic minorities that have instead become the main drivers of a debate that commonly incorporates questions of immigration control, asylum regimes, migrant integration and general references to national identities and ethnic diversity (Buonfino 2004; Triadafilopoulos/Zaslove 2006; Givens 2007).

In this contemporary context, discourse between political parties has played a driving role in the debate, both reflecting and intensifying public contention over issues of migration and ethnic relations. Political parties have become important advocates for the perspectives they represent both on immigration as well as, more generally, on social models, whether of multiculturalism or ethnic homogeneity. This intersection of party politics with migration and ethnic relations thus constitutes an important research area for understanding the dynamics of public contention on these questions. Party politicization plays a key role for several reasons. Above all, it is capable of manipulating the agendas of both the media and the electorate by systematically putting issues up for public debate. In addition, the policy frames that parties adopt in their politicization offer schemes of interpretation that can structure and influence commonly held perceptions and preferences. Furthermore, politicization gives indications of the policies and regulations that will be implemented by the legislature once parties are endowed with the power to govern. Last but not least, party politicization serves the important function in party competition itself of signaling preferences to opponents, and thus it influences parties' expectations in planning electoral campaign strategies (Adams et al. 2005; Benoit/Laver 2006; Triadafilopoulos/Zaslove 2006; Andrews/Money 2009).

Despite this crucial role played by party politics in the political processing of migration and ethnic relations issues, its scholarly examination has remained somewhat one-sided. While much research has been dedicated to anti-immigrant radical right parties and their colonization of the discourse on migration and ethnic relations, less attention has been given to other party types and their politicization of these delicate issues. Only in recent years has the scope of research activity widened as a number of authors began to study the impact of radical right parties' success on the behavior of other party types, especially mainstream parties on the center-right (Eatwell 2000; Downs 2001; Bale 2003; 2005; Boswell/Hough 2008) and more lately also the center-left (Art 2007; Bale et al.

2010). However, most of these studies of the intersection of immigration and party politics have selectively focused on explaining the behavior of a specific party type (i.e. radical right, center-right, or center-left). Only a few exceptions (e.g. Meguid 2008) have attempted a comprehensive comparison of all the relevant parties within a competitive context, integrating a variety of framework conditions and motives into a single coherent model of party politicization.

The purpose of this book

The present study was aimed at filling this lacuna and contributing to the contemporary debate on party behavior vis-à-vis migration and ethnic relations. It suggested an explanatory framework for party politicization, integrating various strands of literature on party motives and party politicization in the context of these issues. While parties were expected to rely on party ideology and issue ownership as the primary basis for their campaign conceptions (Carmines/Stimson 1993; Ansolabehere/Iyengar 1994; Petrocik 1996), vote maximization and coalition considerations were theorized to acquire greater importance as the party system becomes more fragmented and dynamic (Strøm 1990, Müller/Strøm 1999), though mainstream parties were expected to differ from niche parties in that regard (Downs 2001; Bale 2003/2008; Meguid 2008; Green-Pedersen/Odmalm 2008; Bale et al. 2010). Since party competition does not take place in a vacuum but rather is embedded in external socio-structural conditions, the impact of these conditions on the overall patterns of politicization was also considered (Lewis-Beck/Mitchell 1993; Betz 1994; Knigge 1998; Givens 2002; Lahav 2004; Givens/Luedtke 2005; Green-Pedersen/Krogstrup 2008).

The second part of the challenge met by this study was to develop an approach for studying the patterns of politicization of migration and ethnic relations. Building on previous scholarly efforts from a variety of disciplines engaged in discourse analysis and content analysis of the debate on migration and ethnic relations (e.g. Buonfino 2004; Fujiwara 2005; van Gorp 2005; Fröhlich/Rüdiger 2006; Nickels 2007; Vliegenthaart 2007; Green-Pedersen/Krogstrup 2008; Krzyzanowski/Wodak 2009), the present study examined the crucial question of the strategic means political parties employ in practicing issue management. The analysis distinguished between three aspects of politicization: the manipulation of issue salience (Budge/Farlie 1983; Carmines/Stimson 1993; Petrocik 1996), the emphasizing of certain topical aspects at the cost of others (van Dijk 1989/1991; Lynch/Simon 2003; Fröhlich/Rüdiger 2006; Jäger/Maier 2009), and the promotion and legitimization of certain policy preferences (Laver/Hunt 1992; Laver/Garry 2000; Budge et al. 2001; Benoit/Laver 2006; Klingemann et al. 2006). Since studies on party politicization have rarely integrated all of these aspects, this book aimed to contribute to the literature on party politicization of migration and ethnic relations by providing a cohesive study that is able to capture both the diversity of party strategies as well as the changes in those strategies over time. It suggested various strategic options of politicization for different types of parties; while niche parties primarily manipulate issue salience while sticking to their policy positions, mainstream parties amend their positions to either accommodate or oppose their main challengers, depending on their electoral priorities.

To pursue both of these research goals, the electoral arena was deemed the best locus for analysis. As crucial nodes of democratic discourse and the apex of party competition, elections create peaks in the attention paid by the electorate and accordingly bring forth parties' strongest efforts to communicate their profiles and goals in a cohesive manner (Norris 2000; Franck 2003; Kriesi et al. 2009). Since the electoral arena is a highly complex environment in which party campaigns must link short-term and long-term needs, parties craft their messages using a variety of campaign channels, each of which has its own logic and role in the campaign process (Strömbäck 2007; Volkens 2007; Burton 2010; de Vreese 2010). The work at hand took this heterogeneity into account by studying party politicization in two very different campaign channels, namely manifestos and press releases, and investigated the differences in politicization between programmatic and day-to-day communication, including whether some parties were more capable of crafting consistent campaigns than others (Maarek 1995; Blumler et al. 1996).

In order to pursue these research goals in a promising and informative context, the case of Austria was chosen for several reasons. Firstly, Austria's history of cultural diversity, reaching back into the Habsburg era, together with the immigration and asylum inflows resulting from its geopolitical situation, presumably paved the way for party politicization of these issues (Fassmann/Münz 1995). Secondly, the Austrian party system is very party-centric and, like many European post-war democracies, it experienced a shift from a tight party spectrum with high party loyalty and partisanship to a more fragmented system with floating voters and increasingly diverse issues of contention (Plasser/Ulram 2006; Müller 2006). These factors suggested that questions of migration and ethnic relations were more likely to become politicized. Thirdly, the high levels of scepticism amidst the Austrian population regarding the questions of migration and ethnic relations were judged to constitute another stimulus for political controversy, in particular from anti-immigrant parties controversy (Rosenberger/Seeber 2011). Finally and most importantly, the rise of the Freedom Party of Austria (FPÖ) to become Europe's strongest populist radical right party, along with its nationalist appeals, has undoubtedly made Austria a heartland for right-wing populist campaigns on migration and ethnic relations issues and thus a standard example for anti-immigrant party research (Luther 2000; Pelinka 2002). In a nutshell, Austria presents a highly informative case for analyzing and evaluating not only radical right politicization, but electoral party politicization of migration and ethnic relations in general.

The nature of politicization of migration and ethnic relations

Above all, this book contributes to current research on party politicization of migration and ethnic relations by offering valuable insight into how politicization of these issues is shaped and which modes of analysis lead to fruitful results. With regard to the units of analysis and their measurement, the study provides evidence that the precision and practicality of measurement techniques based on word counts offer some advantage over other salience metrics (e.g., those based on quasi-sentences), especially in comparative studies that consider different types of text and periods in time or that focus on multiple regional or language contexts. More importantly, the development of coding schemes for subtopics and policy frames on migration and ethnic relations that was undertaken in this study not only systematized and integrated recent approaches, but also resulted in substantial empirical findings. The distinction between subtopics of migration and ethnic relations corresponding to the different government portfolios accords with the distinctions in political discourse and provides a tool for identifying parties' particular focuses. The inductive extension of deductively derived frames on migration and ethnic relations allowed the present study to track the diversity of issue positions over time and contributed to a field of ongoing research. Thus both the subtopics and frames developed in this study may constitute a solid foundation for future research on migration and ethnic relations.

As the study's findings demonstrate, the distinction between three dimensions of politicization, namely issue salience, subtopics and frames, reveals considerable differences between parties and from election to election, pointing to the independent role of each of these dimensions for party politicization. First and foremost, as salience theory suggests, parties strategically emphasize or deemphasize political issues in order to manipulate the visibility of issues to the electorate and political observers in the media, thus using emphasis as another tool for politicization. However, once a party decides to engage in competition over an issue such as migration and ethnic relations, the choice of its subtopical focus becomes its initial tactical means for competition (and allows it to avoid direct confrontation). Hence a party employs politicization to carve out those aspects of a given policy field in which it possesses a certain reputation of credibility, reproducing the strategy of selective emphasis on another, finer, subtopical level. The gap between the subtopics addressed by the liberal or left-libertarian parties (Greens, LIF) and those emphasized by the radical right parties (FPÖ, BZÖ) is striking in the Austrian case, as is the finding that the mainstream parties (SPÖ, ÖVP) have evidently been influenced more effectively by the radical right, with which they share considerably more overlap. While the radical right and mainstream parties stressed subtopics such as "labor" and "crime & border control" most heavily in their campaigns, the left put more emphasis on "asylum procedures", "societal models" and "xenophobia". Ultimately, beyond these subtopical focuses party politicization is shaped by distinct policy frames, which divide the Austrian party spectrum even more clearly and which open up positional competition. Thus parties differ even more clearly with regard to the policy frames they present on these subtopics. Of course, while the poles of the framing spectrum are covered by niche parties (with the restrictive end belonging to the FPÖ and BZÖ and the liberal end belonging to the Greens and LIF), the mainstream parties present a more balanced set of frames, though they are still subject to change in the course of the examination period, e.g. between the 1990s and the post-millennial period. While the center-left SPÖ moved from a balanced set of frames to a predominantly liberal one including the "rights", "participation" and "solidarity" frames, the center-right ÖVP shifted from a slightly restrictive stance to a more restrictive one most prominently emphasizing the "security" and "relief" frames in the first post-millenial decade.

This demonstrates that, as Green-Pedersen (2007a) mentions, positional competition and selective emphasis are not mutually exclusive but can each characterize parties' politicization strategies at a different level of analysis and, more importantly, in a different period of electoral competition. Each individual party will encounter different strategic opportunities and constraints, allowing it to stick to its strategy of de-/emphasis or requiring it to shift its policy position, though the last option is available primarily to those parties that are not ideologically bound to a particular position. This variety of options available in party politicization makes it imperative to consider the web of opportunities and constraints in which a party finds itself at any particular point in time.

Integrating the drivers behind party politicization strategies

The second contribution of this study was to suggest an explanatory framework capable of predicting which of the strategies of politicization outlined above would be adopted by individual parties, and how those strategies would change over time. The evidence produced by the longitudinal analysis of party politicization in the Austrian electoral arena sheds light on the role that migration and ethnic relations play in parties' strategic considerations in electoral competition. It demonstrates how parties with differing motives adapt their politicization strategies in response to changing conditions.

This study has clearly documented the importance of *party ideology* and *issue ownership* as predictors of party politicization. Politicization strategies depend heavily on parties' ideological roots, particularly in competitive conditions characterized by stability and a narrow party spectrum. This is the main reason why, in the early 1970s, issues of migration and ethnic relations received no electoral emphasis whatsoever from the three Austrian parties competing at the time, despite the guest worker programs and increasing labor migration that characterized the period. Since both mainstream parties, the SPÖ and ÖVP, lacked any ownership of issues such as immigration and asylum, they had little interest in transferring them from the backstage of consociational negotiations to the public

stage of electoral competition. Even the FPÖ refrained from making strong electoral appeals, as its goal of becoming a more acceptable alternative for the electorate obviously prohibited any aggressive campaign on migration and ethnic
relations issues. These circumstances resulted in nearly total depoliticization of
the issues until the mid-1980s, when the party spectrum began to change. From
then on, the issues steadily increased in importance, initially thanks to the presence of new or reformed niche parties aiming to identify winning issues that cut
across the traditional cleavages owned by the established mainstream parties.
Attempting to occupy vacant spots in the political spectrum, niche parties took
fringe positions on these emerging issues that were in line with their ideological
core values. Curiously, the strongest emphasis at first came from the pro-
immigrant side of the spectrum, the Greens, while the anti-immigrant FPÖ did
not reach salience scores characteristic of radical right parties until 1990. This
evidence weighs against two commonly made assumptions. Not only does it
show that the FPÖ was never reducible to a single-issue, anti-immigrant party
(instead, migration and ethnic relations gradually rose on the party's agenda); it
also proves that pro-immigrant party politicization in Austria was not a reaction
to anti-immigrant party success, but rather had already been prominent in its
own right before.

The selective, piecemeal increase in the involvement of the mainstream parties
surpasses the explanations of cleavage theory and issue ownership and points to
the role of issue evolution. With migration and ethnic relations turning into permanent campaign issues for increasingly successful niche parties, mainstream
parties were compelled to abandon their detached behavior. Confronted with
niche parties constantly wooing away their voters, stopping the voter exodus
emerged as a more important, vote-seeking motive for mainstream parties. This
led them to engage more strongly with niche parties' campaign issues in their
politicization. Programmatically at least, both mainstream parties showed increasing emphasis on such issues starting in the mid-1990s, and in the post-
millennial period their salience levels were near those of niche parties, though
they continued to avoid strong engagement in their day-to-day communication.
However, mainstream parties appeared to respond most notably to the pressures
caused by growing radical right, as the comparison of the subtopics emphasized
by each party revealed. A striking similarity among the topic choices of populist
radical right parties, conservatives, and social democrats contrasted with the
subtopics stressed by left-libertarian and liberal parties. In terms of framing
strategies, mainstream parties generally differed from niche parties in their more
balanced selection of frames. After the turn of the millennium, however, both
mainstream parties clearly altered their approaches, as the SPÖ moved from balanced framing to a predominantly liberal set of frames while the ÖVP shifted its
stance to be even more restrictive than before. Thus the ÖVP, in particular, acted
in line with the vote-seeking motive predicted by a number of authors (Eatwell

2000, Downs 2001, Bale 2003/2008) by accommodating the radical right with its politicization, a strategy which it escalated after 2002.

The center-left mainstream (SPÖ) party's strategy conformed to this pattern of radical right accommodation only during the 1990s; after the turn of the millennium it became increasingly liberal and distanced itself even more from the populist radical right parties. This finding contradicts predictions based on a purely vote-seeking motive (Bale et al. 2010) and instead bespeaks another crucial party motive: *coalition considerations*. The increasingly liberal politicization of the SPÖ resulted from the nearly bipolar shape of Austrian party competition after the turn of the millennium as well as from the growing menace of the right's numerical advantage materializing in an actual right-bloc government, ousting the SPÖ from power for the first time since 1970. With the right-bloc government colonizing the restrictive side of the positional spectrum (where they were joined in 2005 by yet a third party), further accommodation of the restrictive spectrum ultimately lost its appeal for the SPÖ, so that the opposite strategy, adversarial politicization against the restrictive approaches of the right bloc coalition, was brought to bear. On the other side of this conflict, the center-right ÖVP itself pursued a coalition friendly approach vis-à-vis its radical right partner by backing a restrictive shift in government policy and, eventually, also adopting a more restrictive electoral approach – which supports the scholarly argument that different party motives are not mutually exclusive and that, at times, they may well result in a similar outcome in politicization. Furthermore, coalition considerations arguably also played a role in the strategies of niche parties, in particular that of the Greens, who lowered the salience of their appeals almost continuously after the millennium in an apparent attempt to present themselves as a more viable coalition option for the two Austrian mainstream parties. This shows that, under certain conditions, parties will indeed sacrifice some of their traditional ownership or vote-maximizing assets in order to increase their chances of gaining executive power.

Finally, speaking of executive power, this study provides evidence for the effect of another factor in party considerations (of mainstream parties in particular) that has been underrated in the literature so far: *ministerial responsibility*. In party-driven democracies, executive responsibility, most notably the distribution of government portfolios, is of vital importance to parties' electoral strategies. For decades the SPÖ's responsibility for the government departments primarily associated with immigration and diversity politics, i.e. the Ministry of Social Affairs and the Ministry of the Interior, shaped its appeals, leading it to raise its politicization in times of actual crisis, such as in 1990, and generally adopt a rather restrictive stance (linked to the policing and security logic of the Ministry of the Interior). Relieved of these responsibilities in 2000, the SPÖ saw incentives and room to adopt alternative strategies of politicization, which materialized in a predominantly liberal framing. Conversely, the center-right ÖVP assumed responsibility for the Ministry of the Interior after the millennium and has since highlighted migration and ethnic relations as central campaign issues in accordance with the policing and security logic associated with this ministry. Thus ministerial considerations encouraged a strategy of greater emphasis and increasingly restrictive framing of migration and ethnic relations. However, the deviation from previous patterns of both mainstream parties in the recent 2013 election campaign, with the ÖVP returning to a more balanced standpoint and the SPÖ drastically cutting the salience of its appeals, may indicate that they have opted for more pragmatic approaches. After establishing a State Secretariat for Integration in 2011, the ÖVP has used the topic of migrant integration to somewhat counterbalance its previously restrictive stances, particularly on asylum. The SPÖ, on the other hand, seems to have depoliticized the issues due to its even more pronounced lack of government responsibility. Whether these strategies will endure or merely constitute a brief interruption remains to be seen.

In a nutshell, these findings demonstrate that only a combination of motivational factors is sufficient to explain the politicization of different party types on a longitudinal basis. Even within the bounds of a single policy field like migration and ethnic relations, analysis of an extended time frame reveals considerable variation in party strategies. A variety of external constraints and elements of the party system reshape the rationales that guide parties' politicization and necessitate that they revise their strategies. Party ideologies and cleavage structures are certainly the most fundamental forces driving party politicization, especially their choices of policy position and issue emphasis. In the long run, however, parties adapt their strategies to changing conditions such as voter migration, changing coalition scenarios, shifts in the balance between government and opposition parties, and the distribution of ministerial responsibilities. For mainstream parties in particular, these environmental factors can bring forth important changes in their politicization, both with respect to emphasis as well as to policy positions, which indicates the comparable importance of vote-seeking and office-seeking motives. Niche parties' politicization, on the other hand, proves to be rather consistent, most notably in regard to issue positions, and systematic changes occur only in the amount of emphasis (i.e. issue salience). Nevertheless, for them, too, coalition considerations become increasingly important the longer they have been established. Another striking finding is the considerable prominence of left-wing politicization, as demonstrated by the important role of the Austrian Greens before the 1990s, when they were the most active party. This strongly suggests that more attention should be paid to the role of left-wing parties in politicizing migration and ethnic relations, since their influence on other parties may be obscured by the widespread and abiding research focus on the role of radical right politicization (the "contagion thesis").

The arena of competition and the channels of politicization

Finally, the study deepens the understanding of the campaign process from a political communication perspective. As the evidence suggests, different campaign channels play different roles in the campaigning process and are used to transmit politicization in considerably different ways. Programmatic politicization is characterized by greater heterogeneity than day-to-day campaign communication, the scope of which is narrowed by the centripetal tendency of public discourse. When parties are constrained by a public agenda from highlighting subtopics as freely as they can when drafting manifestos, subtopics vary much more in programmatic discourse than in day-to-day campaigns, which mostly circulate around a few subtopics that dominate the electoral debate. Another characteristic of manifestos is that, since they are used to construct cohesive narrations and overarching storylines into which the day-to-day debate can be embedded, they often contain broad generalizations. Conversely, press releases are short in length and narrow in scope, putting ideology in concrete terms, articulating specific suggestions for political action, and incorporating statistics, individual example cases, legislative references, and direct responses to opponents. Interestingly, the longer the issues of migration and ethnic relations remain politicized, the more diverse the frames in parties' policy preferences become as parties adapt to the developments in this policy field. Furthermore, the different campaign channels appear to play different roles in parties' engagement with the competition, since mainstream parties in particular seem to prefer to address new issues that are orthogonal to their traditional competences on a programmatic basis rather than in day-to-day communications, as is indicated by the lower salience scores for their press releases throughout the study period. Obviously mainstream parties avoid getting tangled up in day-to-day skirmishes over issues and details from which they have little to gain.

Taken together, these findings evidence the need to differentiate between the campaign channels in analyses of electoral competition, since their differing communicational functions lead to substantially different forms of party discourse. In fact, these general differences between campaign channels are valid for all party types to some extent, as little evidence could be found to support the theory that niche parties are generally more consistent in their politicization than mainstream parties. The only two deviations from the usual pattern that were recorded may instead be attributed to other factors: liberal and left-libertarian parties' divergence from the rest in their subtopic choices being due to their organizational structure, and radical right parties' showing greater consistency in their framing resulting from their populist nature.

Thus, the distinction between electoral communication channels is crucial for our understanding of electoral campaigns. Not only is the selection of issue emphasis subject to different constraints in different channels, but the options for politicizing these issues (in terms of both subtopics and frames) are heavily influenced as well. This should be an important pointer for scholars of party competition to expand the common research focus on programmatic communication, given that manifestos are less sensitive to short-term objectives and to centripetal effects in public and media debate. Thus this book encourages greater consideration of differences between campaign channels in future research on electoral politicization, since day-to-day electoral communication can follow markedly different paths than those outlined in programmatic appeals. In light of the fact that it is primarily the daily media coverage rather than the actual contents of party manifestos that shapes voters' perceptions in pre-election periods, it is vital that these differences in politicization be carefully accounted for.

Limitations and prospects

To conclude, the limitations of this study evidently must be acknowledged as well. First and foremost, these stem from the limited availability of longitudinal data on the socio-structural circumstances of migration and ethnic relations and of the demand-side factors in party competition. The negative and contradictory findings produced by the selective examination afforded by the available data might perhaps be reinforced by more detailed data on voter demands in particular segments of the electorate or by more nuanced socio-structural indicators. Unfortunately, however, longitudinal data of this detail is not available for the Austrian case. Thus wile there are substantive findings regarding the explanatory factors internal to party competition provided by this study, the external dimension of socio-structural and public opinion should be considered more thoroughly in future research, given that data availability is steadily increasing.

Another disregarded dimension that is vital for the understanding of electoral politicization of migration and ethnic relations concerns the role of parties' media coverage environment, or to speak more broadly, of parties' discursive opportunity structures (Marx-Feree 2003; Marx-Feree et al. 2003; Gamson 2004; Koopmans/Olzak 2004). Thus, if the dominant patterns of the media debate, of public discourse and of everyday conversation are leaning into a particular direction, parties might find substantial opportunities and constraints that will influence their strategic considerations in electoral contexts. Although these discursive opportunity structures might largely be a mediator for the effects of public opinion, they nonetheless are worthy to be considered autonomously.

As regards the role of campaign consistency, this study was only able to scratch the surface of a question that apparently depends on a much wider array of factors than just the party's mainstream or niche character. While organizational and ideological patterns have emerged as potential explanations for parties' ability to stick to coherent campaigns, future research should dig much deeper into further factors that are relevant in this process of campaign management. These insights would be highly relevant to gather a deeper understanding of the complex processes that structure the nature of election campaigning.

Finally, and most importantly, the focus on a single country obviously places limitations on the generalizability of the study's results. Not only does the limited number of observations restrict the options of quantitative data analysis, also with regard to country particularities some restrictions apply: While Austrian parties are arguably prototypical examples of party families common in Western democracies, the national context can have many and far-reaching effects on parties' behavior and campaign strategies. Thus a comparative longitudinal study of party documents would be required to corroborate the findings that are discussed in this study. However, the conscious decision to focus on competition in the heartland of the radical right lends considerable substance to the evidence gathered, even outside the national context of the Austrian party system. The central role of a strong radical right presence in structuring competition over migration and ethnic relations, the varying strategies of mainstream parties trying to cope with this pressure and the underrated but nonetheless important role of pro-immigrant parties in these contentious debates are characteristics that resemble those of a great number of European countries. Accordingly, this makes for a systematic study that not only furthers understanding of the development of the Austrian case in particular, but contributes to the advancement of transnational approaches for the study of politicization on migration and ethnic relations, a research area that will certainly retain its importance in years to come.

References

(APSA), American Political Science Association (1950): Toward a more responsible Two-party system. A report of the Committee on Political Parties. In: *American Political Science Review*, Vol. 44, Nr. 3, Supplement.

Adams, James (2001): A Theory of Spatial Competition with Biased Voters: Party Policies Viewed Temporally and Comparatively. In: *British Journal of Political Science*, Vol. 31, Nr. 1, pp. 121-158.

Adams, James (2012): Causes and Electoral Consequences of Party Policy Shifts in Multiparty Elections: Theoretical Results and Empirical Evidence. In: *Annual Review of Political Science*, Vol. 15, pp. 401-419.

Adams, James/Merril, Samuel, III (1999): Modeling Party Strategies and Policy Representation in Multiparty Elections: Why Are Strategies so Extreme? In: *American Journal of Political Science*, Vol. 43, Nr. 3, pp. 765-791.

Adams, James/Clark, Michael/Ezrow, Lawrence/Glasgow, Garrett (2004): Understanding Change and Stability in Party Ideologies: Do Parties Respond to Public Opinion or to Past Election Results? In: *British Journal of Political Science*, Vol. 34, Nr. 4, pp. 589-610.

Adams, James /Clark, Michael/Ezrow, Lawrence/Glasgow, Garrett (2006): Are Niche Parties Fundamentally Different from Mainstream Parties? The Causes and the Electoral Consequences of Western European Parties' Policy Shifts. In: *American Journal of Political Science*, Vol. 50, Nr. 3, pp. 513-529.

Aldrich, John A./Griffin, John D. (2003): The presidency and the campaign: Creating voter priorities in the 2000 election. In: Nelson, M. (Ed.), *The presidency and the political system*. Washington, DC: CQ Press, pp. 239-256.

Alonso, Sonja/Claro da Fonseca, Saro (2011): Immigration, left and right. In: *Party Politics, Online first, May 2011.*

Andrews, Josephine T./Money, Jeannette (2009): The Spatial Structure of Party Competition: Party Dispersion within a Finite Policy Space. In: *British Journal of Political Science*, Vol. 39, Nr. 4, pp. 805-824.

Ansolabehere, Stephen/Iyengar, Shanto (1994): Riding the Wave and Claiming Ownership Over Issues: The Joint Effects of Advertising and News Coverage in Campaigns. In: *The Public Opinion Quarterly*, Vol. 58, Nr. 3, pp. 335-357.

Antalovsky, Eugen/Wolffhardt, Alexander (2002): Migration und Integration. Final report of the research project „Migration und Integration" of the Europaforum Wien. Municial department 18, Vienna

Arceneaux, Kevin (2005): Do Campaigns Help Voters Learn? A Cross-National Analysis. In: *British Journal of Political Science*, Vol. 36, Nr. 1, pp. 159-173.

Art, David (2007): Reacting to the Radical Right: Lessons from Germany and Austria. In: *Party Politics*, Vol. 13, pp. 331-349.

Arzheimer, Kai/Carter, Elisabeth (2006): Political Opportunity Structures and Right-Wing Extremist Party Success. In: *European Journal of Political Research*, Vol. 45, Nr. 3, pp. 419-443.

Balabanova, Ekaterina/Balch, Alex (2010): Sending and receiving: The ethical framing of intra-EU migration in the European press. In: *European Journal of Communication*, Vol. 25, Nr. 4, pp. 382-397.

Bale, Tim (2003): Cinderella and her ugly sisters: the mainstream and extreme right in Europe's bipolarising party systems. In: *West European Politics*, Vol. 26, Nr. 3, pp. 67-90.

Bale, Tim (2008a): Turning round the telescope. Centre-right parties and immigration and integration policy in Europe. In: *Journal of European Policy*, Vol. 15, Nr. 3, pp. 315-330.

Bale, Tim (2008b): Politics matters: a conclusion. In: *Journal of European Public Policy*, Vol. 15, Nr. 3, pp. 453-464.

Bale, Tim/Green-Pedersen, Christoffer/Krouwel, André/Luther, Kurt R./Sitter, Nick (2010): If You Can't Beat Them, Join Them? Explaining Social Democratic Responses to the Challenge from the Populist Radical Right in Western Europe. In: *Political Studies*, Vol. 58, Nr. 3, pp. 410-426.

Bara, Judith/Weale, Albert (Eds.) (2006): *Democratic Politics and Party Competition*, Routledge, New York.

Bauböck, Rainer (1996): »Nach Rasse und Sprache verschieden«. Migrationspolitik in Österreich von der Monarchie bis heute, in *Reihe Politikwissenschaft*, edited by Studien, Institut für Höhere, Wien.

Bauböck, Rainer/Perchinig, Bernhard (2006): Migrations- und Integrationspolitik. In: Dachs, Herbert/Gerlich, Peter/Gottweis, Herbert/Kramer, Helmut/Lauber, Volkmar/Müller, Wolfgang Claudius/Tálos, Emmerich (Eds.): *Politik in Österreich*. Vienna: Manz, pp. 726-742.

Behnke, Joachim (2005): Lassen sich Signifikanztests auf Vollerhebungen anwenden? Einige essayistische Bemerkungen. In: *Politische Vierteljahresschrift*, Vol. 46, Nr. 1, pp. O1-O15.

Behr, Royl L./Iyengar, Shanto (1985): Television News, Real-World Cues, and Changes in the Public Agenda. In: *The Public Opinion Quarterly*, Vol. 49, Nr. 1, pp. 38-57.

Bell, Daniel (1973): The Coming of Post-Industrial Society. A Venture in Social Forecasting. New York, NY: Basic Books.

Benford, Robert D. (1993): Frame Disputes within the Nuclear Disarmament Movement. In: *Social Forces*, Vol. 71, Nr. 3, pp. 677-701.

Benford, Robert. D./Snow, David A. (1988): Ideology, Frame Resonance, and Participant Mobilization. In: *International Social Movement Research*, Vol. 1, pp. 197-217.

Benford, Robert D./Snow, David A. (1992): Master Frames and Cycles of Protest. In: Morris, Aldon D./McClurg Mueller, Carol (Eds.): *Frontiers in Social Movement Theory*. New York, NY: Vail-Ballou Press, pp. 133-155.

Benford, Robert D./Snow, David A. (2000): Framing Processes and Social Movements: An Overview and Assessment. In: *Annual Review of Sociology*, Vol. 26, pp. 11-39.

Benoit, Kenneth/Laver, Michael (2006): *Party Policy in Modern Democracies*. London (u.a.): Routledge.

Benoit, Kenneth/Laver, Michael (2007): Estimating party policy positions: Comparing expert surveys and hand-coded content analysis. In: *Electoral Studies*, Vol. 26, Nr. 1, pp. 90-107.

Berk, Richard A./Western, Bruce/Weiss, Robert E. (1995): Statistical Inference for Apparent Populations. In: *Sociological Methodology*, Vol. 25, pp. 421-458.

Berkhout, Jost/Sudulich, Laura (2011): Codebook for Political Claims Analysis. *SOM Working Papers: 2011-02*. Retrieved from: http://www.som-project.eu/ [accessed 16th November 2012].

Betz, Hans-Georg (1993): The New Politics of Resentment: Radical Right-Wing Populist Parties in Western Europe. In: *Comparative Politics*, Vol. 25, Nr. 4, pp. 413-427.

Betz, Hans-Georg (1994): *Radical right-wing populism in Western Europe*. Basingstoke (u.a.): Macmillan.

Bigo, Didier (2002): Security and Immigration: Toward a Critique of the Governmentality of Unease. In: *Alternatives: Global, Local, Political*, Vol. 27, Nr. 1, pp. 63-92.

Bijl, Rob/Verweij, Arien (2012): Measuring and monitoring immigrant integration in Europe: facts and views. In: Bijl, Rob/Verweij, Arien (Eds.): *Measuring and monitoring immigrant integration in Europe. Integration policies and monitoring efforts in 17 European countries*. The Hague: Netherlands Institute for Social Research, pp. 5-42.

Blondel, Jean (1968): Party Systems and Patterns of Government in Western Democracies. In: *Canadian Journal of Political Science* Vol. 1, Nr. 2, pp. 180-203.

Blumler, Jay G./Kavanagh, Dennis/Nossiter, T. J. (1996): Modern communication versus traditional politics in Britain. In: Swanson, David L./Mancini, Paolo (Eds.): *Politics, Media and Modern Democracy*. Westport (CT): Praeger, pp. 49-72

Bonfadelli, Heinz/Bucher, Priska/Piga, Andrea/Signer, Sara/Friedmann, Reto/Weyand, Jan/Vasella, Lucia (2008): Migration, Medien und Integration. Der Integrationsbeitrag des öffentlich-rechtlichen, kommerziellen und komplementären Rundfunks in der Schweiz. University of Zurich, Zurich. Retrieved from: http://www.klippklang.ch/bisher/forschung/pdfs/Schlussbericht _BAKOM.pdf [accessed 3rd December 2011].

Boomgaarden, Hajo G./Vliegenthart, Rens (2007): Explaining the rise of anti-immigrant parties: The role of news media content. In: *Electoral Studies*, Vol. 26, pp. 404-417.

Borkert, Maren/Penninx, Rinus (2011): Policymaking in the field of migration and integration in Europe: An introduction. In: Zincone, Giovana/Borkert, Maren/Penninx, Rinus (Eds.): *Migration Policymaking in Europe. The Dy-

namics of Actors and Contexts in Past and Present. Amsterdam: University Press, pp. 7-17.

Bortz, Jürgen/Schuster, Christof (2010): *Statistik für Human- und Sozialwissenschaftler*. 7th edition, Wiesbaden: VS Verlag.

Boswell, Christina/Hough, Dan (2008): Politicizing migration: opportunity or liability for the centre-right in Germany? In: *Journal of European Public Policy*, Vol. 15, Nr. 3, pp. 331-348.

Brandenburg, Heinz (2006): Party Strategy and Media Bias: A Quantitative Analysis of the 2005 UK Election Campaign. In: *Journal of Elections, Public Opinion & Parties*, Vol. 16, Nr. 2, pp. 157-178.

Broscheid, Andreas (2009): Bayesianische Ansätze zur Analyse kleiner Fallzahlen. In: Kriwy, Peter/Gross, Christiane (Eds.) *Klein aber fein! Quantitative empirische Sozialforschung mit kleinen Fallzahlen*. Wiesbaden: VS Verlag, pp.43-64.

Broscheid, Andreas/Gschwend, Thomas (2003): Augäpfel, Murmeltiere und Bayes: Zur Auswertung stochastischer Daten aus Vollerhebungen. Max Planck Institute for the Study of Societies, working paper No. 03/7. Retrieved from: http://hdl.handle.net/10419/44278 [accessed 21st October 2011].

Broscheid, Andreas/Gschwend, Thomas (2005): Zur statistischen Analyse von Vollerhebungen. In: *Politische Vierteljahresschrift*, Vol. 46, Nr. 1, pp. O16-O26.

Budge, Ian (1987): The Internal Analysis of Election Programmes. In: Budge, Ian/Robertson, David/Hearl, Derek (Eds.): *Ideology, Strategy and Party Change: Spatial Analysis of Post-War Election Programmes in 19 Democracies*. New York, NY: Cambridge University Press, pp. 15-38.

Budge, Ian (1994): A new Spatial Theory of Party Competition: Uncertainty, Ideology and Policy Equilibria Viewed Comparatively and Temporally. In: *British Journal of Political Science*, Vol. 24, Nr. 4, pp. 443-467.

Budge, Ian (2006): Identifying dimensions and locating parties: Methodological and conceptual problems. In: Katz, Richard S./Crotty, William J. (Eds.): *Handbook of Party Politics*. London, Thousand Oaks, New Delhi: Sage, pp. 422-433.

Budge, Ian/Farlie, Dennis J. (1977): *Voting and Party Competition*. London: Wiley.

Budge, Ian/Farlie, Dennis J. (1983): Party Competition – Selective Emphasis or Direct Confrontation? An Alternative View with Data. In: Daalder, Hans/Mair, Peter (Eds.): *Western European Party Systems. Continuity and Change*. London: Sage, pp. 267-306.

Budge, Ian/Laver, Michael (1986): Office Seeking and Policy Pursuit in Coalition Theory. In: *Legislative Studies Quarterly*, Vol. 11, Nr. 4, pp. 485-506.

Budge, Ian/Klingemann, Hans-Dieter/Volkens, Andrea/Bara, Judith/Tanenbaum, Eric (Eds.) (2001): *Mapping policy preferences. Estimates for parties, electors, and governments; 1945-1998*, 1. publ. ed., X, 274 S. pp., Oxford University Press, Oxford.

Buonfino, Alessandra (2004): Between unity and plurality: the politicization and securitization of the discourse of immigration in Europe. In: *New Political Science*, Vol. 26, Nr. 1, pp. 23-49.

Burke, Edmund (1899): Thoughts on the cause of the present discontents, in *The Works of the Right Honourable Edmund Burke*, edited, pp. 433-537, J.C. Nimmo, London.

Burton, Michael J./Shea, Daniel M. (2010): Campaign Craft. The Strategies, tactics, and art of political campaign management. Westport, Conn. (u.a.): Praeger.

Butschek, Felix (1992): Der österreichische Arbeitsmarkt - von der Industrialisierung bis zur Gegenwart. Stuttgart: Fischer.

Caramani, Daniele (2007): Party Systems. In: Caramani, Daniele (Ed.), *Comparative Politics*. Oxford: Oxford University Press, pp. 318-347.

Carmines, Edward G./Stimson, James A. (1986): On the Structure and Sequence of Issue Evolution. In: *The American Political Science Review*, Vol. 80, Nr. 3, pp. 901-920.

Carmines, Edward G./Stimson, James A. (1989): *Issue Evolution: Race and the Transformation of American Politics*. Princeton, NJ: Princeton University Press.

Carmines, Edward G./Stimson, James A. (1993): On the evolution of Political Issues. In: Riker, William H. (Ed.), *Agenda Formation*. Ann Arbor: University of Michigan Press, pp. 151-168.

Carmines, Edward G./Wagner, Michael W. (2006): Political issues and Party alignments: Assessing the Issue Evolution Perspective. In: *Annual Review of Political Science*, Vol. 9, pp. 67-81.

Carsey, Thomas M./Jackson, Robert A./Stewart, Melissa/Nelson, James P. (2011): Strategic Candidates, Campaign Dynamics, and Campaign Advertising in Gubernatorial Races. In: *State Politics & Policy Quarterly*, Vol. 11, Nr. 3, pp. 269-298.

Clarke, Harold D./Stewart, Marianne C. (1998): The decline of parties in the minds of citizens. In: *Annual Review of Political Science*, Vol. 1, pp. 357-378.

Converse, Philip E. (1975): Public Opinion and Voting Behavior. In: Greenstein, Fred I./Polsby, Nelson W. (Eds.): *Handbook of Political Science*. Reading, MA: Addison, pp. 75-169.

Crotty, William (2006): Party origins and evolution in the United States. In: Katz, Richard S./Crotty, William (Eds.): *Handbook of Party Politics*. London, Thousand Oaks, New Delhi: SAGE, pp. 25-33.

Dalton, Russell J. (1985): Political Parties and Political Representation. Party Supporters and Party Elites in Nine Nations. In: *Comparative Political Studies*, Vol. 18, pp. 267-299.

Dalton, Russell J./Flanagan, Scott/Alt, James E./Beck, Paul Allen (Eds.) (1984): *Electoral change in advanced industrial democracies. Realignment or dealignment?*, Princeton University Press, Princeton, NJ.

D'Angelo, Paul (2002): News Framing as a Multiparadigmatic Research Program: A Response to Entman. In: *Journal of Communication*, Vol. 52, Nr. 4, pp. 870-888.

Daviter, Falk (2007): Policy Framing in the European Union. In: *Journal of European Public Policy*, Vol. 14, Nr. 4, pp. 654-666.

Davy, Ulrike/Çinar, Dilek (2001): Österreich. In: Davy, Ulrike (Ed.), *Die Integration von Einwanderern. Rechtliche Regelungen im europäischen Vergleich*. Frankfurt: Campus, pp. 567-708.

de Lange, Sarah (2007): A New Winning Formula?: The Programmatic Appeal of the Radical Right. In: *Party Politics*, Vol. 13, Nr. 4, pp. 411-435.

de Lange, Sarah L. (2012): New Alliances: Why Mainstream Parties Govern with Radical Right-Wing Populist Parties. In: *Political Studies*, Vol. 60, Nr. 4, pp. 899-918.

de Vreese, Claes H. (2005): News framing: Theory and typology. In: *Information Design Journal + Document Design*, Vol. 13, Nr. 1, pp. 48-59.

de Vreese, Claes (2010): Campaign Communication and the Media. In: LeDuc, Lawrence/Niemi, Richard G./Norris, Pippa (Eds.): *Comparing Democracies. Elections and Voting in the 21st century*. Los Angeles: SAGE, pp. 118-140.

de Vries, Catherine E./Hobolt, Sara B. (2012): When dimensions collide: The electoral success of issue entrepreneurs. In: *European Union Politics*, Vol. 13, Nr. 2, pp. 246-268.

de Wilde, Pieter/Zürn, Michael (2012): Can the Politicization of European Integration be Reversed? In: *Journal of Common Market Studies*, Vol. 50, Nr. S1, pp. 137-153.

Dearing, James W./Rogers, Everett M. (1996): *Agenda-setting*. Thousand Oaks, CA: Sage.

Dolezal, Martin (2005): Globalisierung und die Transformation des Parteienwettbewerbs in Österreich. Eine Analyse der Angebotsseite. In: *Österreichische Zeitschrift für Politikwissenschaft*, Vol. 34, Nr. 2, pp. 163-176.

Donati, Paolo A. (2001): Die Rahmenanalyse politischer Diskurse. In: Keller, Rainer/Hirseland, Andreas/Schneider, Werner/Viehöver, Willy (Eds.): *Handbuch Sozialwissenschaftliche Diskursanalyse*. Opladen: Leske+Budrich, pp. 145-175.

Downs, Anthony (1957): *An economic theory of democracy*. New York, NY: Harper & Row.

Downs, William M. (2001): Pariahs in their midst: Belgian and Norwegian parties react to extremist threats. In: *West European Politics*, Vol. 24, Nr. 3, pp. 23-42.

Drummond, Andrew J. (2006): Electoral Volatility and Party Decline in Western Democracies: 1970–1995. In: *Political Studies*, Vol. 54, Nr. 3, pp. 628-647.

Duncan, Fraser/van Hecke, Steven (2008): Immigration and the transnational European centre-right: a common programmatic response? In: *Journal of European Public Policy*, Vol. 15, Nr. 3, pp. 431-451.

Duverger, Maurice (1954): Political Parties. Their organization and activity in the modern state. London: Methuen.

Eatwell, Roger (2000): The Rebirth of the 'Extreme Right' in Western Europe? In: *Parliamentary Affairs*, Vol. 53, pp. 407-425.

Enelow, James M./Hinich, Melvin J. (1984): *The spatial theory of voting. An introduction*. Cambridge [u.a.]: Cambridge Univ. Press.

Entman, Robert M. (1993): Framing: Toward Clarification of a Fractured Paradigm. In: *Journal of Communication*, Vol. 43, Nr. 4, pp. 51-58.

Epstein, Lee/Segal, Jeffrey A. (2000): Measuring Issue Salience. In: *American Journal of Political Science*, Vol. 44, Nr. 1, pp. 66-83.

Esser, Frank (2000): Massenmedien und Fremdenfeindlichkeit im Ländervergleich. In: Schatz, Heribert/Nieland, Jörg-Uwe (Eds.): *Migranten und Medien. Neue Herausforderungen an die Integrationsfunktion von Presse und Rundfunk*. Wiesbaden: Westdeutscher Verlag, pp. 82-105.

(EUMC), European Monitoring Centre on Racism and Xenophobia (2005): Majorities' Attitudes towards minorities: Key findings from the Eurobarometer and the European Social Survey. Retrieved from: http://www.mediadiversity.org [accessed 16th September 2012].

Ezrow, Lawrence (2010): Linking Citizens and Parties. How Electoral Systems Matter for Electoral Representation. Oxford: Oxford University Press.

Farrell, David. M (1996): Campaign strategies and tactics. In: LeDuc, Lawrence/Niemi, Richard G./Norris, Pippa (Eds.): *Comparing Democracies: Elections and Voting in Global Perspective*. Thousand Oaks (CA): SAGE, pp. 160-183.

Farrell, David M./Webb, Paul (2000): Political Parties as Campaign Organizations. In: Dalton, Russell J./Wattenberg, Martin P. (Eds.): *Parties without Partisans. Political Chance in Advanced Industrial Democracies*. Oxford: Oxford University Press, pp. 102-128.

Fassmann, Heinz/Münz, Rainer (1995): *Einwanderungsland Österreich*. Vienna: Jugend & Volk.

Favell, Adrian/Hansen, Randall (2002): Markets against politics: Migration, EU enlargement and the idea of Europe. In: *Journal of Ethnic and Migration Studies*, Vol. 28, Nr. 4, pp. 581-601.

Filzmaier, Peter/Hofinger, Christoph/Perlot, Flooh/Ptaszyñska, Aleksandra (2009): Die Nationalratswahl 2008: Ergebnisse und Wahlverhalten. In: Filzmaier, Peter/Plaikner, Peter/Duffek, Karl A. (Eds.): *Stichwort Wählen*. Cologne, Weimar: Böhlau, pp. 13-40.

Franck, Georg (2003): *Ökonomie der Aufmerksamkeit. Ein Entwurf*. Munich, Vienna: Hanser.

Freeman, Gary P. (1995): Modes of Immigration Politics in Liberal Democratic States. In: *International Migration Review*, Vol. 29, Nr. 4, pp. 881-902.

Friesl, Christian/Polak, Regina/Hamachers-Zuba, Ursula (2009): *Die Österreicher innen. Wertewandel 1990-2008*. Wien: Czernin.

Fröhlich, Romy/Rüdiger, Burkart (2006): Framing political public relations: Measuring success of political communication strategies in Germany. In: *Public Relations Review*, Vol. 32, Nr. 1, pp. 18-25.

Fröhlich-Steffen, Susanne (2004): Die Identitätspolitik der FPÖ: Vom Deutschnationalismus zum Österreich-Patriotismus. In: *Österreichische Zeitschrift für Politikwissenschaft*, Vol. 33, Nr. 3, pp. 281-295.

Früh, Werner (2007): *Inhaltsanalyse*. Konstanz: UVK.

Fujiwara, Lynn H. (2005): Immigrant Rights Are Human Rights: The Reframing of Immigrant Entitlement and Welfare. In: *Social Problems*, Vol. 52, Nr. 1, pp. 79-101.

Gabel, Matthew J./Huber, John D. (2000): Putting Parties in Their Place: Inferring Party Left-Right Ideological Positions from Party Manifestos Data. In: *American Journal of Political Science*, Vol. 44, Nr. 1, pp. 94-103.

Gächter, August (2000): Austria: Protecting Indigenous Workers from Immigrants. In: Penninx, Rinus/Roosblad, Judith (Eds.): *Trade Unions, Immigration, and Immigrants in Europe, 1960-1993. A Comparative Study of the Attitudes and Actions of Trade Unions in Seven West European Countries*. New York, NY: Berghahn Books, pp. 65-89.

Gamson, William A. (1989): News as Framing: Comments on Graber. In: *The American Behavioral Scientist*, Vol. 33, Nr. 2, pp. 157-161.

Gamson, William A. (1992): The social psychology of collective action. In: Morris, Aldon D./Mc Clurg Mueller, Carol (Eds.): *Frontiers in Social Movement Theory*. New Haven, CT: Yale University Press, pp. 53-76.

Gamson, William A. (2004): Bystanders, Public Opinion, and the Media. In: Snow, David A./Soule, Sarah A./Kriesi, Hanspeter (Eds.): *The Blackwell companion to social movements*. Malden, MA: Blackwell, pp. 242-261.

Gamson, William A./Modigliani, Andre (1987): The changing culture of affirmative action. In: Braungart, Richard G./Braungart, Margaret M. (Eds.): *Research in Political Sociology*. Greenwich, CT: JAI Press, pp. 137-177.

Gamson, William A./Modigliani, Andre (1989): Media Discourse and Public Opinion on Nuclear Power: A Constructionist Approach. In: *American Journal of Sociology*, Vol. 95, Nr. 1, pp. 1-37.

Gans, Herbert J. (1980): Deciding What's News. A Study of CBS Evening News, NBC Nightly News, Newsweek and Time. New York, NY: Vintage.

Garner, Steve (2005): The Racialisation of Mainstream Politics. In: *Ethical Perspectives*, Vol. 12, Nr. 2, pp. 123-140.

Gehmacher, Ernst/Birk, Franz/Ogris, Günther (1988): 1986 - The Year of Election Surprises. In: Pelinka, Anton/Plasser, Fritz (Eds.): *The Austrian Party-System*. Boulder, CO: Westview Press, pp. 93-116.

George, Alexander L./Bennet, Andrew (2005): *Case studies and theory development in the social sciences*. Cambridge, MA: MIT Press.

Gerring, John (2004): What Is a Case Study and What Is It Good for? In: *American Political Science Review*, Vol. 98, Nr. 2, pp. 341-354.

Gibson, Rachel K./Römmele, Andrea (2001): Changing Campaign Communications. A Party-Centered Theory of Professionalized Campaigning. In: *The Harvard International Journal of Press/Politics*, Vol. 6, Nr. 4, pp. 31-43.

Givens, Terri (2002): The Role of Socio-Economic Factors in the Success of Extreme Right Parties. In: Schain, Martin/Zolberg, Aristide/Hossay, Patrick (Eds.): *Shadows over Europe: The Development and Impact of the Extreme Right in Western Europe*. New York, NY: Palgrave MacMillan, pp. 137-158.

Givens, Terri (2007): Immigrant Integration in Europe: Empirical Research. In: *Annual Review of Political Science*, Vol. 10, pp. 67-83.

Givens, Terri/Luedtke, Adam (2005): European Immigration Policies in Comparative Perspective: Issue Salience, Partisanship and Immigrant Rights. In: *Comparative European Politics*, Vol. 3, Nr. 1, pp. 1-22.

Goffmann, Erving (1977): Rahmen-Analyse. Ein Versuch über die Organisation von Alltagserfahrungen. Frankfurt: Suhrkamp.

Golder, Matt (2003): Explaining Variation In The Success Of Extreme Right Parties In Western Europe. In: *Comparative Political Studies*, Vol. 36, Nr. 4, pp. 432-466.

Gottschlich, Maximilian (1989): Regierungserklärungen als Modellfälle politischer Kommunikation. In: Gottschlich, Maximilian/Panagl, Oswald/Welan, Manfried (Eds.): *Was die Kanzler sagten. Regierungserklärungen der Zweiten Republik, 1945-1987*. Vienna, Cologne: Böhlau, pp. 33-68.

Green, Donald/Shapiro, Ian (1994): Pathologies of Rational Choice Theory: A Critique of Applications in Political Science. New Haven (CT): Yale University Press.

Green-Pedersen, Christoffer (2007a): The Growing Importance of Issue Competition: The Changing Nature of Party Competition in Western Europe. In: *Political Studies*, Vol. 55, Nr. 4, pp. 607-628.

Green-Pedersen, Christoffer (2007b): The Conflict of Conflicts in Comparative Perspective: Euthanasia as a Political Issue in Denmark, Belgium, and the Netherlands. In: *Comparative Politics*, Vol. 39, Nr. 3, pp. 273-291.

Green-Pedersen, Christoffer/Odmalm, Pontus (2008): Going different ways? Right-wing Parties and the Immigrant Issue in Denmark and Sweden. In: *Journal of European Public Policy*, Vol. 15, Nr. 3, pp. 367-381.

Green-Pedersen, Christoffer /Krogstrup, Jesper (2008): Immigration as a political issue in Denmark and Sweden. In: *European Journal of Political Research*, Vol. 47, Nr. 5, pp. 610-634.

Green-Pedersen, Christoffer/Mortensen, Peter B. (2010): Who sets the agenda and who responds to it in the Danish parliament? A new model of issue competition and agenda-setting. In: *European Journal of Political Research*, Vol. 49, Nr. 2, pp. 257-281.

Grofman, Bernard (2004): Downs and Two-Party Convergence. In: *Annual Review of Political Science*, Vol. 7, pp. 25-46.

Hajer, Maarten A. (1993): Discourse coalitions and the Institutionalisation of Practice. The case of acid rain in Britain. In: Forester, John/Fischer, Frank

(Eds.): *The Argumentative Turn in Policy and Planning*. Durham, NC: Duke University Press, pp. 43-76.

Hammar, Thomas (1985): *European Immigration Policy. A comparative study*. Cambridge: Cambridge University Press.

Harmel, Robert/Svasand, Lars (1997): The Influence of New Parties on Old Parties' Platforms: The Cases of the Progress Parties and the Conservative Parties of Denmark and Norway. In: *Party Politics*, Vol. 3, Nr. 3, pp. 315-340.

Hayes, Danny (2008): Does the message matter? Candidate-media agenda convergence and its effects on voter issue salience. In: *Political Research Quarterly*, Vol. 61, Nr. 1, pp. 134-146.

Haynes, Audrey A./Flowers, Julianne (2002): News Norms and the Strategic Timing and Content of Candidate Messages. In: *Journal of Political Marketing*, Vol. 1, Nr. 4, pp. 1-21.

Heiss, Gernot/Rathkolb, Oliver (Eds.) (1995): Asylland wider Willen. Flüchtlinge in Österreich im europäischen Kontext seit 1914, Jugend & Volk, Vienna.

Helbling, Marc (2013): Framing Immigration in Western Europe. In: *Journal of Ethnic and Migration Studies*, Vol. 40, Nr. 1, pp. 21-41.

Hell, Matthias (2005): Einwanderungsland Deutschland? Die Zuwanderungsdiskussion 1998-2002: Wandel und Kontinuität in der politischen Diskussion zur Zuwanderung 1998-2002. Eine Diskursanalyse. Wiesbaden: VS Verlag.

Hertog, James K. /McLeod, Douglas M. (2001): A multiperspectival approach to framing analysis: A field guide. Framing public life: Perspectives on media and our understanding of the social world. In: Reese, Stephen D./Gandy, Oscar J./Grant, August E. (Eds.): *Framing public life. Perspectives on Media and Our Understanding of the Social World*. Mahwah, NJ: Lawrence Erlbaum Associates, pp. 139-161.

Hinich, Melvin J./Munger, Michael C. (1997): *Analytical Politics*. Cambridge: Cambridge University Press.

Hinich, Melvin J./Henning, Christian H.C.A./Shikano, Susumu (2004): Proximity versus Directional Models of Voting: Different Conepts but one Theory. In: Henning, Christian H.C.A./Melbeck, Christian (Eds.): *Interdisziplinäre Sozialforschung. Theorie und empirische Anwendungen*. Frankfurt: Campus, pp. 37-56.

Hofinger, Christoph/Ogris, Günther (1996): Wählerwanderungen. Ein Vergleich fünf verschiedener Wählerstromanalysen anläßlich der Nationalratswahl 1995. In: Plasser, Fritz/Ulram, Peter A./Ogris, Günther (Eds.): *Wahlkampf und Wählerentscheidung. Analysen zur Nationalratswahl 1995*. Vienna: Signum, pp. 315-341.

Hofinger, Christoph/Ogris, Günther/Breitenfelder, Ursula (2000): Ein Jahr der Kontraste. Die Wählerströme bei den Nationalratswahlen am 3. Oktober, bei den Wahlen zum Europäischen Parlament und bei den Landtagswahlen in Kärnten, Salzburg und Tirol am 7. März. In: Khol, Andreas/Ofner, Günther/Burkert-Dottolo, Günther/Karner, Stefan (Eds.): *Österreichisches Jahr-*

buch für Politik 1999. Vienna, Munich: Verlag für Geschichte und Politik, pp. 119-145.

Hofinger, Christoph/Ogris, Günther/Thalhammer, Eva (2003): Der Jahrhundertstrom: Wahlkampfverlauf, Wahlmotive und Wählerströme im Kontext der Nationalratswahl 2002,. In: Plasser, Fritz/Ulram, Peter A. (Eds.): *Wahlverhalten in Bewegung. Analysen zur Nationalratswahl 2002*. Vienna:: WUV-Universitätsverlag, pp. 159-190.

Hofinger, Christoph/Ogris, Günther/Salfinger, Brigitte (2007): What goes up must come down. Wählerströme und Wahlmotive bei der Nationalratswahl 2006. In: Plasser, Fritz/Ulram, Peter A. (Eds.): *Wechselwahlen. Analysen zur Nationalratswahl 2006*. Vienna: Facultas, pp. 195-211.

Hooghe, Liesbet/Marks, Gary (2008): A Postfunctionalist Theory of European Integration: From Permissive Consensus to Constraining Dissensus. In: *British Journal of Political Science*, Vol. 39, Nr. 1, pp. 1-23.

Hopmann, David Nicolas/Elmelund-Praestekaer, Christian/Vliegenthart, Rens/de Vreese, Claes H./Albaek, Erik (2010): Party media agenda-setting: How parties influence election news coverage. In: *Party Politics*.

Hotelling, Harold (1929): Stability in Competition. In: *The Economic Journal*, Vol. 39, pp. 41-57.

Huysmans, Jef (2000): The European Union and the Securitization of Migration. In: *Journal of Common Market Studies*, Vol. 38, Nr. 5, pp. 751-777.

Huysmans, Jef/Squire, Vicki (2009): Migration and Security. In: Cavelty, Myriam D./Mauer, Victor (Eds.): *Handbook of Security Studies*. London: Routledge, pp. 169-179.

Ickes, Andreas (2008): Parteiprogramme: Sprachliche Gestalt und Textgebrauch. Darmstadt: Büchner.

Ignazi, Piero (2003): *Extreme Right Parties in Western Europe*. Oxford: Oxford University Press.

Inglehart, Ronald (1990): *Culture Shift in Advanced Industrial Society*. Princeton: University Press.

Ivarsflaten, Elisabeth (2005): Threatened by diversity: Why restrictive asylum and immigration policies appeal to western Europeans. In: *Journal of Elections, Public Opinion & Parties*, Vol. 15, Nr. 1, pp. 21-45.

Iversen, Torben (1994): Political Leadership and Representation in West European Democracies: A Test of three models of Voting. In: *American Journal of Political Science*, Vol. 38, pp. 45-74.

Iyengar, Shanto (1991): *Is anyone responsible? How television frames political issues*. Chicago: University of Chicago Press.

Jäger, Siegfried/Maier, Florentine (2009): Theoretical and Methodological Aspects of Foucauldian Critical Discourse Analysis and Dispositive Analysis. In: Wodak, Ruth/Meyer, Michael (Eds.): *Methods for Critical Discourse Analysis*. London: Sage, pp. 34-61.

John, Michael/Lichtblau, Albert (Eds.) (1993): Schmelztiegel Wien - einst und jetzt. Zur Geschichte und Gegenwart von Zuwanderung und Minderheiten, Böhlau, Vienna.

Joppke, Christian (2007): Transformation of Immigrant Integration in Western Europe: Civic Integration and Antidiscrimination Policies in the Netherlands, France, and Germany. In: *World Politics*, Vol. 59, Nr. 2, pp. 243-273.

Kahneman, Daniel/Tversky, Amos (1981): The Framing of Decisions and the Psychology of Choice. In: *Science*, Vol. 211, Nr. 4481, pp. 453-458.

Kahneman, Daniel/Tversky, Amos (1984): Choices, values and frames. American Psychologist. In: *American Psychologist*, Vol. 39, Nr. 4, pp. 341-350.

Karp, Jeffrey A./Banducci, Susan A. (2002): Issues and Party Competition Under Alternative Electoral Systems. In: *Party Politics*, Vol. 8, pp. 123-141.

Kitschelt, Herbert (2001): Politische Konfliktlinien in westlichen Demokratien: Ethnisch-kulturelle und wirtschaftliche Verteilungskonflikte. In: Loch, Dietmar/Heitmeyer, Wilhelm (Eds.): *Schattenseiten der Globalisierung*. Frankfurt am Main: Suhrkamp, pp. 418-442.

Kitschelt, Herbert/McGann, Anthony (1997): The Contemporary Radical Right: An Interpretive and Explanatory Framework. In: Kitschelt, Herbert/McGann, Anthony (Eds.): *The Radical Right in Western Europe. A comparative analysis*. Michigan: University of Michigan Press, pp. 1-46.

Klemmensen, Robert /Binzer Hobolt, Sara/Hansen, Martin E. (2007): Estimating policy positions using political texts: An evaluation of the Wordscores approach. In: *Electoral Studies*, Vol. 26, Nr. 4, pp. 746-755.

Klingemann, Hans-Dieter (1987): Electoral Programmes in West Germany 1949-1980. Explorations in the nature of political controversy. . In: Budge, Ian (Ed.), *Ideology, Strategy, and Party Change: Spatial Analyzes of Post-War Election Programmes in 19 Democracies*. New York, NY: Cambridge University Press, pp. 294-323

Klingemann, Hans-Dieter (1989): Die programmatischen Profile der politischen Parteien in der Bundesrepublik Deutschland. Eine quantitative Inhaltsanalyze der Wahlprogramme von SPD, FDP und CDU von 1949 bis 1987. In: Herzog, Dietrich/Weßels, Bernhard (Eds.): *Konfliktpotentiale und Konsensstrategien. Beiträge zur politischen Soziologie der Bundesrepublik*. Opladen: Westdeutscher Verlag, pp. 98-115.

Klingemann, Hans-Dieter/Volkens, Andrea/Bara, Judith/Budge, Ian (Eds.) (2006): *Mapping Policy Preferences II: Estimates for Parties, Electors and Governments in Central and Eastern Europe*, Oxford University Press, Oxford.

Knigge, Pia (1998): The ecological correlates of right-wing extremism in Western Europe. In: *European Journal of Political Research*, Vol. 34, Nr. 2, pp. 249-279.

Köhler, Thomas (2008): *Statistische Einzelfallanalyse. Eine Einführung mit Rechenbeispielen*. Weinheim: Beltz.

Koenig, Thomas (2004): Routinizing Frame Analysis through the Use of CAQDAS. Paper presented at RC33 Sixth International Conference on Social Science Methodology, Amsterdam. Retrieved from: http://www.restore.ac.uk/lboro/research/methods/routinizing_frame_analysis_ RC33.pdf [accessed 28th July 2010].

Konstantinidis, Ioannis (2008): Who Sets the Agenda? Parties and Media Competing for the Electorate's Main Topic of Political Discussion. In: *Journal of Political Marketing*, Vol. 7, Nr. 3, pp. 323-337.

Koopmans, Ruud/Statham, Paul (1999): Ethnic and Civic Conceptions of Nationhood and the Differential Success of the Extreme Right in Germany and Italy. In: Giugni, Marco/McAdam, Doug/Tilly, Charles (Eds.): *How Social Movements Matter*. Minneapolis, MN: University of Minnesota Press, pp. 225-251.

Koopmans, Ruud/Olzak, Susan (2004): Discursive opportunities and the evolution of right-wing violence in Germany. In: *American Journal of Sociology*, Vol. 110, Nr. 1, pp. 198-230.

Koopmans, Ruud/Statham, Paul/Giugni, Marco/Passy, Florence (2005): *Contested Citizenship: Immigration and Cultural Diversity in Europe*. Minneapolis, London: University of Minnesota Press.

Kraler, Albert/Reichel, David (2010): Quantitative data in the area of migration, integration and discrimination in Europe - an overview. ICMPD, Vienna

Kraler, Albert/Hollomey, Christina/Wöger, Alfred (2009): Austria. Country Report on national data collection systems and practices. PROMINSTAT. Retrieved from: www.prominstat.eu [accessed 5th April 2011].

Kretsedemas, Philip (2012): The Immigration Crucible: Transforming Race, Nation and the Limits of the Law. New York, NY: Columbia University Press.

Kriesi, Hanspeter/Bernhard, Laurent/Hänggli, Regula (2009): The Politics of Campaigning – Dimensions of Strategic Action. In: Marcinkowski, Frank/Pfetsch, Barbara (Eds.): *Politik in der Mediendemokratie*. Wiesbaden: VS Verlag für Sozialwissenschaften, pp. 345-365.

Kriesi, Hanspeter/Grande, Edgar/Lachat, Romain/Dolezal, Martin/Bornschier, Simon/Frey, Timotheus (2006): Globalization and the transformation of the national political space: Six European countries compared. In: *European Journal of Political Research*, Vol. 45, Nr. 6, pp. 921-956.

Krouwel, André (2006): Party models. In: Katz, Richard S./Crotty, William (Eds.): *Handbook of Party Politics*. London; Thousand Oaks; New Delhi: SAGE, pp. 249-269.

Krouwel, André (2012): *Party transformations in European democracies*. Albany, NY: State of New York Press.

Krzyzanowski, Michal/Wodak, Ruth (2008): *The Politics of Exclusion: Debating Migration in Austria*. New Brunswick, NJ: Transaction Publishers.

Kymlicka, Will (1995): Liberalism and the politicization of ethnicity. In: Stapleton, Julia (Ed.), *Group Rights: Perspectives Since 1900*. Bristol: Thoemmes Press, pp. 233-257.

Kytir, Josef/Lebhart, Gustav/Neustädter, Christian (2005): Von der Bevölkerungsfortschreibung zum Bevölkerungsregister. Datengrundlagen, Konzepte und methodische Ansätze des neuen bevölkerungsstatistischen Systems. In: *Statistische Nachrichten*, Nr. 3, pp. 203-210.

Lahav, Gallya (2004): Immigration and Politics in the New Europe: Reinventing Borders. Cambridge: Cambridge University Press.

Lakoff, George (2004): *Don't Think of an Elephant: Know Your Values and Frame the Debate.* White River Junction, VT: Chelsea Green Publishing.

Lakoff, George/Ferguson, Sam (2006): The Framing of Immigration. Retrieved from: http://www.rockridgeinstitute.org/research/rockridge/immigration [accessed 12th January 2009].

Larsen, Knud S./Krumov, Krum /Van Le, Hao/Ommundsen, Reidar/van der Veer, Kees (2009): Threat Perception and Attitudes Toward Documented and Undocumented Immigrants in the United States: Framing the Debate and Conflict Resolution. In: *European Journal of Social Sciences*, Vol. 7, Nr. 4, pp. 115-134.

Lavenex, Sandra (2005): National Frames in Migration Research: the Tacit Political Agenda. In: Bommes, Michael/Morawska, Ewa T. (Eds.): *International Migration Research: Constructions Omissions and the Promises of Interdisciplinarity*. Aldershot: Ashgate, pp. 243-264.

Laver, Michael/Hunt, W. B. (1992): *Policy and party competition.* New York, NY [u.a.]: Routledge.

Laver, Michael/Garry, John (2000): Estimating Policy Positions from Political Texts. In: *American Journal of Political Science*, Vol. 44, Nr. 3, pp. 619-634.

Laver, Michael/Benoit, Kenneth/Garry, John (2003): Extracting Policy Positions from Political Texts Using Words as Data. American Political Science Review. In: *American Political Science Review*, Vol. 97, Nr. 2, pp. 311-331.

Lebhart, Gustav/Münz, Rainer (1999): Migration und Fremdenfeindlichkeit. Schriften des Instituts für Demographie 13. Institut für Demographie, Wien

Lebhart, Gustav/Münz, Rainer (2003): Migration und Fremdenfeindlichkeit in Österreich - Perzeption und Perspektiven. In: Faßmann, Heinz/Stacher, Irene (Eds.): *Lebhart, G., & Münz, R. (2003). Migration und Fremdenfeindlichkeit in Österreich - Perzeption und Perspektiven. In H. Faßmann & I. Stacher (Eds.), Österreichischer Migrations- und Integrationsbericht. Demographische Entwicklungen - sozioökonomische Strukturen - rechtliche Rahmenbedingungen (pp. 343-355). Klagenfurt/Celovec: Drava.* Klagenfurt/Celovec: Drava, pp. 343-355.

Lebhart, Gustav/Marik-Lebeck, Stephan (2007): Zuwanderung nach Österreich. Aktuelle Trends. In: Fassmann, Heinz (Ed.), 2. Österreichischer Migrations- und Integrationsbericht 2001-2006. Rechtliche Rahmenbedingungen, demographische Entwicklungen, sozioökonomische Strukturen. Klagenfurt/Celovec: Drava, pp. 145-163.

Lewis-Beck, Michael S./Mitchell, Glenn E. (1993): French electoral theory: the national front test. In: *Electoral Studies*, Vol. 12, Nr. 2, pp. 112-127.

Lilly, William S. (1900): The Price of Party Government. In: *Fortnightly Review*, Vol. 73, pp. 925-932.

Lipset, Seymor M./Rokkan, Stein (1967): Cleavage structures, party systems, and voter alignments: an introduction *Party systems and voter alignments: Cross-national perspectives*. New York: Free Press, pp. 1-64.

Lubbers, Marcel/Scheepers, Peer/Wester, Fred (1998): Ethnic minorities in Dutch newspapers 1990-1995, results of systematic content analyzes. In: *International Journal for Communication Studies Gazette*, Vol. 60, Nr. 5, pp. 415-431.

Luntz, Frank (2007): Words That Work: It's Not What You Say, It's What People Hear. New York, NY: Hyperion.

Luther, Kurth Richard (1999): Austria: From Moderate to Polarized Pluralism? In: Broughton, David/Donovan, Mark (Eds.): *Changing Party Systems in Western Europe*, pp. 118-142.

Luther, Kurth Richard (2008): The 2006 Austrian Parliamentary Election: From Bipolarism to Forced Marriage. In: *West European Politics*, Vol. 31, Nr. 5, pp. 1004-1015.

Lynch, James P./Simon, Rita J. (2003): *Immigration the World Over: Statutes, Policies, and Practices*. Lanham: Rowman & Littlefield.

Maarek, Phillip J. (1995): *Political Marketing and Communication*. London: John Libbey.

MacDonald, Stuart Elaine/Listhaug, Ola/Rabinowitz, George (1991): Issues and Party Support in Multiparty Systems. In: *The American Political Science Review*, Vol. 85, Nr. 4, pp. 1107-1131.

Mahnig, Hans/Wimmer, Andreas (2000): Country-Specific or Convergent? A Typology of Immigrant Policies in Western Europe. In: *Journal of International Migration and Integration*, Vol. 1, Nr. 2, pp. 177-204.

Mainwaring, Scott/Torcal, Mariano (2006): Party system institutionalization and party system theory after the third wave of democratization. In: Katz, Richard S./Crotty, William (Eds.): *Handbook of Party Politics*. London; Thousand Oaks; New Delhi: Sage, pp. 204-227.

Mair, Peter (Ed.), (1990): *The West European party system*, University Press, Oxford.

Mair, Peter (2006): Cleavages. In: Katz, Richard S./Crotty, William (Eds.): *Handbook of Party Politics*. London; Thousand Oaks; New Delhi: Sage, pp. 371-375.

Mair, Peter/Mudde, Cas (1998): The party family and its study. In: *Annual Review of Political Science*, Vol. 1, pp. 211-229.

Mair, Peter/Müller, Wolfgang C./Plasser, Fritz (2004): Introduction: Electoral Challenges and Party Responses. In: Mair, Peter/Müller, Wolfgang C./Plasser, Fritz (Eds.): *Political Parties and Electoral Change*. London: Sage, pp. 1-19.

Marx-Ferree, Myra (2003): Resonance and Radicalism: Feminist Framing in the Abortion Debates of the United States and Germany. In: *American Journal of Sociology*, Vol. 109, Nr. 2, pp. 304-344.

Marx-Ferree, Myra/Gamson, William A./Gerhards, Jürgen/Rucht, Dieter (Eds.) (2002): *Shaping abortion discourse: Democracy and the public sphere in Germany and the United States*, University Press, Cambridge.

Matthes, Jörg (2007): Framing-Effekte. Zum Einfluss der Politikberichterstattung auf die Einstellungen der Rezipienten. München: Verlag Reinhard Fischer.

Matthes, Jörg (2010): Frames in Political Communication: Toward Clarification of a Research Program. In: Allan, Stuart (Ed.), *Rethinking Communication: Keywords in Communication Research*. Cresskill, NJ: Hampton Press, pp. 123-136.

Matthews, Steven A. (1979): A simple directional model of electoral competition. In: *Public Choice*, Vol. 34, pp. 141-156.

Matuschek, Helga (1985): Ausländerpolitik in Österreich. 1962-1985. Der Kampf um und gegen die ausländische Arbeitskraft. In: *Journal für Sozialforschung*, Vol. 25, Nr. 2, pp. 159-198.

Mazzoleni, Gianpetro/Schulz, Winfried (1999): "Mediatization" of Politics: A Challenge for Democracy? In: *Political Communication*, Vol. 16, Nr. 3, pp. 247-261.

McCombs, Maxwell E. (2008): *Setting the agenda: the mass media and public opinion*. Cambridge: Polity Press.

McDonald, Michael D./Budge, Ian/Mendes, Silvia M. (2004a): What Are Elections For? Conferring the Median Mandate. In: *British Journal of Political Science*, Vol. 34, pp. 1-26.

McDonald, Michael D./Budge, Ian/Pennings, Paul (2004b): Choice versus sensitivity. Party reactions to public concerns. In: *European Journal of Political Research*, Vol. 43, pp. 845-868.

McGann, Anthony J./Kitschelt, Herbert (2005): The Radical Right in the Alps: Evolution of Support for the Swiss SVP and Austrian FPÖ. In: *Party Politics*, Vol. 11, Nr. 2, pp. 147-171.

Meguid, Bonnie M. (2005): Competition Between Unequals: The Role of Mainstream Party Strategy in Niche Party Success. In: *American Political Science Review*, Vol. 99, Nr. 03, pp. 347-359.

Meguid, Bonnie M. (2008): Party competition between unequals. Strategies and electoral fortunes in Western Europe. Cambridge (u.a.): Cambridge University Press.

Merrill, Samuel/Grofman, Bernard (1999): *A unified theory of voting. Directional and proximity spatial models*. Cambridge [u.a.]: Cambridge University Press.

Messina, Anthony M. (2007): *The Logics and Politics of Post-WWII Migration to Western Europe*. Cambridge: Cambridge University Press.

Meyer, Sarah/Peintinger, Teresa (2011): Pro-immigrantische Akteure im Nachteil? Zivilgesellschaftliche Gegenmobilisierung im Kontext österreichischer Migrationpolitik. In: Dahlvik, Julia/Fassmann, Heinz/Sievers, Wiebke (Eds.):

Migration und Integration - wissenschaftliche Perspektiven aus Österreich.
Vienna: Vienna University Press, pp. 143-161.

Meyer, Thomas M./Miller, Bernhard (2013): The niche party concept and its measurement. In: *Party Politics, Online first, Jan 2013.*

Minkenberg, Michael (2001): The Radical Right in Public Office: Agenda-Setting and Policy Effects. In: *West European Politics*, Vol. 24, Nr. 4, pp. 1-21.

Minkenberg, Michael (2002): The New Radical Right in the Political Process: Interaction Effects in France and Germany. In: Schain, Martin/Zolberg, Aristide/Hossay, Patrick (Eds.): *Shadows over Europe: The Development and Impact of the Extreme Right in Western Europe.* New York: Macmillan, pp. 245-268.

Mohrmann, Günther (1979): Der Prozeß der Programmkonstruktion in der Bremer SPD, CDU und FDP. In: Roth, Reinhold/Seibt, Peter (Eds.): *Etablierte Parteien im Wahlkampf. Studien zur Bremer Bürgerschaftswahl 1975.* Meisenheim am Glan: Verlag Anton Hain, pp. 173-304.

Morse, Anson D. (1891): The Place of Party in the Political System. In: *Annals of the American Academy of Political and Social Science*, Vol. 2, Nr. 3, pp. 12-20.

Mourão Permoser, Julia/Rosenberger, Sieglinde (2012): Integration Policy in Austria. In: Frideres, James/Biles, John (Eds.): *International Perspectives: Integration and Inclusion.* Montreal: McGill-Queens University Press, pp. 39-58.

Mudde, Cas (1999): The single-issue party thesis: Extreme right parties and the immigration issue. In: *West European Politics*, Vol. 22, Nr. 3, pp. 182-197.

Müller, Wolfgang C. (1997): Das Parteiensystem. In: Dachs, Herbert et. al. (Ed.), *Handbuch des politischen Systems Österreichs.* Wien: Manz, pp. 215-234.

Müller, Wolfgang C. (1998): Das Parteiensystem in der Zweiten Republik: Entwicklungsphasen und Dynamik seit 1986. In: Kriechbaumer, Robert (Ed.), *Österreichische Nationalgeschichte nach 1945.* Wien; Köln; Weimar: Böhlau, pp. 199-230.

Müller, Wolfgang Claudius (2000): Das österreichische Parteiensystem: Periodisierung und Perspektiven. In: Pelinka, Anton/Plasser, Fritz/Meixner, Wolfgang (Eds.): *Die Zukunft der österreichischen Demokratie.* Vienna: Signum, pp. 281-309.

Müller, Wolfgang C./Strøm, Kaare (1999): Policy, office, or votes? How political parties in Western Europe make hard decisions. Cambridge [u.a.]: Cambridge Univ. Press.

Müller, Wolfgang Claudius/Fallend, Franz (2004): Changing Patterns of Party Competition in Austria: From Multipolar to Bipolar System. In: *West European Politics*, Vol. 27, Nr. 5, pp. 801-835.

Münz, Rainer/Zuser, Peter/Kytir, Josef (2003): Grenzüberschreitende Wanderungen und ausländische Wohnbevölkerung. Struktur und Entwicklung. In:

Fassmann, Heinz/Stacher, Irene (Eds.): *Österreichischer Migrations- und Integrationsbericht. Demographische Entwicklungen – sozio-ökonomische Strukturen – rechtliche Rahmenbedingungen.* Klagenfurt/Celovec: Drava, pp. 20-61.

Nadeau, Richard/Pétry, Francois/Bélanger, Éric (2010): Issue-Based Strategies in Election Campaigns: The Case of Health Care in the 2000 Canadian Federal Election. In: *Political Communication*, Vol. 27, Nr. 4, pp. 367-388.

Nelson, Thomas E./Oxley, Zoe M. (1999): Issue Framing Effects on Belief Importance and Opinion. In: *Journal of Politics*, Vol. 61, Nr. 4, pp. 1040-1067.

Nelson, Thomas E./Willey, Elain A. (2003): Issue frames that strike a value balance: A political psychology perspective. In: Reese, Stephen D./Gandy, Oscar H. G./Grant, August E. (Eds.): *Framing public life: Perspectives on media and our understanding of the social world.* Mahwah, NJ: Lawrence Erlbaum, pp. 245-266.

Nickels, Henri Charles (2007): Framing Asylum Discourse in Luxembourg. In: *Journal of Refugee Studies*, Vol. 20, Nr. 1, pp. 37-59.

Norris, Pippa (2000): A Virtuous Circle. Political Communications in Post-Industrial Societies. New York: Cambridge University Press.

Norris, Pippa (2005): *Radical right. Voters and parties in the electoral market.* Cambridge: Cambridge University Press.

Ogris, Günther (1991): Ebenbild oder Kontrastprogramm. Eine Analyse des Wahlkampfes und des Wahlverhaltens bei der Nationalratswahl im Oktober 1990. In: Khol, Andreas/Ofner, Günther/Stirnemann, Alfred (Eds.): *Österreichisches Jahrbuch für Politik 1990.* Vienna, Munich: Verlag für Geschichte und Politik.

Olzak, Susan (1984): Contemporary Ethnic Mobilization. In: *Annual Review of Sociology*, Vol. 9, pp. 355-374.

Pan, Zhongdang/Kosicki, Gerald M. (2003): Framing as a strategic action in public deliberation. In: Reese, Stephen D./Gandy, Oscar H. G./Grant, August E. (Eds.): *Framing public life: Perspectives on media and our understanding of the social world.* Mahwah, NJ: Lawrence Erlbaum, pp. 35-65.

Panebianco, Angelo (1988): *Political Parties. Organization and Power.* Cambridge: Cambridge University Press.

Pardos-Prado, Sergi (2011): Framing attitudes towards immigrants in Europe: when competition does not matter. In: *Journal of Ethnic and Migration Studies*, Vol. 37, Nr. 7, pp. 999-1015.

Peintinger, Teresa (2011): Demographics of Immigration: Austria. *SOM Working Papers*: 2011-4. Retrieved from: http://www.som-project.eu/ [accessed 26th November 2011].

Pelinka, Anton (1979): Funktionen von Parteiprogrammen. In: Pelinka, Anton/Kadan, Albert (Eds.): *Die Grundsatzprogramme der österreichischen Parteien. Dokumentation und Analyse.* St.Pölten: NÖ Pressehaus, pp. 7-17.

Pelinka, Anton (1998): *Austria: out of the shadow of the past.* Boulder, CO: Westview Press.

Pelinka, Anton (2002): Die FPÖ in der vergleichenden Parteienforschung. Zur typologischen Einordnung der Freiheitlichen Partei Österreichs. In: *Österreichische Zeitschrift für Politikwissenschaft*, Vol. 31, Nr. 3, pp. 281-290.

Pelinka, Anton/Rosenberger, Sieglinde (2000): *Österreichische Politik. Grundlagen - Strukturen - Trends*. Vienna: WUV.

Pelinka, Anton/Plasser, Fritz/Meixner, Wolfgang (2000): Von der Konsen- zur Konfliktdemokratie? Österreich nach dem Regierungs- und Koalitionswechsel. In: Pelinka, Anton /Plasser, Fritz /Meixner, Wolfgang (Eds.): *Die Zukunft der österreichischen Demokratie. Trends, Prognosen und Szenarien*. Vienna: Signum, pp. 439-464.

Pelizzo, Ricardo (2003): Party positions or party direction? An analysis of Party Manifesto Data. In: *West European Politics*, Vol. 26, Nr. 2, pp. 67-89.

Perchinig, Bernhard (2009): Von der Fremdarbeit zur Integration? (Arbeits)migrations- und Integrationspolitik in der Zweiten Republik. In: *Österreich in Geschichte und Literatur*, Vol. 53, Nr. 3, pp. 228-246.

Perlmutter, Ted (1996): Bringing Parties Back In: Comments on 'Modes of Immigration Politics in Liberal Democratic Societies'. In: *International Migration Review*, Vol. 30, Nr. 1, pp. 375-388.

Perlmutter, Ted (2002): The Politics of Restriction: The Effect of Xenophobic Parties on Italian Immigration Policy and German Asylum Policy. In: Schain, Martin/Hossay, Patrick/Zolberg, Aristide (Eds.): *Shadows over Europe: The Development and Impact of the Extreme Right in Western Europe*. London: Palgrave Macmillan, pp. 269-298.

Petrocik, John R. (1996): Issue Ownership in Presidential Elections, with a 1980 Case Study. In: *American Journal of Political Science*, Vol. 40, Nr. 3, pp. 825-850.

Pettigrew, Thomas F. (1998): Reactions Toward the New Minorities of Western Europe. In: *Annual Review of Sociology*, Vol. 24, Nr. 1, pp. 77-103.

Picker, Ruth/Salfinger, Brigitte/Zeglovits, Eva (2004): Aufstieg und Fall der FPÖ aus der Perspektive der Empirischen Wahlforschung: Eine Langzeitanalyse (1986–2004). In: *Österreichische Zeitschrift für Politikwissenschaft*, Vol. 33, Nr. 3, pp. 263-279.

Plasser, Fritz/Ulram, Peter A. (1987): Das Jahr der Wechselwähler. Wahlen und Neustrukturierung des österreichischen Parteiensystems 1986. In: Khol, Andreas/Ofner, Günther/Stirnemann, Alfred (Eds.): *Österreichisches Jahrbuch für Politik 1986*. Vienna, Munich: R. Oldenbourg Verlag, pp. 31-80.

Plasser, Fritz/Ulram, Peter (1991): "Die Ausländer kommen!". Empirische Notizen zur Karriere eines Themas und der Bewußtseinslage "im Herzen Europas". In: Ofner, Günther/Khol, Andreas/Stirnemann, Alfred (Eds.): *Österreichisches Jahrbuch für Politik*. Wien; München, pp. 311-324.

Plasser, Fritz/Ulram, Peter (2000): Parteien ohne Stammwähler? Zerfall der Parteibindungen und Neuausrichtung des österreichischen Wahlverhaltens. In: Pelinka, Anton/Plasser, Fritz/Meixner, Wolfgang (Eds.): *Die Zukunft der österreichischen Demokratie*. Vienna: Signum, pp. 169-202.

Plasser, Fritz/Plasser, Gunda (2002): Global Political Campaigning. A Worldwide Analysis of Campaign Professionals and Their Practices. Westport (CT): Praeger.

Plasser, Fritz/Ulram, Peter (2006): Das Parteiensystem Österreichs. In: Niedermayer, Oskar/Stöss, Richard/Haas, Melanie (Eds.): *Die Parteiensysteme Westeuropas*. Wiesbaden: VS-Verlag, pp. 351-372.

Plasser, Fritz/Sommer, Franz/Ulram, Peter A. (1991): Eine Kanzler- und Protestwahl. Wählerverhalten und Wählermotive bei der Nationalratswahl 1990. In: Ofner, Günther/Khol, Andreas/Stirnemann, Alfred (Eds.): *Österreichisches Jahrbuch für Politik 1990*. Vienna, Munich: R. Oldenbourg Verlag, pp. 95-150.

Plasser, Fritz/Sommer, Franz/Ulram, Peter A. (1995): Ende des traditionellen Parteiensystems? Analyse der Nationalratswahl 1994. In: Khol, Andreas/Ofner, Günther/Burkert-Dottolo, Günther/Karner, Stefan (Eds.): *Österreichisches Jahrbuch für Politik*. Wien, München: Verlag für Geschichte und Politik, pp. 51-123.

Plasser, Fritz/Sommer, Franz/Ulram, Peter A. (2000): Nationalratswahl 1999: Transformationen des österreichischen Wahlverhaltens. In: Khol, Andreas/Ofner, Günther/Burkert-Dottolo, Günther/Karner, Stefan (Eds.): *Österreichisches Jahrbuch für Politik 1999*. Vienna, Munich: R. Oldenbourg Verlag, pp. 49-87.

Plasser, Fritz/Ulram, Peter A./Seeber, Gilg (2003): Erdrutschwahlen: Momentum, Motive und neue Muster im Wahlverhalten. In: Plasser, Fritz/Ulram, Peter A. (Eds.): *Wahlverhalten in Bewegung. Analyzen zur Nationalratswahl 2002*. Vienna: WUV-Universitätsverlag, pp. 97-157.

Plasser, Fritz/Ulram, Peter A./Seeber, Gilg (2007): Was Wähler(innen) bewegt: Parteien-, Themen- und Kandidatenorientierungen 2006. In: Plasser, Fritz/Ulram, Peter A. (Eds.): *Wechselwahlen. Analyzen zur Nationalratswahl 2006*. Vienna: WUV-Universitätsverlag, pp. 155-194.

Popkin, Samuel L. (1994): The Reasoning Voter: Communication and Persuasión in Presidential Campaigns. Chicago, IL: University of Chicago Press.

Price, Vincent/Tewksbury, David (1997): News Values and Public Opinion: A Theoretical Account of Media Priming and Framing. In: Barnett, George A./Boster, Frank J. (Eds.): *Progress in Communication Sciences: Advances in Persuasion*. Greenwich, CT: Greenwood Publishing Group, pp. 172-212.

Rabinowitz, George/MacDonald, Stuart Elaine (1989): A Directional Theory of Issue Voting. In: *American Political Science Review*, Vol. 83, pp. 93-121.

Ray, Samirendra N. (2004): Modern Comparative Politics: Approaches, Methods and Issues. New Delhi: Prentice Hall.

Reeger, Ursula (2008): Austria. In: Fassmann, Heinz/Reeger, Ursula/Sievers, Wiebke (Eds.): *Statistics and Reality: Concepts and Measurements of migration in Europe*. Amsterdam: Amsterdam University Press, pp. 111-130.

Reese, Stephen D. (2003): Prologue - Framing Public Life: A Bridging Model for Media Research. In: Reese, Stephen D./Gandy, Oscar H. G./Grant, August

E. (Eds.): *Framing public life: Perspectives on media and our understanding of the social world*. Mahwah, NJ: Lawrence Erlbaum, pp. 7-32.

Rein, Martin/Schön, Donald (1993): Reframing Policy Discourse. In: Fischer, Frank/Forester, John (Eds.): *The Argumentative Turn in Policy Analysis and Planning*. London: UCL Press Limited and Duke University Press, pp. 145-166.

Rein, Martin/Schön, Donald (1996): Frame-critical policy analysis and frame-reflective policy practice. In: *Knowledge and Policy*, Vol. 9, Nr. 1, pp. 85-104.

Reisigl, Martin/Wodak, Ruth (2001): Discourse and Discrimination: Rhetorics of Racism and Antisemitism. New York, NY: Routledge.

Richardson, Charles (1892): Party government. In: *Annals of the American Academy of Political and Social Science*, Vol. 2, Nr. 4, pp. 86-89.

Riker, William H. (1986): *The art of political manipulation*. New Haven: Yale University Press.

Riker, William H. (1996): The strategy of rhetoric: Campaigning for the American Constitution. New Haven, CT: Yale University Press.

Robertson, David (1976): *A Theory of Party Competition*. London; New York, Sydney; Toronto: John Wiley & Sons.

Roggeband, Conny/Verloo, Mieke (2007): Dutch Women are Liberated, Migrant Women are a Problem: The Evolution of Policy Frames on Gender and Migration in the Netherlands, 1995-2005. In: *Social Policy & Administration*, Vol. 41, Nr. 3, pp. 271-288.

Ronge, Volker (2003): The Politicization of administration in advanced capitalist societies. In: *Political Studies*, Vol. 22, Nr. 1, pp. 86-93.

Rosenberger, Sieglinde/Seeber, Gilg (2011): Kritische Einstellungen: BürgerInnen zu Demokratie, Politik, Migration. In: Polak, Regina (Ed.), *Zukunft. Werte. Europa. Die Europäische Wertestudie 1990-2010: Österreich im Vergleich*. Vienna, Cologne, Weimar: Böhlau, pp. 165-190.

Rothschild, Joseph (1981): Ethnopolitics. A conceptual framework. New York: Columbia University Press. New York, NY: Columbia University Press.

Ruedin, Didier (2013): Obtaining Party Positions on Immigration in Switzerland: Comparing Different Methods. In: *Swiss Political Science Review*, Vol. 19, Nr. 1, pp. 84-105.

Ruedin, Didier/Morales, Laura (2012): Obtaining Party Positions on Immigration from Party Manifestos. Paper presented at Elections, Public Opinion and Parties (EPOP) Conference, Oxford, 7th of September.

Safran, William (2009): The catch-all-party revisited. Reflections of a Kirchheimer student. In: *Party Politics*, Vol. 15, Nr. 5, pp. 543-554.

Sartori, Giovanni (1976): *Parties and party systems. A framework for analysis*. Cambridge [u.a.]: Cambridge Univ. Press.

Sartori, Giovanni (1990): The Sociology of Parties: A Critical Review. In: Mair, Peter (Ed.), *The West European Party System*. Oxford: University Press, pp. 150-182.

Schain, Martin A. (1987): The National Front in France and the Construction of Political Legitimacy. In: *West European Politics*, Vol. 10, Nr. 2, pp. 229-252.

Schain, Martin A. (2006): The Extreme-Right and Immigration Policy-Making: Measuring Direct and Indirect Effects. In: *West European Politics*, Vol. 29, Nr. 2, pp. 270-289.

Schain, Martin A. (2008): Commentary: Why political parties matter. In: *Journal of European Public Policy*, Vol. 15, Nr. 3, pp. 465-470.

Schain, Martin A./Zolberg, Aristide/Hossay, Patrick (Eds.) (2002): *Shadows over Europe. The development and impact of the extreme right in Western Europe*, 1. publ. ed., XIII, 397 S. pp., Palgrave, New York [u.a.].

Schattschneider, Elmer E. (1942): *Party government*. New York: Holt, Rinehart and Winston.

Scheufele, Dietram A./Tewksbury, David (2007): Framing, agenda setting, and priming: The evolution of three media effects models. In: *Journal of Communication*, Vol. 57, Nr. 1, pp. 9-20.

Scholten, Peter (2011): Framing Immigrant Integration. Dutch Research-Policy Dialogues in Comparative Perspective. Amsterdam: Amsterdam University Press.

Schulz, Winfried (2008): Politische Kommunikation: Theoretische Ansätze und Ergebnisse empirischer Forschung. Wiesbaden: VS Verlag für Sozialwissenschaften.

Schulze, Detlef G. (2006): Das Politische und das Juridische als Produkte performativer Praxis. Überlegungen zu einer anti-essentialistischen Reformulierung des Verrechtlichungs-Begriffs. In: Schulze, Detlef G./Berghahn, Sabine/Wolf, Frieder O. (Eds.): *Politisierung und Ent-Politisierung als performative Praxis*. Münster: Westfälisches Dampfboot, pp. 22-41.

Semetko, Holli A./Schoenbach, Klaus (1999): Parties, leaders and issues in the news. In: *German Politics*, Vol. 8, Nr. 2, pp. 72-87.

Semetko, Holli A./Valkenburg, Patti M. (2000): Framing European Politics: A Content Analysis of Press and Television News. In: *Journal of Communication*, Vol. 50, Nr. 2, pp. 93-109.

Siaroff, Alan (2000): Comparative European party systems. An analysis of parliamentary elections since 1945. New York [u.a.]: Garland.

Sides, John (2006): The Origins of Campaign Agendas. In: *British Journal of Political Science*, Vol. 36, Nr. 3, pp. 407-436.

Sigelman, Lee/Buell, Emmet H. (2004): Avoidance or Engagement? Issue Convergence in U.S. Presidential Campaigns, 1960–2000. In: *American Journal of Political Science*, Vol. 48, Nr. 4, pp. 650-661.

Signer, Sara/Puppis, Manuel/Piga, Andrea (2011): Minorities, integration and the media: Media regulation and media performance in multicultural and multilingual Switzerland. In: *International Communication Gazette*, Vol. 73, Nr. 5, pp. 419-439.

Smithies, Arthur (1941): Optimum Location in Spatial Competition. In: *The Journal of Political Economy*, Vol. 49, pp. 423-439.

Snow, David A./Rochefort, Burke E./Worden, Steven K./Benford, Robert D. (1986): Frame Alignment Process, Micromobilization and Movement Participation. In: *American Sociological Review*, Vol. 51, Nr. 4, pp. 464-481.

Soysal, Yasemine (1994): Limits of Citizenship: Migrants and Postnational Membership in Europe. Chicago: Chicago University Press.

Stadler, Ulrike (1995): Kleine Bemerkungen zu vermischten Ziffern. Die österreichische Asylwerberstatistik in der bis Ende 1994 erhobenen Form. In: Heiss, Gernot/Rathkolb, Oliver (Eds.): *Asylland wider Willen. Flüchtlinge in Österreich im europäischen Kontext seit 1914*. Vienna: Jugend & Volk, pp. 239-247.

Statham, Paul (2003): Understanding the Anti-Asylum Rhetoric: Restrictive Politics or Racist Publics? In: *Political Quarterly*, Vol. 74, Nr. 1, pp. 163-177.

Strøm, Kaare (1990): A Behavioral Theory of Competitive Political Parties. In: *American Journal of Political Science*, Vol. 34, Nr. 2, pp. 565-598.

Strömbäck, Jesper (2007): Political Marketing and Professionalized Campaigning. In: *Journal of Political Marketing*, Vol. 6, Nr. 2, pp. 49-67.

Strömbäck, Jesper (2008): Four Phases of Mediatization: An Analysis of the Mediatization of Politics. In: *The International Journal of Press/Politics*, Vol. 13, Nr. 3, pp. 228-246.

Strömbäck, Jesper (2010): A framework for comparing political market-orientation. In: Lees-Marshment, Jennifer /Strömbäck, Jesper/Rudd, Chris (Eds.): *Global Political Marketing*. London: Routledge, pp. 16-33.

Strömbäck, Jesper/Nord, Lars W. (2006): Do Politicans lead the Tango? A Study of the Relationship between Swedish Journalists and their Political Sources in the Context of Election Campaigns. In: *European Journal of Communication*, Vol. 21, pp. 147-164.

Strömbäck, Jesper/Maier, Michaela/Kaid, Lynda Lee (Eds.). (2011). *Political Communication in European Parliamentary Elections*. Farnham: Ashgate.

Tarrow, Sidney (1992): Mentalities, Political Cultures, and Collective Action Frames. In: Morris, Aldon D./McClurg Mueller, Carol (Eds.): *Frontiers in Social Movement Theory*. New Haven, CT: Yale University Press, pp. 174-202.

Tedesco, John C. (2001): Issue and Strategy Agenda-Setting in the 2000 Presidential Primaries. In: *American behavioral scientist*, Vol. 44, Nr. 12, pp. 2048-2067.

Tenscher, Jens (2013): First- and second-order campaigning: Evidence from Germany. In: *European Journal of Communication*, Vol. 28, Nr. 3, pp. 241-258.

Triadafilopoulos, Triadafilos/Zaslove, Andrej (2006): Influencing Migration Policy from Inside: Political Parties. In: Giugni, Marco/Passy, Florence (Eds.): *Dialogues on Migration Policy*. Lanham, MD: Lexington Books, pp. 171-191.

Triandafyllidou, Anna (2002): Religious Diversity and Multiculturalism in Southern Europe: The Italian Mosque Debate. In: *Sociological Research Online*, Vol. 7, Nr. 1.

Triandafyllidou, Anna/Fotiou, Anastasios (1998): Sustainability and Modernity in the European Union: A Frame Theory Approach to Policy-Making. In: *Sociological Research Online*, Vol. 3, Nr. 1.

Ulram, Peter A. (2008): Ein verspielter Sieg und eine siegreiche Zeitungspartei – zur Analyze der Nationalratswahl 2008. In: Khol, Andreas/Ofner, Günther/Burkert-Dottolo, Günther/Karner, Stefan (Eds.): *Österreichisches Jahrbuch für Politik 2008*. Vienna, Munich: Verlag R. Oldenbourg, pp. 3-21.

van Biezen, Ingrid/Mair, Peter/Poguntke, Thomas (2012): Going, going,...gone? The decline of party membership in contemporary Europe. In: *European Journal of Political Research*, Vol. 51, Nr. 1, pp. 24-56.

van de Wardt, Marc (2011): The impact of Societal Factors, Mainstream Parties and Niche Parties on the Politicization of Niche Party Issues: The Danish Case. Paper presented at 6th ECPR General Conference, Reykjavik, Iceland

van der Brug, Wouter (2001): Analysing party dynamics by taking partially overlapping snap-shots. In: Laver, Michael (Ed.), *Estimating the policy position of political actors*. London: Routledge, pp. 115-132.

van der Brug, Wouter /Fennema, Meindert /Tillie, Jean (2005): Why Some Anti-Immigrant Parties Fail and Others Succeed: A Two-Step Model of Aggregate Electoral Support. In: *Comparative Political Studies*, Vol. 38, Nr. 5, pp. 537-573.

van Dijk, Teun A. (1989): Mediating Racism: 'The role of media in the Reproduction of Racism'. In: Wodak, Ruth (Ed.), *Language, Power and Ideology*. Amsterdam: John Benjamins, pp. 199-225.

van Dijk, Teun A. (1991): *Racism and the Press*. London: Routledge.

van Gorp, Baldwin (2005): Where is the frame? Victims and intruders in the Belgian press coverage of the asylum issue. In: *European Journal of Communication*, Vol. 20, Nr. 4, pp. 484-507.

van Gorp, Baldwin (2007): The Constructionist Approach to Framing: Bringing Culture Back In. In: *Journal of Communication*, Vol. 57, Nr. 1, pp. 60-78.

van Kersbergen, Kees/Krouwel, André (2008): A double-edged sword! The Dutch centre-right and the 'foreigners issue'. In: *Journal of European Public Policy*, Vol. 15, Nr. 3, pp. 398-414.

van Spanje, Joost (2010): Contagious Parties: Anti-Immigration Parties and Their Impact on Other Parties' Immigration Stances in Contemporary Western Europe. In: *Party Politics*, Vol. 16, Nr. 5, pp. 1-24.

van Spanje, Joost/van Der Brug, Wouter (2007): The Party as Pariah: The Exclusion of Anti-Immigration Parties and its Effect on their Ideological Positions. In: *West European Politics*, Vol. 30, Nr. 5, pp. 1022-1040.

Vanden, Harry E. (2003): Globalization in a Time of Neoliberalism: Politicized Social Movements and the Latin American Response. In: *Journal of Developing Societies*, Vol. 19, Nr. 2-3, pp. 308-333.

Vassallo, Francesca/Wilcox, Clyde (2006): Party as carrier of ideas. In: Katz, Richard S./Crotty, William J. (Eds.): *Handbook of Political Parties*. London, Thousand Oaks, New Delhi: Sage, pp. 413-421.

Vasta, Ellie (2010): The controllability of difference. Social cohesion and the new politics of solidarity. In: *Ethnicities*, Vol.10, Nr. 4, pp. 503-521.

Verloo, Mieke (2005): Mainstreaming Gender Equality in Europe. A critical frame analysis approach. In: *The Greek Review of Social Research*, Vol. 117, Nr. B, pp. 11-34.

Vliegenthart, Rens (2007): Framing Immigration and Integration. Facts, Parliament, Media and Anti-Immigrant Party Support in the Netherlands, Dissertation thesis, Vrije Universiteit, Amsterdam.

Vogl, Mathias (2007): Die jüngere Entwicklung im Bereich des Asyl- und Fremdenrechts. In: Fassmann, Heinz (Ed.), *2. Österreichischer Migrations- und Integrationsbericht*. Klagenfurt/Celovec: Drava, pp. 19-46.

Volkens, Andrea (2007): Strengths and weaknesses of approaches to measuring policy positions of parties. In: *Electoral Studies*, Vol. 26, Nr. 1, pp. 108-120.

Volkens, Andrea/Bara, Judith/Budge, Ian/McDonald, Michael/Klingemann, Hans-Dieter (Eds.) (2013): *Mapping Policy Preferences from Texts: Statistical Solutions for Manifesto Analysts*, Oxford University Press, Oxford.

Wagner, Markus (2012): Defining and measuring niche parties. In: *Party Politics*, Vol. 18, Nr. 6, pp. 845-864.

Walgrave, Stefaan/Van Aelst, Peter (2006): The Contingency of the Mass Media's Political Agenda Setting Power. Towards A Preliminary Theory. In: *Journal of Communication*, Vol. 56, Nr. 1, pp. 88-109.

Walgrave, Stefaan/De Swert, Knut (2007): Where Does Issue Ownership Come From? From the Party or from the Media? Issue-party Identifications in Belgium, 1991-2005. In: *The Harvard International Journal of Press/Politics*, Vol. 12, Nr. 1, pp. 37-67.

Walters, Timothy N. /Walters, Lynne M. /Gray, Roger (1996): Agenda Building in the 1992 Presidential Campaign. In: *Public Relations Review*, Vol. 22, Nr. 1, pp. 9-24.

Weaver, David/McCombs, Maxwell E./Shaw, Donald L. (2004): Agenda-Setting Research: Issues, Attributes, and Influences. In: Kaid (Ed.), *Handbook of Political Communication Research*. London: Lawrence Erlbaum Associates, pp. 257-281.

Weigl, Andreas (2009): *Migration und Integration. Eine widersprüchliche Geschichte*. Innsbruck, Vienna, Bozen: Studienverlag.

Wengeler, Martin (2003): Topos und Diskurs: Begründung einer argumentationsanalytischen Methode und ihre Anwendung auf den Migrationsdiskurs (1960 - 1985). Tübingen: Niemeyer.

White, John K. (2006): What is a poltical party? In: Katz, Richard S./Crotty, William (Eds.): *Handbook of Political Parties*. London; Thousand Oaks; New Delhi: SAGE, pp. 5-15.

Whiteley, Paul F. (2011): Is the party over? The decline of party activism and membership across the democratic world. In: *Party Politics*, Vol. 17, Nr. 1, pp. 21-44.

Williams, Michelle H. (2009): Catch-All in the Twenty-First Century? Revisiting Kirchheimer's Thesis 40 Years Later: An Introduction. In: *Party Politics*, Vol. 15, Nr. 5, pp. 539-541.

Wlezien, Christopher (2005): On the salience of political issues. The problem with 'most important problem'. In: *Electoral Studies*, Vol. 24, Nr. 4, pp. 555-579.

Wlezien, Christopher (2010): Election Campaigns. In: LeDuc, Lawrence (Ed.), *Comparing democracies. Elections and voting in the 21st century* Los Angeles (u.a.): SAGE, pp. 98-117.

Wodak, Ruth (2008): Introduction: Discourse Studies. Important Concepts and Terms. In: Wodak, Ruth/Krzyzanowski, Michal (Eds.): *Qualitative Discourse Analysis in The Social Sciences*. Basingstoke: Palgrave MacMillan.

Wolinetz, Steven B. (1988): *Parties and Party Systems in Liberal Democracies*. London: Routledge.

Wolinetz, Steven B. (2002): Beyond the Catch-All Party. Approaches to the Study of Parties and Party Organization in Contemporary Democracies. In: Gunther, Richard/Montero, José R./Linz, Juan (Eds.): *Political Parties. Old Concepts and New Challenges*. Oxford: Oxford University Press, pp. 136-166.

Wolinetz, Steven B. (2006): Party systems and party system types. In: Katz, Richard S./Crotty, William (Eds.): *Handbook of Party Politics*. London; Thousand Oaks; New Delhi: Sage, pp. 51-62.

Yanow, Dvora (2006): *Conducting interpretive policy analysis*. London, Thousand Oaks, New Delhi: Sage.

Zapata-Barrero, Ricard/Triandafyllidou, Anna (2012): *Addressing tolerance and diversity discourses in Europe. A Comparative Overview of 16 European Countries*. Barcelona: CIDOB. Barcelona Center for International Affairs.

Zürn, Michael (2011): Politisierung als Konzept der Internationalen Beziehungen. In: Zürn, Michael/Ecker-Ehrhardt, Matthias (Eds.): *Gesellschaftliche Politisierung und Internationale Institutionen*. Frankfurt: Suhrkamp, pp. 7-35.

Zulianello, Mattia (2013): Analyzing party competition through the comparative manifesto data: some theoretical and methodological considerations. In: *Quality & Quantity, May 2013*, pp. 1-15.

Zuser, Peter (1996): Die Konstruktion der Ausländerfrage in Österreich. Eine Analyse des öffentlichen Diskurses 1990. Institute for Advanced Studies, Vienna. *Political Science Series: 35*

Appendices

Appendix 1: Issue-salience of migration and ethnic relations (in % and number of words), 1971-2013

		SPÖ		ÖVP		FPÖ		Greens		LIF		BZÖ		Stronach		NEOS		Avg.	
		MF	PA	MF	PA	MF	PA	MF	PA	MF	PA	MF	PA	MF	PA	MF	PA	MF	PA
1971	%	0.0	0.1	1.2	0.8	1.8	0.8	-	-	-	-	-	-	-	-	-	-	1.0	0.4
	words	0	72	37	140	71	10	-	-	-	-	-	-	-	-	-	-		
1975	%	0.3	0.3	2.9	0.3	0.0	0.3	-	-	-	-	-	-	-	-	-	-	1.1	0.3
	words	13	301	163	351	0	5	-	-	-	-	-	-	-	-	-	-		
1979	%	0.9	0.0	0.0	0.0	2.3	0.0	-	-	-	-	-	-	-	-	-	-	1.1	0.1
	words	73	68	0	277	69	0	-	-	-	-	-	-	-	-	-	-		
1983	%	1.0	0.3	0.0	2.2	3.3	2.2	-	-	-	-	-	-	-	-	-	-	1.4	1.0
	words	129	419	0	408	235	56	-	-	-	-	-	-	-	-	-	-		
1986	%	0.6	0.8	0.0	0.4	0.0	0.4	6.6	-	-	-	-	-	-	-	-	-	1.8	0.5
	words	49	1229	0	459	0	133	397	-	-	-	-	-	-	-	-	-		
1990	%	4.5	6.0	2.7	14.1	7.9	14.1	13.1	9.1	-	-	-	-	-	-	-	-	7.1	7.9
	words	565	9304	208	3593	850	5417	3542	1567	-	-	-	-	-	-	-	-		
1994	%	5.2	2.3	8.8	5.7	7.1	5.7	25.8	32.5	5.1	5.4	-	-	-	-	-	-	10.4	9.6
	words	569	2966	1687	2618	878	4258	2879	3304	133	962	-	-	-	-	-	-		
1999	%	1.6	2.5	5.5	9.6	11.7	9.6	10.3	8.0	8.2	9.0	-	-	-	-	-	-	7.4	6.2
	words	143	4452	1646	1818	1557	8421	1056	1857	248	2615	-	-	-	-	-	-		
2002	%	6.1	3.6	10.9	6.7	8.4	6.7	7.9	10.3	-	-	-	-	-	-	-	-	8.3	6.0
	words	737	7493	2465	4690	2312	3269	552	2729	-	-	-	-	-	-	-	-		
2006	%	9.4	5.8	6.3	16.2	27.4	16.2	8.2	8.9	-	-	15.8	11.2	-	-	-	-	13.4	9.4
	words	672	11120	1173	4296	1040	9932	669	2253	-	-	1145	5395	-	-	-	-		
2008	%	5.6	3.0	14.8	9.1	20.9	9.1	6.7	7.4	-	-	14.0	7.8	-	-	-	-	12.4	6.1
	words	713	4401	863	5022	1036	5656	367	2642	-	-	557	4367	-	-	-	-		
2013	%	2.3	2.4	4.4	3.7	35	8.8	6.5	8.1	-	-	0	0.5	2.3	0	7.6	0	8.3	3.4
	words	317	2312	829	2228	514	5479	2571	2337	-	-	0	144	426	0	1305	0		

Note: MF stands for Manifestos, PR stands for Press releases.

Appendix 2: National and non-national population in Austria by citizenship, 1951-2011

Citizenship	1951	1961	1971	1981	1991	2001	2011
Total	**6.933.905**	**7.073.807**	**7.491.526**	**7.555.338**	**7.795.786**	**8.032.926**	**8.401.940**
Nationals	6.611.307	6.971.648	7.279.630	7.263.890	7.278.096	7.322.000	7.461.953
Non-nationals	322.598	102.159	211.896	291.448	517.690	710.926	939.987
in % of population	4,7	1,4	2,8	3,9	6,6	8,9	11,2
Non-nationals by citizenship							
Europe[1]	75.424	75.149	186.799	260.708	467.013	642.969	824.217
Bulgaria	742	326	489	432	3.582	4.217	12.073
Germany	23.667	43.944	47.087	40.987	57.310	72.218	148.160
Former Yugoslavia	14.948	4.565	93.337	125.890	197.886	322.261	302.069
Former Sovjet union[1]	1.955	226	192	495	2.112	7.247	26.493[3]
Former Czechoslov.	4754	741	2991	2032	11.318	15.052	31.174
France	950	1.116	1.387	1.623	2.178	4.044	6.492
Italy	9.847	8.662	7.778	6.681	8.636	10.064	15.912
Netherlands	552	759	1.478	1.764	2.617	3.910	7.086
Poland	3.705	539	774	5.911	18.321	21.841	41.509
Romania	2.798	262	397	1.253	18.536	17.470	46.288
Switzerland	2.474	3.307	3.860	3.569	4.901	5.962	7.209
Turkey	112	217	16.423	59.900	118.579	127.226	112.774
Hungary	5985	4956	2691	2526	10.556	12.729	28.372
United Kingdom	954	1520	2341	2666	3.427	5.447	8.432
Other europ. States	1.981	4.009	5.574	4.979	7.054	13.281	68.698
Afrika	29	626	1279	3127	8.515	14.223	22.844
Asia[2]	294	1630	4254	12304	25.677	34.978	68.698
America	788	2717	6000	6305	9.516	12.313	17.653
U.S.A.	647	2.082	4.422	4.171	5.770	6.108	6.902
Australia & Oceania	9	99	570	555	738	1.026	1.286
Stateless, unknown	246.054	21.938	12.994	8.449	6.231	5.417	5.289

Source: Statistics Austria

Note: Population census from 1951 to 2011.
[1] Including Asian part of former Soviet Union
[2] Excluding Asian part of former Soviet Union
[3] Only Russian Federation

Appendix 3:   List of Manifestos in data-set

SPÖ

1971	'Für ein modernes Österreich und seine Menschen'
1975	'Sicherheit und eine gute Zukunft für Österreich'
1979	'Der österreichische Weg in die 80er Jahre'
1983	Wahlprogramm der SPÖ
1986	Das Vranitzky-Programm 'Vor uns liegt das neue Österreich'
1990	'Das Österreich von morgen. Wie die SPÖ in den nächsten vier Jahren Österreich erneuern will'
1994	'Es geht um viel, es geht um Österreich'
1999	'Der richtige Weg für Österreich'
2002	'Faire Chancen für alle!'
2006	Den Wohlstand gerecht verteilen. 20 Projekte für mehr Fairness in Österreich.
2008	Wahlmanifest der Sozialdemokratischen Partei Österreichs. Nationalratswahl 2008.
2013	111 Projekte für Österreich. SPÖ-Wahlprogramm 2013

ÖVP

1971	'107 Vorschläge für Österreich'
1975	'Herausforderung 75', Wahlprogramm der ÖVP
1979	'Für einen neuen Frühling in Österreich'
1983	'Jetzt mit Mock'
1986	'Österreich zuerst. Das Mock-Programm für eine Wende zum Besseren'
1990	'Den Aufschwung wählen! Mit uns ist er sicher. ÖVP. Mehr Zukunft, weniger Sozialismus'
1994	'Die Erhard-Busek-Pläne für Österreich'
1999	'Der Bessere Weg'
2002	'Das Österreich-Programm der Volkspartei'
2006	'Kursbuch Zukunft. Modern. Sicher. Menschlich.'
2008	'Neustart für Österreich!'
2013	Zukunftsweisend. Österreich 2018: Das Programm der ÖVP zur Nationalratswahl 2013

FPÖ

1971	'FPÖ-Schwerpunkte im neuen Nationalrat'
1975	Wahlplattform der FPÖ
1979	'Frei sein statt abhängig'
1983	Die Wahlplattform 1983 der Freiheitlichen Partei 'Am 24. April für Österreich. Die Freiheitlichen'
1986	'Unser Österreich. Jörg Haider. Ein Politiker der neuen Art.'
1990	'Blaue Markierungen'. Schwerpunkte Freiheitlicher Erneuerungspolitik für Österreich. 1990 freiheitlich.'
1994	'Österreich-Erklärung. Dr. Jörg Haider'
1999	Das Programm der Freiheitlichen Partei Österreichs
2002	'Wir gestalten Österreich'
2006	'Wahlprogramm der Freiheitlichen Partei Österreichs. FPÖ.'
2008	'Österreich im Wort. Auswahl und Zusammenfassung inhaltlicher Ziele der Freiheitlichen Partei Österreichs für die neue Legislaturperiode'
2013	Liebe deinen Nächsten. Für mich sind das unsere Österreicher

Greens

1986	'Grüne Alternativen für ein neues Österreich. Offenes Kurzprogramm'
1990	Leitlinien Grüner Politik zu den Themen Umwelt - Demokratie - soziale Gerechtigkeit
1994	'Alpeninitiative für Österreich'
1999	'Kompetent. Engagiert. Grüne Positionen für eine neue Politik'
2002	'Österreich braucht jetzt die Grünen'
2006	'Zeit für Grün. Das Grüne Programm'
2008	'neu beginnen! das grüne programm für einen neubeginn'
2013	Saubere Umwelt. Saubere Politik. Wahlprogramm der Grünen. Nationalratswahl 2013

LIF

1994   'Die Politik des Liberalen Forums'
1999   'Das Buch zur Wahl. Liberale Antworten. Nationalratswahl 1999'

BZÖ

2006   Wahlprogramm – Liste Westenthaler
2008   'Deinetwegen. Österreich'. Das Wahlprogramm des BZÖ
2013   Die moderne Mitte. Das BZÖ-Wirtschafts- und Sozialprogramm

Stronach

2013   Team Stronach. Grundsatzprogramm

NEOS

2013   NEOS – Das Neue Österreich. Pläne für ein neues Österreich

---

Note: For elections between 1971 and 1999, manifestos have been collected via the CMP-data-base with support from the Leibniz-Institut für Sozialwissenschaten (GESIS). For the remaining elections the original manifestos have been collected by the author.

Studien zur politischen Kommunikation
hrsg. von PD Dr. Jens Tenscher (Universität Trier)

Peter Maurer
Medieneinfluss aus der Sicht von Politikern und Journalisten
Ein deutsch-französischer Vergleich
Die vorliegende Untersuchung nimmt den scheinbaren Widerspruch zwischen Theorien zur voranschreitenden „Medialisierung" der Politik und den allenfalls moderaten empirischen Befunden zum Anlass einer empirischen Neubestimmung des politischen Einflusses der Medien. Sie konfrontiert die bisher vorliegenden Ergebnisse mit den Wahrnehmungen von Politikern und Journalisten in Deutschland und Frankreich. Auf Basis der geäußerten Einschätzungen der Betroffenen und der „Verursacher" von Medieneinfluss werden Divergenzen im Ländervergleich aufgedeckt, die mit der Wirkung politisch-institutioneller Rahmenbedingungen erklärt werden können.
Bd. 8, 2013, 200 S., 29,90 €, br., ISBN 978-3-643-12145-5

Benedikt Porzelt
Politik und Komik
‚Fake-Politiker' im Bundestagswahlkampf
Der Komik wird häufig etwas Unernstes zugesprochen. Doch tatsächlich stellt sie eine wichtige Kommunikationsform zur unterhaltsamen Informationsvermittlung und Kritik an politischen Missständen dar. Besonders deutlich wurde dies im Bundestagswahljahr 2009, in dem drei Komiker mit ihrem Auftreten als angebliche Politiker die Grenze zwischen Fiktion und Realität einrissen und medienwirksam mit realen politischen Akteuren interagierten. Anhand dieses Phänomens werden in der vorliegenden Studie die gesellschaftlichen Potentiale, aber auch Risiken eines komischen Umgangs mit Politik untersucht.
Bd. 10, 2013, 320 S., 34,90 €, br., ISBN 978-3-643-12390-9

LIT Verlag Berlin – Münster – Wien – Zürich – London
Auslieferung Deutschland / Österreich / Schweiz: siehe Impressumsseite